TEACHING the BRIGHT and GIFTED

TEACHING

the

BRIGHT and GIFTED,

NORMA E. **CUTTS, PH.D.**

Director of Graduate Studies
New Haven State Teachers College

NICHOLAS MOSELEY, PH.D.
Educational Consultant

1957
Englewood Cliffs, N. J.
PRENTICE-HALL, INC.

Prentice-Hall Psychology Series
Arthur T. Jersild, *editor*

Grateful acknowledgment is made to the following for the pictures used as illustrations: Michael F. Hannon, New Haven State Teachers College; the Major Work Classes, Cleveland, Ohio, Public Schools; Robert J. Cyr, Meriden, Conn., Public Schools; the Peabody Museum of Natural History, Yale University; Leo E. Garrepy, the Yale-Norfolk Summer Art School, Ellen Battell Stoeckel Trust, Yale University.

PRINTED IN THE UNITED STATES OF AMERICA

89614

To the Memory of
Lewis Madison Terman
Gifted Leader in the Study of the Gifted

Preface

America's greatest resource is her bright children. The need today is to discover every bright child, challenge him to work to his full capacity, and see that he receives all the education from which he can profit.

Teaching the Bright and Gifted is designed to give practical help to classroom teachers in elementary and secondary schools and to teachers in training. It has grown out of many years of experience in teaching courses on the gifted and in counseling bright students and their parents. Materials have been contributed by well over a thousand teachers, parents, and pupils, and quotations from these materials have been liberally used to provide true-to-life illustrations. Valuable information that has hitherto been available only in scattered magazines and books has been gathered together and organized to provide answers to the questions that teachers commonly raise. The appendixes contain annotated references to books and pamphlets about the bright and talented, to tests, and to books on materials and methods in the subjects that are commonly taught in the various grades. There is a list of problems into which further research is needed, and this list also provides topics for group discussion.

We hope that the book will help teachers identify and understand their bright and gifted pupils, increase the teachers' satisfaction in their work, and stimulate them to new efforts and new discoveries. There is hardly a field in education where there are greater rewards—for the pupil, for society, and for the teacher himself.

Norma E. Cutts
Nicholas Moseley

Table of Contents

I
Calling All Teachers, 1

DEFINITIONS, 2; WANTED: EDUCATED MANPOWER, 4; REASONS FOR THE SHORTAGE OF PROFESSIONAL PERSONNEL, 6; THE INDIVIDUAL'S NEED, 7; NEGLECT OF THE GIFTED, 9; THE VITAL ROLE OF THE CLASSROOM TEACHER, 10.

II
Identification, 12

EARLY IDENTIFICATION, 13; HINDRANCES TO A SOUND AP-PRAISAL, 14; SYSTEMATIC OBSERVATION, 17; GENERAL CHAR-ACTERISTICS OF BRIGHT CHILDREN, 18; QUALITY, 26; OUT-OF-SCHOOL ACTIVITIES, 27; PRESCHOOL DEVELOPMENT, 29; THE USE AND ABUSE OF TEST RESULTS, 30; TESTING BY THE CLASS-ROOM TEACHER, 33; PSYCHOLOGICAL SERVICES, 34; CUMULA-TIVE RECORDS, 35.

III
Enrichment: Purposes and Plans, 37

MAJOR FACTORS, 37; A COMMON PRACTICE, 38; A NECES-SITY, 38; HINDRANCES, 39; GENERAL OBJECTIVES, 42; THE

ix

IV

Enrichment: Methods and Content, 55

V

Utilizing Community Resources, 72

VI

Special Groups, 89

VII

Acceleration, 102

VIII

The Fundamentals, 117

IX

Motivating the Underachievers, 131

X

Mental Hygiene, 153

XI

Character Development, 176

XII

Educational Guidance, 191

TEACHING the BRIGHT and GIFTED

I

Calling All Teachers

*In my school and in many I know, it is up to the
classroom teacher to identify the bright and gifted children and to plan their programs. In the past, I didn't
go as far as I might. I was afraid of going over their
heads—and my own! Now I think, "The sky is the
limit." I will not let lack of knowledge on my part
interfere with my attempts to challenge these youngsters, to enrich their studies, and to instigate research.
I'll learn with them—and tell them so.*
                                                    —*A Teacher.*

What do you do to help the bright and gifted in your classes?

Almost every teacher of whom we have asked this question feels that he has an obligation to identify his bright pupils,
to help them to fulfill their capacity to profit from education,
and to guide them into careers where their high abilities will
serve their country and the world. He is eager to give and to
gain information about the best methods of teaching the bright
and gifted.

But enough teachers make remarks like, "I haven't any
bright pupils this year," and, "I never had a gifted child in my
room," to show that they have a mistaken concept of what constitutes "brightness," "giftedness," and "talent." There are also
a good many who agree with one teacher who wrote, "I feel the
gifted and above-average children can do their work with minimum directions. Therefore, most of my spare time is involved
in helping those who I feel need help." There is obviously room

1

for more understanding of who the bright are and why each of them deserves his share of his teachers' time.

DEFINITIONS

There are no standard definitions of brightness and giftedness. Many of those adopted by individual research workers, by school systems, and by community committees on the gifted are based on the IQ. You can find the lower limit stated as low as 110 and as high as 150. Any lower limit is arbitrary and raises several difficulties. Once a figure has been set, the tendency is to rule out all children with a score even one point below the arbitrary figure, though there may be very grave doubts about the validity of the test score upon which the decision was made. The use of the IQ alone makes no allowance for the character and the motivation of the youngster. There is also the question of children who do not have the stated IQ but who are obviously talented in art or music or leadership or some other field. Such considerations show the wisdom of Paul Witty's proposal that "a child be referred to as 'gifted' when his performance in a worth-while type of human endeavor is *consistently remarkable*." [1]

Actually a close definition is neither necessary nor desirable. You are interested in all the pupils in your class. You wish to help each of them, the slow, the average, and the bright. Knowing a child's approximate IQ helps you adjust the curriculum to his ability and decide whether he is learning as he should. You do not expect your slower pupils to go as far or as fast as your average pupils, and you expect your brighter pupils to go further and faster. Your primary problem with your brighter pupils is to see that they are not held back, to be sure you are using methods which help them capitalize on whatever capabilities they have. Then, as they progress, you guide them toward fields which will give full scope to their abilities and you help each individual set a worthy goal for himself. Your role is not determined by anything so simple as giving your pupils an intelligence test. You have to use enlightened judgment, based on your general and professional knowledge and your knowledge of the particular individual's capabilities and temperament.

In this book, therefore, you will find us treating the words "bright," "gifted," and "talented" rather loosely, though not synonymously. In general, we think of bright pupils as those capable of profiting from a college education and of doing well in any career which they may choose. When we speak of the gifted, we mean pupils whose potentialities may be greater than those of the bright, but we do not separate the bright from the gifted in any hard or fast manner. The talented, in our use of the phrase, are all pupils who show unusual ability along non-academic lines and are capable of profiting from advanced instruction and of making a career in their special field. The common denominator is the capacity for superior achievement and superior service.

It is essential to keep a sane perspective when you are thinking about the bright and gifted. Reflect that you yourself are at least bright. You are presumably a college graduate. You are engaged in a professional career. You are rendering superior service. You associate on equal terms with others who are bright and gifted.

Remember also that bright and gifted children do not spring full grown from Zeus's brow like Athena, the goddess of wisdom. They are children, subject to the frailties and insufficiencies of childhood. Like all children, they lack knowledge, they lack experience, they lack judgment, they are physically and socially immature. Given proper care at home and skilled teaching in school, they do develop physically and mentally more quickly than other children, and eventually they may surpass their parents and teachers in knowledge and achievement. But attaining full development is a long process for even the most gifted child. Like your other pupils, your bright and gifted need your affection and support. Give them these and they will be grateful.

WANTED: EDUCATED MANPOWER

The widespread emphasis on the need to identify all bright pupils and to see that they continue their education is the result of acute and growing shortages of professional personnel. Most prominence has been given to the shortage of scientists, mathematicians, engineers, and technicians, because this shortage poses a twofold threat to our way of life. First, we are increasingly dependent on science for feeding our population, maintaining health, and developing industry. Second, if we are to win the conflict between democracy and communism, we require great numbers of highly trained professional people and technicians not only for defense but also to serve the backward nations of the world and thus incline them to our point of view.

We have apparently been overconfident of our leadership in technology. The United States Central Intelligence Agency estimated that in 1956 Russia was training four men to our three, and training them as well or better. Admiral Strauss, chairman of the Atomic Energy Commission, told a Senate committee in 1956 that the United States needs 45,000 to 50,000 new engineers each year and is getting less than 25,000. The big corporations are so short of scientists and engineers, both for defense work and for industrial development, that there are at the moment four vacancies for each person taking a degree in engineering or science.

Because of the critical situation, President Eisenhower in 1956 set up a Committee for the Development of Scientists and Engineers to "foster the development of more highly qualified technological manpower." To this committee he appointed leaders from the fields of engineering, science, education, industry, labor, government, and the humanities. But committees and commissions can merely point the way. As the President said, "Although the government has a responsibility for increasing the supply and improving the quality of our technological personnel, the basic responsibility for solution of the problem lies

4

in concerted action of citizens and citizens' groups organized to act effectively."

The importance of scientists and engineers to the defense effort tends to obscure shortages in other fields. These shortages are very great. For example, in 1956 the State of New Jersey had 1,500 vacancies in well-paid positions which require college training or its equivalent. Most sorely needed, a state official said, were "apprentice social case workers, psychiatrists, psychologists, nurses, and accountants," as well as engineers.

A shortage of teachers is perhaps the most serious of all the shortages because it is the most fundamental. Until every pupil in elementary school and high school, and every student in college and graduate school, has teachers who are trained to perform their specific duties, our manpower is doomed to be deficient in quality as well as in quantity. In 1955 we were short 140,000 qualified teachers in elementary and secondary schools. In the crucial field of science, the number of qualified teachers had actually decreased 53 per cent since 1950 while the high-school enrollment was increasing 16 per cent. Largely because of a lack of teachers, more than half of our high schools did not offer either physics or chemistry to their students. The prospects for overcoming the shortages are not good. We need each year about 200,000 new elementary- and secondary-school teachers and 20,000 college teachers to take care of increasing enrollments and to replace teachers leaving the profession.[2]

The appalling problem of where we are to find enough teachers carries over to other types of school personnel. A school administrator has said, not altogether jokingly, that the only surplus is in administrators. Of special concern to you in your work with bright and gifted children is the shortage of qualified school psychologists and guidance counselors. A report of the American Psychological Association, *School Psychologists at Mid-Century,* estimates the potential demand at 15,000 school psychologists but states that only a small fraction of this number are available.[3] Dr. Edwin Van Kleeck, New York State assistant commissioner of education, has said that in his state in 1955 there were 161 public high schools with no specific counseling service whatever and 118 more where there was very little. Three-fourths of the counselors in the state, he said, needed further training.

REASONS FOR THE SHORTAGE
OF PROFESSIONAL PERSONNEL

Part of the reason for the shortage of scientists, teachers, and other personnel is the low birth rate in the 1930's and the rapid increase in our population since then. For example, the relatively small number of people maturing in 1955 who were qualified to be teachers might have been ample if the number of births had remained stable instead of almost doubling. It is as though a stream of water flowing from a small spring had to supply the large and thirsty population of a big city many miles away.

The increasing complexity of modern life likewise demands an ever greater number of highly trained specialists to maintain the advantages it gives—and we insist upon. For example, the time has passed when a farmer simply raised what he could as he could and sold it directly to the consumer or a local dealer. Today the process of feeding our population involves the geneticist who breeds seed, the chemist and the bacteriologist who specialize in soils, the entomologist who controls insect pests, the technician in the public-health laboratory who guards against residues from lethal sprays, the engineer who designs and supervises packaging machinery, the economist who studies market trends, and, not least, the dietitian who tells us what not to eat if we do not wish to get too fat. All of these specialists and more must be experts in fields where only good students can qualify. And the farmer himself, if he is to take full advantage of the experts' knowledge, must be a graduate of an agricultural college and must have studied under many skilled teachers.

But even the combination of the low birth rate of the Thirties and the increased demands would not have created shortages as extensive as those that have developed if so many superior individuals had not been diverted into barren fields before they completed their education. The waste is still continuing. Various surveys of national manpower, including one by a commission of the National Education Association, show that each year 500,000 individuals who have the ability to graduate from college do not do so. Of these, 100,000 drop out of high school before the end of senior year, 200,000 graduate from high school but do not go to college, and another 200,000 drop out of college. Less than 5 per cent of those who do graduate from college go on to study for the Ph.D. degree.

Investigation has shown that about half of the young people who discontinue their education cannot afford, or think they cannot afford, the cost of college. Governmental officials and industrial leaders are now considering how to provide scholarships for many if not all who deserve them. The cost, certainly $250,000,000 a year and perhaps twice that, staggers a teacher's financial imagination. But so do the billions spent on defense, billions that must be spent by intelligent specialists if they are not to be wasted.

The other half of the superior students who do not complete their education lack motivation. These are the pupils who have not learned to exercise foresight, to study hard to achieve a goal, and to exert themselves to the full in the service of others. Not a few of them actually dislike school. Many do so badly in their studies that their true abilities are never discovered. Even when they do "well enough," they have no abiding interest in education. If the crisis in manpower is to be survived, you must learn to discover these bright children and teach them and guide them to make the most of their abilities.

THE INDIVIDUAL'S NEED

You serve the bright pupil himself as well as the world when you challenge him to work hard and to prepare himself for employment that will use his capabilities to the full. If he

7

continues merely to do "well enough," he is on the way to missing much that he might and ought to gain out of life. And there is more than a chance that he will not continue to do "well enough" but will do very badly.

Our collection of case histories of bright children has many examples of pupils who were so given either to daydreaming or to aggressive disorder in school that their teachers thought them stupid. When their high intelligence was discovered and they were given work which challenged their power, the change in behavior was often miraculous. But there are many cases where the discovery came only after the pupil had developed such faulty habits of work and such an antisocial attitude that the school could do little or nothing to help. The world is full of intelligent adults who are futile dreamers or actively discontented as a result of not having been trained to qualify for work which would interest them and use their skills. Unfortunately, most of these people have passed the point of no return. They have to continue in their dull routine, no matter how bitterly they resent it, because it is too late for them to go back and secure the prerequisite education for a more challenging occupation.

Many recruits to communism (and many clever criminals) are young people who know that they have the ability to excel in a profession but feel they have been discriminated against because of poverty or because of racial background. We do not wish to exaggerate this aspect of the neglect of our brightest pupils. Our democratic tradition is so strong and so loyally served by our school teachers that, in contrast with most other countries, our young people show relatively little opposition to their government. But the danger is there, and communist agents are aware of it. In America there are surely no grounds for denying equal opportunity for full development to any boy or girl.

The child who is endowed with unusual talent has as much need of self-fulfillment as the one whose gifts are mainly intellectual, and he may have fewer opportunities. Many teachers share the fear of one who wrote, "Creative music has always scared me—but I will add ballroom and square dancing!" But great artists often owe their start to a teacher who, although not talented himself, noticed their unusual ability, planted ambition in their minds, and guided them in seeking training.

NEGLECT OF THE GIFTED

You may see the need to do more for your brightest pupils but feel that the demands made on you by their slower classmates just do not leave you time. A slow pupil may cause you more trouble than a bright one, but for that very reason he seems more of a challenge. One teacher writes, "I started the year with three pupils who really couldn't read. I've worked hard with them and they're now almost up to grade level. They and their parents are very pleased, and I guess I'm proud of myself. Anyway, I'd hate to take time from my weaklings to give to my three or four bright youngsters, who seem to have done very well by themselves."

Some teachers and administrators think it undemocratic to give bright pupils special attention, and still more undemocratic to segregate them in special classes. There are also some who object to any identification of a pupil as bright. They think this smacks of class distinction, especially when some other pupils, equally bright, may be overlooked. The answer to these doubts is that the bright pupil, in all fairness, deserves as much of his teachers' time as any other pupil. He and the slow pupil both deserve the opportunity to make the most of themselves. Both are better served when their teachers use methods which help them develop as individuals.

A few teachers undoubtedly resent the bright child's superiority. Theoretically we should all welcome students who learn more than we teach and in the end come to know more about our subjects than we do. For a teacher's success is measured by his pupil's success. But, actually, few of us find it easy to say to a questing student, "I don't know—but let's find out." It

9

takes humility to maintain the attitude: "I will not let lack of knowledge on my part interfere with my attempts to challenge these youngsters. . . . I'll learn with them—and tell them so." But you will soon gain courage when you meet the welcome which bright boys and girls give you as a partner in learning.

THE VITAL ROLE
OF THE CLASSROOM TEACHER

You and your fellow teachers are the only agents of society who have contact with all children. You are, therefore, the only ones who have the full opportunity to discover the bright and gifted in the rising generation. The lack of school psychologists and guidance counselors, especially at the elementary-school level, means that more often than not you yourself will have to make the decision as to whether a pupil is working up to his ability. The long years that a child attends school give you and the pupil's other teachers ample time to test your conclusions. But if the education of a bright child is left to chance, if he is challenged only part of the time, if he is allowed to start each year far below his level of achievement, he will surely be handicapped in his development. So your obligation is not only to do what you can for him in your own classroom but also to co-operate with his later teachers. The guidance of the gifted is a project for the whole faculty. And, because parents may not be aware of a child's true abilities or of how those abilities might be developed to serve the common good, you will have to do what you can to help them exercise foresight and make wise decisions.

We hope that this chapter has alerted you to the situation and has given you the feeling that you would like to help. The rest of the book is planned to provide you with ways of making a start and to suggest principles and procedures. Most of the details you will want to work out for yourself. That is part of the fun, but only part. Classroom teachers with whom we have worked as they began to give the bright pupil his fair share of attention have found every phase of their teaching more interesting. The bright pupil stimulates your interest. You find yourself sharing his pleasure as he discovers the world of the mind and progresses in knowledge and in skill. He is quick to respond to your efforts to help him, and quick to show gratitude. One of the world's great scientists and teachers, Carolus Linnaeus, said two hundred years ago: "A teacher can never better distinguish himself in his work than by encouraging a clever pupil, for the true discoverers are among them, as comets amongst the stars."

II

Identification

Jane came to us from an out-of-town school and brought no record. But she showed immediately that she was superior. When an assignment was given, she'd first think about it and then go ahead with economy of time and motion. She never needed to be told how to arrange her work. She was quick to make her own deductions and generalizations whenever the class started to discuss a passage they had read. She had the best sense of humor in the class. She was constantly bringing in cartoons from the Saturday Evening Post *to share with me, and her laughter was infectious. Her favorite program was "Mr. Wizard," and she was able to explain to the class the facts he related. When the Kuhlmann-Anderson was given, her IQ was estimated as 130.*

—A Teacher.

I know I have some bright pupils, but how bright? Are they gifted?

—A Teacher.

If you were asked to name some of the brightest pupils in a class you had taught for a month or two, you would have no difficulty. And if you thought over the way you teach these pupils, you would find several differences from the way you teach their slower classmates. Why, then, should you be concerned with specific methods of identification?

There are two main answers to this question. First, you want to be sure that you are not missing any pupils who might, if you gave them their share of attention, contribute more to your class now and eventually to the world. Second, you want to gauge how far above average each of your bright pupils is so that you know what to expect of him.

The principal means of discovering all your bright pupils is systematic observation on your part. You will also want all the assistance you can obtain from cumulative records, test results, marks, and other teachers. In practice, you will use more or less together all of the sources available to you. But inasmuch as we have to discuss the methods one by one, we are leaving records and psychological services till the end of the chapter, because these are essentially checks on the teacher's judgment. They are an aid to, rather than a substitute for, personal interest in each pupil.

EARLY IDENTIFICATION

Early and accurate determination of a pupil's real abilities has advantages for everyone concerned. If, from the beginning of his education, teachers challenge the child to do his best, he learns good study habits and keeps his interest in school. His teachers, alert to the fact that he is bright, watch to gauge the range of his abilities, help him explore his interests and talents, and help him and his parents plan for his future education. If an unusual talent or a powerful interest appears early, there is time to develop both it and other interests. The latter will test the strength of the major interest and round out the pupil's personality.

Civilization owes much to young people whose abilities and talents have developed early in life. Newton conceived his doctrine of light and color (the spectrum) before he was 20. Orville Wright was only in his teens, but already a skilled mechanic, when he built his first glider, and he and Wilbur Wright achieved powered flight in their early thirties. Mme. Curie worked in her father's laboratory when she was in her teens and discovered radium when she was 31. Marian Anderson was a concert singer at 17.   Yehudi Menuhin made his debut with the San Francisco Symphony when he was 7, and by the age of 21 was described as "a mature artist, in the first rank of violinists."

Today, because of increasing knowledge and the practical necessity of a college education, it takes longer and longer to acquire the fundamentals in any field.   But creativity, the power to generate new ideas, is at its height before the age of thirty.

James B. Conant, formerly President of Harvard, has stressed the need to identify bright pupils early.   In his book *The Citadel of Learning,* writing about the failure to educate more mathematicians and scientists, he says, ". . . the difficulty is in no small part due to our failure to identify at a relatively young age those boys and girls who have more than the average talent for mathematics.   If such pupils were identified (and tests for this purpose seem to be at hand) and then were stimulated to proceed relatively rapidly with their studies, a respectable fraction of the incoming freshmen of the better colleges would have sufficient mathematical aptitude to tackle the physics and chemistry courses with both enthusiasm and success." [1]

HINDRANCES TO A SOUND APPRAISAL

Large classes make sound appraisal difficult.   You just cannot know all of your pupils well enough.   And for the secondary-school teacher who meets 150 or more students every day in periods that are only about forty-five minutes long, the difficulty is compounded.   For example, even if you study the cumulative records, you are unlikely to remember the chronological ages of all your students and so may not realize that one who seems to be doing merely average work is competing with students who are two or three years older.   When your room is overcrowded you mainly notice students who compel your attention.   Too often, the activator is not good work, but bad work or bad behavior.   In such cases, you know you have to take action.   In the meantime, a brilliant student may be hidden in the crowd.

Identification

Bright children, as one high-school dean observes, are not all little angels. If they are bored or if they feel they are wasting time, they are more than likely to make trouble. They may have acquired bad work habits or be impatient with routine and so fail to do their lessons. You may judge them on the basis of behavior or performance and never discover their true abilities. Or, unconsciously, you may be glad to emphasize their faults in order to avoid recognizing their superiority. A psychologist, investigating the school history of a boy in Grade II whose score on an individual psychological test indicated an IQ of 185, found the following report from the teacher: "Jack is only happy when he is in a leadership role, and finds it difficult not to take the initiative in activities. He bites his pencil and gets lead on his face, hands, and arms, which, when he smears it on his paper, makes an untidy paper. His number work is just average. I would like to see development in this area and neatness and promptness in finishing work." An achievement test given by the psychologist put Jack's arithmetic on the fifth-grade level and his science on the eighth.

An emotionally disturbed child may daydream so continuously, or, contrariwise, be so overaggressive, as to do little or no schoolwork. Emotional blocks actually interfere with the working of the mind. Erik Erikson, a child psychiatrist, has spoken of children whose IQ's rose more than twenty points after psychotherapy.

Minor degrees of deafness and some types of visual defect can be discovered only by specialists. Such defects go undetected by the ordinary school physical examination, but they interfere with schoolwork and may make a bright child seem stupid.

Reading difficulties are far from uncommon in bright children and are often ascribed to low intelligence rather than to the true causes.

Whenever a number of teachers are asked to identify the gifted children in their classes, some balk. The unwillingness here is not entirely due to difficulties of definition. These teachers quite rightly dislike pinning a label on a child. They

15

agree with the Vassar member of Phi Beta Kappa whose family gave her a gold chain so she could wear the key as a pendant. "I might as well wear a millstone," was her response. And a high-school sophomore used almost the same words when he was discussing transfer to the fastest section. "I'd rather tie a millstone round my neck and jump in the pond than be called 'gifted.'" Teachers also fear that they may identify one student as gifted and miss others who are equally bright. This worry becomes acute when assignment to a special group is at stake. At such times there is great comfort in sharing responsibility by talking over the decision with several teachers who know the pupil. In a case in which a decision must be made, all the evidence should be weighed and the individual should be given the benefit of any reasonable doubt.

All judgments of brightness are subject to the principle: *A high rating with regard to one or several criteria generally indicates high ability, but a low rating does not necessarily indicate low ability.* Einstein learned to talk later than the average child, and was late in learning to read.

On the other hand, a child who is well dressed, has good manners, speaks correctly, and is healthy and nice looking may seem so much brighter than he is that everybody's judgment is warped. Psychologists call this "the halo effect." It occurs most frequently in the cases of children of well-educated parents, but Personality with a capital P is not confined to upper-class children.

The safeguard against inaccurate appraisal is to develop such a firm mental set to identify the bright children in your class that you will systematically weigh all of the evidence you can find. If you and your fellow teachers have such a set, and if your principal co-operates, you will improve your chances of discovering the bright and gifted children in your school and of gauging their abilities with fairness.

Each June [writes a teacher] every teacher in our school talks over his next year's class with their current teacher. We take all the cumulative records and run through them together. This way I learn a lot about each child's character, behavior, work habits, and interests that never gets into the records. I have brief conferences with my prospective pupils, usually in groups of five or six, and talk over their summer plans. In the fall, just before school opens, I go over the records again. When the children come in we feel we know each other and we get off to a flying start. Then, at one of the early faculty meetings, the principal asks us to discuss the children on his "special list." The list includes those who have difficult problems of any kind and those who are thought very bright. I almost always learn something new about my bright pupils and how to work with them.

In one high school, the guidance director keeps a list of superior students and calls the teachers' attention to them. Early in the year, the teachers send him a brief report on the work of each of these students, and in May each teacher prepares a special report for the next teacher in his subject.

SYSTEMATIC OBSERVATION

The purpose of systematic observation is to make sure that you are not missing any clues to brightness. It involves knowing what information you would like to have about each pupil and then deliberately checking his performance under conditions which yield the information. The process sounds formidable, but it does not require much additional work, because the day-by-day life of the classroom is made up of activities that afford you ample ground for judgment.

If you take your class list and the list of characteristics given below, you will probably find that you already have information to help you judge how strong a child is with respect to a given trait. For example, success on tests and examinations evinces memory and ability to reason. The words a pupil uses in conversation and in his written work are an indication of the size of his vocabulary. If you have any doubts about how a pupil rates on a trait, think what activities would give him occasion to display it and make a point of watching him the next time one of these activities is under way.

You must remember that not every bright child rates well

on every trait and that even when he possesses a trait to a high degree, he may not reveal it. But almost every bright child will give you some means of discovering his abilities. If you systematically check each child on each trait, you are less likely to overlook any signs of brightness.

In taking stock of your pupils you will be tempted to think in generalities, like, "Frank has a good sense of humor." It's better to think of a typical incident. One teacher writes: "Elsie asked in all sincerity how her friend's camel's-hair coat could be red when a camel was not. Quickly Frank said, 'Perhaps the camel came from the Painted Desert,' and Johnny added in a flash, 'Perhaps he fell in the Red Sea.'" The specific anecdote of this type helps you think objectively, and makes convincing material if you have to defend your judgment.

GENERAL CHARACTERISTICS
OF BRIGHT CHILDREN

Bright children as a group are superior in physique and in emotional and social adjustment. This superiority is maintained into adulthood, as Terman has shown.[2] Granted a good start, continued superiority is logical in view of the intelligence which bright individuals can be expected to apply to keeping in good condition and to solving personal problems. One high-school teacher writes: "Brian is valedictorian of his class and captain of the football team. His nickname is 'the iron man' because he played every minute of every game last fall."

In addition to superiority in physique and in emotional and social adjustment, bright children are generally characterized by superiority in certain intellectual achievements and processes. Those most readily discernible in the classroom are discussed below.

Size of vocabulary and accurate use of words. Language ability is often said to be the best single indicator of brightness, though one must remember that children with limited backgrounds are under a handicap in learning words. Jim, a 5-year-old kindergartner (who is the source of many of our examples in this chapter), was devoted to dinosaurs and knew and used names like "brontosaurus," "stegosaurus," and "ichthyosaurus," as well as words like "fossil" and "petrified." Sibyl, Grade V, IQ 133, achieved the norm for Grade XII on a vocabulary test. A high-school sophomore, starting the study of French, worked out on his own initiative a comparative dictionary of French, Latin, and English words.

Ability to make generalizations. This rests upon seeing common elements in situations and deducing, or trying to deduce, general principles. A kindergartner, after a trip to the beach, asked, "Is the water in swimming pools salt?" A junior-high-school student deduced the rhyme scheme of the Italian sonnet from reading sonnets in *The Golden Treasury.*

Abstract thinking. In a way, all thought is abstract. Metaphorical language is more difficult to comprehend than words printed below a picture in a mail-order catalogue, though even there the word and the picture are both symbols. A visitor to a language-arts class, which was discussing semantics, told the class, "I. A. Richards says all language is metaphorical." A sophomore girl thought a moment and said, "I see. The word is not the thing."

You can check on older pupils' abilities to think abstractly by having them write a paper on a generalization which is stated in abstract words. The Declaration of Independence contains many examples, and working on them and thinking about them will benefit the whole class. Try the class on, "How the following phrase from the Declaration of Independence applies to our school: 'Governments . . . instituted among Men, deriving their just powers from the consent of the governed.' " See if they distinguish between men and teen-agers.

Insight into problems. Insight has a connotation of sympathetic understanding. The bright child is often quick to discover why another child is sorrowful or happy or bossy, and to make allowances. One day when Fred, the bad boy of Grade

III, was absent, the rest of the class began to discuss his behavior and how much they disliked him. Tommy volunteered, "I think he wants to be liked. We ought to try to be nice to him." The teacher then asked if Fred did anything that the others liked. With Tommy pointing the way, they found Fred had several good points and decided how to help him capitalize on these. Insight like Tommy's is valuable in every field—human relations, science, poetry. It helps individuals to discover the essentials of a problem and so to reach a sound solution quickly.

Reasoning. The power of seeing logical relationships and drawing correct inferences marks man as "the reasoning animal." Superior individuals have this power to a superior degree. A high-school Latin teacher made a practice of calling on inattentive Latin pupils to translate. Sally was looking dreamily out of the window, but, when called, knew the exact place and was letter perfect in her translation. The teacher, not to be outdone in reasoning, called on her again a few minutes later. The first passage was the only part of the lesson Sally had prepared. Reasoning involves forming an explanatory hypothesis and testing it out. It requires selection of pertinent facts, trial arrangement of possible cause-effect relationships, and the selection of the one which best explains the situation or problem about which you are reasoning. Any question that asks, "Why?" is a test of reasoning powers, provided the student does not already know the answer.

Problem solving. This involves reasoning and all of the other abilities so far discussed. Practically every classroom exercise requires the pupils to solve problems. Perhaps the easiest basis for comparing all pupils is success in solving mathematics problems which involve remembering and applying two or more processes. Unfortunately, some bright students, particularly in the upper grades, are relatively poor in mathematics, just as some are poorer in reading or mechanics or art. Therefore classes should be asked to tackle problems in other fields, too. An excellent practical approach is to have them write suggestions for overcoming some problem of order in the room or building, for example, crowded corridors, and then discuss their proposals.

Speed of learning; speed of completing intellectual tasks. These are the standard classroom gauges of intellectual superiority, and certainly they are among the best. Almost any class assignment serves as a means of observation. The ideal task is one which combines learning new materials and applying them; for example, learning the spelling and meaning of words and using them in sentences. But you must remember that a very brilliant mind may work very slowly. The individual may be temperamentally cautious and have the habit of checking every detail. He may be aware of so many possibilities and implications that he needs extra time to choose the answer which he thinks exactly right.

Persistence. Catharine Cox [Miles], in her book *The Early Mental Traits of Three Hundred Geniuses,* gives prominent place to the ability to persist in the face of difficulties and discouragement.[3] Paul F. Brandwein, in *The Gifted Student as Future Scientist,* calls persistence a major characteristic of successful young scientists.[4] Teachers of young children cite a child's *attention span* as an indicator of his intellectual development.

Many factors, especially that of interest, influence the length of time during which a pupil will concentrate on a task. Both the slow pupil who cannot comprehend the meaning of a chapter and the bright pupil who knows it already are easily distracted. But the bright pupil who has a reason for working can keep at work for an extraordinarily long time. Moreover, the bright youngster will continue to strive toward a goal, whether it is a stamp he wants for his collection or success in building his own TV receiver, through months of failure.

Memory. Many a bright student claims to have no memory powers. This is a regular phenomenon after an examination which a student has thought he could take in his stride and so has failed to study for. There are undoubted individual differences in memory power which are not directly in proportion to intellectual power.   But the bright student generally has little trouble memorizing materials which he knows he is going to use, and no trouble remembering those which he does use with fair frequency.   A first-grade teacher reports that his first intimation that a girl was very bright was the speed with which she memorized long passages of a play.   Testing showed an IQ of 145.   A practical clue is the relative success with which students answer factual questions about materials which they studied weeks or months previously.

Foresight.   The ability to profit from experience, including one's mistakes, and to foresee what may happen in similar circumstances shows both intelligence and common sense.   It involves memory and reasoning.   Jim's teacher reports: "His mother told me that when Jim hears that a certain young friend who is rather destructive is coming to visit, he puts his mechanical train away and takes out some of his older toys.   If anything is broken he says philosophically, 'Oh well, it was an old toy anyway.' "   A junior-high-school teacher writes: "Caleb was elected to carry the flag ahead of the school platoon in the Memorial Day parade.   The week before the parade, he checked to be sure of the weight of the flag, that it was securely fastened in case of wind, and had a waterproof cover in case of rain." You can discern foresight by noticing which pupils plan their own activities skillfully.   When the class is planning together, the pupil with foresight has good reasons for his suggestions and for his objections to others' ideas.

Humor and wit.   Superior intelligence does not endow a person with the gift of laughter, but a clever joke or pun reveals brightness.   When Jim had had his tonsils removed, his teacher went to see him and asked him how he felt.   He replied, "I feel dinosaurish.   That means I feel like a beast."   One 11-year-old thrives on a business of writing a comic dictionary.   (He sells sheets of fifty-four lines, neatly typed, for ten cents a sheet.) Here are four definitions from the first sheet.   "Abbey—a monk's hangout.   Abbot—the guy who sticks with Costello. Achilles—this guy was killed by a real heel.   Adam—this guy started something." You might profitably use an English period for word study and have your class attempt some comic definitions.

Range of interests and curiosity. The typical bright child is interested in everything. He really wants to know the answers to the multitude of questions which he asks. Jim's teacher reports: "He has all the interests of an ordinary 5-year-old—cowboys, TV, cartoons, his record player, and his friends. He's also interested in airplanes, rockets, space travel, and all-consumingly in dinosaurs. He has a collection of 'fossils' (beautiful stones which he has found) and right now is campaigning for a trip to Arizona to visit the Flaming Cliffs. Asked what he wants to be when he grows up, he replies, 'a paleontologist.' " A seventh-grade teacher writes:

Mat, age 13, IQ 126, has listed all the educational programs on TV. In class discussions, he has quoted programs on science, medicine, travel, animals, inventions, history, and gathering news. Bernard, age 12, IQ 124, has a bump of curiosity that often leads to trouble. He is so interested in what everyone else is doing that he neglects his own work. But he can turn it to good account. Someone brought in a clipping about a bear. "What kind?" asked Bernard. No one could tell him so he started out to study bears and ended up with an excellent report on black, white, brown, and grizzly bears, their traits and habitats.

Alertness and keenness of observation. The bright child is quick to notice anything that is new to him and he has an eye for detail. A seventh-grade teacher writes: "My social-studies class visited the historical museum, which is in a house built in 1760. I was amazed by the details the brightest pupils noticed and remembered: modern cement pointing in the chimney, the appliquéd pattern of a quilt, the 'mineral-red' paint on a chest." After a visit to the Museum of Natural History, Jim and his mother were looking at pictures of dinosaurs. His mother said, "That's a nice pterodactyl." With some annoyance Jim corrected her, "No, Mommy, that's a pteranodon. Don't you see how its head is shaped?" (Alertness and observation of detail

23

mark not only the bright child but also the creative adult. The classic example is that of Sir Alexander Fleming, who discovered penicillin when he noticed that mold on a laboratory dish destroyed the bacteria in a culture.)

Initiative. A bright child is quick to see when something needs to be done and to take the matter in hand. And if he does not have the knowledge he needs for action, he sets out to acquire it. One teacher put his bright pupils in charge of the room library. Without saying anything to him, they went to the school librarian to learn how to catalogue and arrange books. They set up a system for their library. Then, after the manner of good librarians everywhere, they started a reading contest to entice the other members of the class to use more books.

Many teachers post on the bulletin board interesting pictures and clippings. Some post a list, "What we would like to know," to which both pupils and teachers add from time to time. Pupils who are quick to notice a new item on the board and then voluntarily find out more about it are probably bright.

Creative ability. Progress, whether in material products and convenience or in human relations, depends on the creative power of individuals. This involves originality, the insight necessary to see where original ideas are called for, and the ability to evaluate the practical application of original ideas.[5] Those who have these powers are our true leaders.

Strangely enough, creativity seems to be more widespread in children than in adults. The world would be a better place if larger numbers of mature artists could have the unshackled imagination of a 6-year-old finger-painter and if our statesmen could be as open-minded as the 10-year-old captain of a space ship. But the youngster's freedom from ties to the accepted makes your judgment of his creativity extremely fallible. When is a child's novel approach due to ignorance and when to creative imagination? And how good, really, are his flaming pictures, off-scale tunes, free verse? Obviously you cannot judge these by adult standards. The answer lies in a comparison of both the quality and the quantity of his productions with the productions of his contemporaries. Both classwork and independent activities should encourage all pupils to creative effort along many lines.

The frequency with which a pupil volunteers or is chosen by his classmates for an activity involving creative work informs you of his interest, and this may be an indication of ability. The young artist will illustrate his reports or be chosen art editor of the school paper. The musician will volunteer to play for the class or try out for the orchestra. The dancer wants a dancing part in the class show. Musical talent may appear in young children as an unusual sense of rhythm, true pitch, and quickness in detecting another child who is singing off key. But if you are not specially qualified yourself, you will want the assistance of your special supervisors or of outside authorities in trying to identify unusual talent. The judge should himself be creative, and he should have expert knowledge of what to expect from children.

In judging creative writing, try not to be misled by the merely "cute." We see hundreds of children's compositions which are, quite properly, admired by teachers and parents but still have not the spark of genius which lights up the work of the superior child. Perhaps the metaphors which the child creates are the best basis of judgment. Are they original with him and both striking and moving; i.e., do they help you see and *feel* what he is trying to convey? In mechanics, the temptation is to think the complicated clever. It may be, in the sense of being deliberately funny, like a Goldberg contraption. But practically, mechanical genius manifests itself in evolving the simplest possible way of doing a task. One student saw a motorist whose right front bumper was hung up on a high curb. The owner of the car was trying to place a jack in position to lift the car up. The boy stepped on the left rear bumper, and his weight on the springs did the trick.

Critical judgment. The ability to answer the questions, "Is it satisfactory? Will it work?" is the hallmark of intelligence. The pupil who thinks through suggestions and foresees results demonstrates to a high degree a power for abstract thought. The same ability is involved in his judgment as to whether or not actual products, his own or a group's, are satisfactory. He has to compare them mentally with others' productions which he recalls accurately or with possible products which he imagines in detail. In every case, he has to see what is wrong or, at its best, still not perfect. Young children who can tell you what's wrong with a picture ("The dog has no tail.") probably have critical ability as well as keenness of observation. Older students can be tried out on samples from the class's papers. ("What's wrong with this paragraph?" "It has six ideas.")

Critical ability can make the owner unpopular. When you see a pupil exercising it you know that he has superior intelligence and that you have an obligation to teach him to use it tactfully and constructively.

Desire to be of service. Reports from teachers on the bright children in their classes mention again and again the way these children volunteer services. When they have finished their own work, they are eager to help slower pupils. They take over the housekeeping chores of the room—cleaning boards, picking up papers, tidying the library table. They collect bank deposits and lunch money, and keep accounts. If you keep track of the pupils who volunteer when you ask for help and who proceed to carry through the task efficiently, you'll have a good start on a list of your bright pupils.

QUALITY

Teachers' descriptions of how they have discovered previously unidentified bright pupils are likely to begin, "I was struck by . . ." Often the arresting fact is an unusual oral or written report by a quiet pupil. Sometimes an individual shows unexpected knowledge. An athlete who got into a discussion about the United Nations was able to cite the Charter and to marshal his arguments effectively. A girl, picking a book from the library shelf, was overheard quoting to herself, "There is no frigate like a book." A boy, when the custodian failed in a struggle to open a window, did the job easily by using a chair back as a fulcrum and the window pole as a lever. Another boy, as soon as he finished his social-studies assignment, always took out his math book; the teacher looked over his shoulder and found he was studying a lesson five months ahead of the class.

Alertness to the quality of anything an individual does which strikes you as unusual will help you identify the bright. Watch for skillful use of words, good sentence structure (especially in an oral report), quickness in making generalizations—in fact, for all the characteristics of a bright child. Whenever you suspect that a pupil may be brighter than you had thought, make a special effort to talk with him privately. He may warm up in response to your attention and reveal abilities which he has hidden out of shyness.

OUT-OF-SCHOOL ACTIVITIES

A pupil's out-of-school activities are a major clue to his interests and abilities. The bright child is an ardent hobbyist. He may shift hobbies as rapidly as other children and in much the same sequence, but he is likely to persist in one or two and to gain a surprisingly expert knowledge in these. Where an average child just collects, a bright child collects and classifies. He goes to the library for books written for specialists in his field, and he spends most of his allowance buying equipment. He hunts out fellow specialists of all ages. (If they rate him well, you can be extra sure of his ability.) Given a chance to talk about his hobby, he does so with excessive, but very healthy, enthusiasm.

You can find out about a pupil's hobbies by having the class fill in an "interest finder" or write a paper on the topic, "What

I most like to do." A hobby exhibit in your classroom may bring some surprise entries. But all you really need to do is to give a hobbyist a chance to convert you.

The books a pupil reads for fun give you a good idea of his ability. Does he read more books than his friends do? Compared with what others of his age are reading, are the books he chooses more intellectual? Specifically, does he read more poetry and nonfiction? Are the books he reads more difficult in vocabulary, abstractness of style, and complexity of subject matter? Children, including bright children, are often not above claiming to have read books when they only know the titles. The best and most pleasant confirmation is to find that a child likes a book which you like also, and to exchange opinions about it. Notice his vocabulary, humor, and critical judgment. When you are in the school library or the public library which the child uses, talk with the librarian about him. The librarian will probably be able to show you a list of the books the child has taken out. And, because children's librarians are friendly, sympathetic people who love their work, they are almost sure to talk with a child about books as he brings them back. A teacher says of the librarian of the public library in his town, "She has recognized by his reading habits many a quiet bright child who has been overlooked by his teachers."

A child who takes private lessons in music, art, dancing, or any other field may or may not be talented. You should certainly know which of your pupils are taking outside lessons, and you should discuss these pupils with their private teachers. Ask your pupils at the beginning of the year to list the information you need, and enter it on the permanent record.

The type of friends made by a child helps you to know what he is like. The healthy bright boy plays football with his gang, but he chooses for his particular friends those who share his intellectual interests. Often the bright child's close friends are somewhat older than he is and so able to meet him on his own intellectual level.

PRESCHOOL DEVELOPMENT

If you can find out about a child's preschool development, you may secure a good deal of information which will help you decide whether or not he is bright. Sometimes kindergarten teachers enter the pertinent facts on the permanent record. If not, you can ask the parents. Their estimates and tales of children's accomplishments often err on the rosy side, but you can make allowances. Perhaps they will have the child's baby-book and, if he is not present to be embarrassed, they may let you read it.

In general, bright children develop faster than average children physically and socially as well as mentally. Some significant landmarks are first words, first sentences, first steps, independent walking, and learning to read. Arnold Gesell's *The Child from Five to Ten* contains "profiles" from babyhood up which facilitate comparisons on these and other items.[6] Again, though rapid development indicates superiority, slow development is not a sign that a child is not superior. Remember Einstein.

We have authentic reports of very bright individuals who started walking alone at ages varying from 12 to 18 months. Jim walked "holding hands" at 10 months, and at 12 months he was walking unassisted. He could say "daddy" and "car" at 8 months, and "mommy" at 9 months. When he was 11 months old his aunt recorded 96 words which he used in conversation. This is an unusual record. The ability to say "mama" and "papa" at 12 months and to talk in sentences at 24 months indicates superiority. Twenty-five words spontaneously used at the age of 18 months make an excellent vocabulary.

We have certain knowledge of bright children who taught themselves to read by the age of 3 and reports of children who read at 2. Any child who, without being forced, learns to read before he is 5 is very bright.

Social development is hard to estimate from parents' reports. But if you have a trustworthy record, compare it with the *Vineland Social Maturity Scale*.[7] If the child's social development has proceeded at a faster pace than that indicated on the scale, he is probably superior in intelligence.

THE USE AND ABUSE OF TEST RESULTS

A great many teachers think that, if they can find a pupil's IQ on the record, all of their troubles of identification are over. And if the IQ is backed up by a couple of scores from achievement tests, they look no further.

Standardized tests, both of intelligence and of achievement, are certainly one of the main means for discovering bright pupils who have previously gone unidentified. A pupil who does well on a modern standardized test is almost surely superior. The tests are so constructed that luck and guessing play little part. Only clerical errors in scoring or recording are likely to give a pupil a higher score than he rates. (Standardized tests of musical, artistic, and mechanical ability are interesting, but authorities disagree as to how good they are as indicators of special aptitudes.)

Unfortunately the intelligence and achievement of many bright pupils are often underestimated because of some limitation in a test they have taken or because of the situation in which the test was given. In other words, the principle that high achievement indicates brightness but low achievement does not necessarily indicate dullness holds in the case of test results as it does for other criteria for judging brightness.

A typical case of the way a group test may underestimate intelligence is described by a principal. The school was to start a class for superior students. The teachers were asked to nominate pupils whom they considered bright, and these pupils were given individual Stanford-Binet tests by the school psychologist. (In general, an individual test given by a qualified psychologist is far more reliable than a group test.) But, because not enough pupils to fill the class were nominated, it was decided to give a group intelligence test to discover if any had been missed. One fourth-grade pupil, picked by his teachers as the brightest in the class, had an IQ of 162 when given the Stanford-Binet test. On the group test his IQ was only 119. This test was devised for Grades I through IV. It did not contain enough difficult material to give this gifted fourth-grader an opportunity to show what he could do.

There are many additional dangers. A pupil may omit a section of a test. He may misinterpret directions. If he has a reading disability there may be large sections of a test which he cannot comprehend. A foreign-born pupil or one from an underprivileged background is at a great disadvantage because he does not know the meaning of all the words and is not familiar with the type of problem presented. A teacher referring to a score may, out of carelessness, haste, or ignorance, confuse percentiles with IQ's, CA with MA, or grade level with CA or MA. (One result was stated as 9.2. Was this grade level, CA, or MA? Actually it was a clerical error for the 92nd percentile!)

The first safeguard against all of these mistakes is to compare test results with your own estimate of a pupil's ability. If the test score is higher than you had expected, fine. Give him the benefit of the doubt. If his test score is lower than you had expected, trust your own estimate until you are sure you, and not the test, are at fault. Examine the paper to be sure that there is no omission. Recalculate the score. Ask the pupil to read the directions to you and to explain what they mean.

Periodic testing by a variety of tests at frequent intervals guards against flukes. A pupil who always scores high is almost surely bright, and there is a good chance that the consistent low scorer is not bright, though there is always a possibility that the low scorer suffers from a reading or other disability. The extent of the testing program will depend on what a school system thinks it can afford. Some schools give Stanford-Binet tests in Grade I or II and a group intelligence test in alternate years thereafter. They test reading every year and give a full battery of achievement tests every second year. When a teacher has reason to believe that a pupil's work is above or below expectation, that pupil is given an examination by a school psychologist.

Granted proper precautions, test results can be an enormous help to you in working with a bright pupil. If they confirm your judgment (or if, after being alerted by the results, your judgment confirms them), you gain valuable confidence in making decisions which affect the pupil's work. A good test lets you compare a pupil's intelligence and achievement with national norms, so you know how he stands not only in relation to the others in your class but also in relation to his age mates elsewhere. If a fourth-grader has an IQ of, say, 125 and achievement-test scores a full grade or more above his age-grade level, you feel justified in expecting him to do really superior work. If a pupil ranks in the top quarter nationally, you will want to encourage him and his family to make long-range plans for his education. If his scores on achievement tests are uneven, you may be able to identify some special ability or some unsuspected weakness, or both. You can then build up his strength and correct his shortcomings. In brief, test results do help you find out how bright a bright pupil is.

A pupil's immediate potential is made clearer by considering both achievement-test results and mental age. Remember that, though the IQ is presumed to remain fairly constant—we will not go into the vexed question of factors that may increase or decrease it over the years—the relative mental age advances as the pupil grows older. A pupil with an IQ of 125 has a mental age 25 per cent greater than his chronological age. That is, when his chronological age is 6, his mental age is 7½, or 1 year and 6 months greater than his chronological age. When his chronological age is 10, his mental age is 12½, or 2 years and 6 months greater than his actual age. A pupil is to some extent underachieving if his scores on achievement tests are below what you would expect from one of his mental age.

TESTING BY THE CLASSROOM TEACHER

Ideally you should have the help of a school psychologist or guidance counselor in the selection, administration, scoring, and interpretation of standardized tests. But if you teach in a system which does not have a well-organized testing program, you will find it valuable to procure some tests and give them yourself. (Appendix II lists a few tests that teachers have found satisfactory and gives the names of some test publishers who issue helpful manuals on testing.) You will, of course, consult your principal. He may be able to advise you and may be able to secure test blanks and manuals from the central office. If tests are to be ordered, ask your principal to send the order on official stationery. Publishers prefer this as a means of preventing the tests from falling into unauthorized hands.

If you have not had training and experience in the use of tests, you must, of course, be doubly cautious about trusting the results. But the value of objective testing as a means of identifying the bright pupils in your class or confirming your judgment of a pupil's abilities more than warrants giving such tests at your discretion.

You can make objective-type tests yourself and sometimes substitute them for other types of examination, or use them to explore a pupil's abilities. Directions for making objective tests are included in most books on tests and measurements, for example, in *How to Improve Classroom Testing*, by Charles Watters Odell.[8] You will find making up your own tests interesting in itself and valuable in giving you insight into the merits and demerits of objective testing. Homemade tests are an easy way of securing additional information for rating pupils in your class. The pupils themselves profit from much experience in taking this type of examination. They may have to take many similar tests at crucial periods in their lives: for college entrance, for placement in the armed forces, and for employment.

Homemade tests serve merely as clues to intelligence, not

as a means of estimating an IQ. Another clue is the way children from 4 to 10 draw a man, particularly the amount of detail which they include. The drawing reflects their intelligence regardless of their artistic ability. This is the basis of the Goodenough test, described in *Measurement of Intelligence by Drawings,* by Florence L. Goodenough.[9] Her book and Beatrice Lantz's *Easel Age Scale* [10] will help you observe signs of intelligence in children's drawings, though you will hardly take time to become expert in the use of the measurements they describe.

PSYCHOLOGICAL SERVICES

The surest method of identifying bright children includes, in addition to systematic observation by the teacher, individual psychological studies of every pupil. An experienced school psychologist is the best person to estimate each child's intelligence and achievement and to explore his aptitudes and personality characteristics. His report and his advice to the teacher contain much more than an estimated IQ.

A few school systems are fortunate enough to be able to arrange for a psychological study of every child on his first entering school, in kindergarten or later, and at least one subsequent study to determine whether expected development is being made. In the interval, these systems give standardized tests, and, when anything unusual about a child is disclosed, he is referred to the psychologist. In most systems, even if a full-time psychologist is employed, the psychological services are customarily devoted to helping pupils who are in difficulty. One teacher of a combined third and fourth grade writes: "All but 2 of the 11 children sent to me as third-grade pupils were marked A in all subjects. Only one of these children has been tested by the psychologist. On the other hand, 10 of the 16 members of the low fourth grade have had Binet tests. Unless a bright child is troublesome, or his parents try to get him into first grade under the ordinary age for admission, he seldom is given an intelligence test."

Identification

Psychologists themselves welcome a change from working with slow children and those with behavior problems. And since it is only fair that bright children should have their share of all services, you may be able to secure psychological help when you wish to know how bright a pupil is and how he is developing. Your principal will know the routine of referral and what information the psychologist will expect from you. Try to give the psychologist all you can of what he wants in the way of records, anecdotes, your opinion of the child, and facts about the child's background. Complete information will help him give you an idea, not only of the child's intelligence, but also of his strengths and weaknesses and his general potential.

If your school system does not offer psychological services, you may be able to refer a bright child to a child-study clinic. The free clinics maintained by cities and states are usually more than busy with problem cases, but, like school psychologists, their staffs might welcome a change. University child-study clinics and vocational-guidance clinics regularly study bright youngsters. They usually charge a fee. You should be familiar with all the child-study clinics within easy reach of your school, what they charge, and the method of referral. Then, when you feel the need of help, your principal or the child's parents may be able to make an appointment for him.

CUMULATIVE RECORDS

If your system has good cumulative records, and if you will study these and talk them over with your pupils' previous teachers, you will have a broad, sound foundation upon which to base your judgment of brightness. And if you are familiar with the records before you first meet your class, you can save yourself and your pupils a great deal of time and many false starts.

Some teachers have a theory that they should not look at the records before they meet a class. They say they want the pupils to come to them with "a clean sheet." Ten of thirty teachers in

35

a graduate class reported that they did not read records until some incident in the classroom or some doubt about their own judgment drove them to it. The subsequent discussion disclosed that all of the teachers did consult the records within a month or two and that twenty-seven found them helpful. One of the remaining three said, "Our records give nothing but marks and attendance and aren't very useful. But in the middle of the year a student entered my class from out of town. His school sent me his record. It was very complete and I found it so helpful that I'm campaigning for a reform in our system."

A good cumulative record helps in identifying bright pupils by including: information about preschool development; results of reading-readiness tests; age of beginning reading; the results of a series of intelligence, achievement, and aptitude tests; marks; information about hobbies and out-of-school lessons; specific anecdotes of incidents that indicate ability, e.g., a pupil's being letter perfect in a long dramatic role; notes of conferences with parents about the pupil's work and about plans for future education; samples of unusual work; and teachers' opinions about work habits, character, and interests. (An occasional weeding out of the materials on the last five items is necessary to keep the record from getting too bulky.) In fact, the record should contain information about all the points that have been discussed in this chapter. If it does, you will be grateful enough to be glad to do your part in seeing that it is up to date when you pass it on.

III

Enrichment: Purposes and Plans

more guidance

My aim for the bright child is more responsibility and less supervision.
—A Teacher.

Enriching the everyday program by directed activities provides the bright child with more opportunities for personality growth, for improving leadership, and for working and sharing with others.
—A Teacher.

"Enrichment" may be defined as the substitution of beneficial learning for needless repetition or harmful idleness. The qualifying adjectives are necessary because not everything that goes under the name of enrichment is beneficial, much drill may be necessary, and not all idleness is harmful.

MAJOR FACTORS

The grade you teach, the methods you use, the amount of detail in the official curriculum, the daily and weekly schedule, the resources of your building and community, the administration's policies, the past experiences of your pupils in and out of school, and the special interests of individual pupils or groups of pupils are some of the major factors that will influence your attitude to enrichment and the means you employ to provide it. If you regularly teach by units of work or in an activity program,

37

enrichment is easily arranged because these methods entail planning by pupils, individual research, creative projects, and evaluation by pupils.   If you are a secondary-school teacher operating on a fixed schedule of short periods and if you are required to give fixed assignments in a basal text, the problem is more difficult but certainly not impossible.

A COMMON PRACTICE

The bright child in the nineteenth-century one-room rural school regularly engaged in many enrichment activities: he recited with, or at least followed, the older pupils; he helped younger children and slower age mates; he engaged in spelling bees that put a premium on his learning as many words as he could.   At Harvard, in the 1870's, Henry Adams did away with history textbooks and "put his students to work for themselves." [1] President James R. Killian, of Massachusetts Institute of Technology, has recently proposed "a complete tutorial system, in which the boys are allowed to develop under the direction of a volunteer group of faculty members, to proceed without requirements to attend classes, and [will] be expected at the end to meet the requirements for graduation." [2]   Secondary-school teachers have for generations used term essays, free choice of books for review, prepared debates, and voluntary participation in dramatics, glee clubs, and art clubs—all excellent means of challenging students to do their best and encouraging them to range both wide and far from the required course of study.

A NECESSITY

People who disapprove of acceleration and ability grouping have seized upon enrichment as a substitute for these.   As a matter of fact, enrichment is basic to all sound teaching and to every plan for providing for bright pupils. However bright pupils are grouped, they remain individuals with varying interests and aptitudes. The best special programs recognize this and are planned to help each pupil make the most of his particular capacities. This purpose is poorly served if the word "enrichment" is used, as so many educational terms have been used, to excuse haphazard planning or lack of planning, or impulsive, superficial following of will-o'-the-wisps.

Holding a bright pupil to stereotyped work which has been planned for the average and trusting him to take care of himself may induce bad intellectual habits. Typically he behaves in one or several of the following ways. He accomplishes the required work so easily that he becomes lazy. Repeating what he already knows, especially when repetition takes the form of routine drill, bores him. He begins to regard all schoolwork as drill and not worth his effort. He becomes restless and seeks excitement in aggressive misbehavior, or he withdraws into a world of daydreams. When he finds himself up against real intellectual competition or is faced with a problem which he can solve only by sustained intellectual effort, he is at a loss and quits. He drops out of high school or college because he has never learned to work. He may become emotionally maladjusted. Jack, the boy with an IQ of 185 who was so badly underrated by his teacher, is a case in point. The anecdotal account of his behavior reads: "Every morning he cried and pleaded not to be sent to school. He took ages to dress and eat. In class one day he stood up and shouted, 'What are you all sitting here for? We're not learning anything.' At home he was reading *Tom Sawyer*. In reading period in school he just sat and looked out the window. At recess he sat alone or tried to break up the others' games."

HINDRANCES

When a basal text determines the curriculum in any subject, and especially when all pupils in a class are expected to study and recite upon the same assignment each day, enrichment is relegated to special periods, homework, or snippets of time "when the regular work is finished." Our observation and our reports from teachers show that the use of basal texts is widespread at all levels, and general in high school and college. The system has the merit of ensuring coverage of the material presented in the text. It provides a logical sequence. It helps the teacher who may not be a specialist in the field. It makes budgeting and supervision easy for the administrator and gives him concrete evidence to use against critics who call his schools "progressive." But the bright pupil who already really knows the materials in the text or can learn them in a fraction of the allotted time is soon bored to complacency or desperation unless the teacher takes steps to liven up the lessons. A junior-high-school teacher reports: "The administration insists that a specific eighth-grade basic reader be used even with my top group (five students who have reading-comprehension and vocabulary ratings far above the rest of the class), but I supplement this with more-advanced and more-mature literature. I use books from my own library, because the administration has limited me in the amount of money I may spend."

Strict departmentalization tends to reduce opportunities for enrichment. Even when the existence of several sections in each subject has resulted in ability grouping and the fast section covers more ground, it is still difficult to provide enrichment activities. Periods are generally short, so there is not much time left when students have finished their regular work. Many teachers may use the same room during different periods of the day, and one who monopolizes the blackboards ("SAVE") and bulletin boards and clutters the window sill with models is not popular. The teachers are subject-matter specialists who think of a student's progress mainly in terms of their own subjects. Only rarely does one find collaboration like that which let students in a Latin II class use some of their shop period to build a model of Caesar's bridge over the Rhine and some of their Latin periods to study the terms used in the health and hygiene course.

40

Enrichment: Purposes and Plans

There are mental hazards about extensive enrichment which hold back teachers who have never tried it. "Won't it be a great deal more work? I'm already more than busy with preparation for my classes, the correction of papers, and a million odd jobs. Where can I find the books, the apparatus, the art materials that will be needed? What about discipline? How can I keep order if some youngsters are typing and others arguing over plans for a field trip? Will the rest of the class pay any attention to their own work? And what happens when they want to study something I don't know anything about?" The last possibility worried one teacher, who wrote, "I like art work and usually I have had only art activities for children to do in their free time. Now I shall use some mathematical tricks and brain teasers, if I can find some that I am able to understand. Arithmetic is not one of my strong subjects."

Experience shows that most of these fears are unwarranted. Discipline definitely improves when the pupils become interested enough in their work to want to keep at it. Visitors to classes where enrichment activities are in progress are always impressed by the *self-control* and *self-direction* the pupils show. There may be noise but there is no disorder. Securing materials, apparatus, and books soon becomes a problem in selection rather than discovery. The teacher learns with the pupils who go out of his field, and he enjoys the adventure.

Enrichment does entail a great deal of time and effort on the teacher's part if it is to be beneficial to each pupil. There must be careful consideration of general objectives and of how these are served by what each pupil does. The teacher must study the shortcomings of each pupil, his capabilities, and his interests and then plan carefully to be sure that he benefits. The pupil must be given a large part in making plans, but the teacher has to take time to confer with him and to check on his progress. All of which means work, enormously interesting and rewarding work.

GENERAL OBJECTIVES

The objectives of enrichment are to:

Challenge the full use of abilities. Progress along any line depends upon the recognition of obstacles and the determination to overcome them. Luckily the drive to advance in the face of difficulties is apparently innate in human beings. The curiosity and range of interests typical of the bright child make it easy to engage his efforts, and his attention span helps him persist in the face of difficulty. He eagerly attacks puzzles, word games, and "originals" in geometry. He welcomes every "Why?" He enjoys using what he knows, and works hard to learn what he sees may be useful. He takes great satisfaction in success for itself and also when it represents a victory either over a temporary failure of his own or over a competitor. In short, challenge stimulates learning.

Broaden the base of knowledge. A broad base of knowledge within one field is a sound foundation for memory of facts, because each fact adds associations. A breadth of knowledge covering many fields helps the bright pupil explore his aptitudes and choose the field which interests him most. He acquires a breadth of vision which keeps him from becoming the kind of specialist who knows more and more about less and less, "who can't see the wood for the trees." Leaders in professional education have for some years cautioned students against narrowness. Engineering schools now include liberal arts in the required curriculum. The Rockefeller Institute's new program for training research workers and teachers of the biological sciences is planned to give students a broad background and outlook. Each fellow's stipend of $3,500 includes $1,000 a year for travel.

Deepen understanding. One of the simplest experiments in educational psychology compares the rate of learning nonsense syllables with the rate of learning meaningful sentences. You can probably repeat verbatim the forty-three syllables in the last sentence, but you would have to spend some time in memorizing

42

a series of forty-three digits, and even longer to learn "doq, qij, zyg," and so forth. The more thorough a student's knowledge of why a thing is so—of why a word is spelled as it is, of why closing a switch starts a current—the more quickly he learns not only that fact but also related facts. And understanding makes for the quick and accurate application of knowledge in new situations. The bright student, because of his ability to think abstractly and to make generalizations, is quick to profit from understanding. The boy who enriched his work in language by making a comparative dictionary was cementing his knowledge of the contributing languages and laying the groundwork for further language study.

Increase the level of skills. Funk and Wagnalls' dictionary defines "skill" as "familiar knowledge . . . shown by dexterity in execution or performance or in its application to practical purposes." Enrichment should foster many more skills than those included in the phrase "skill subjects," meaning arithmetic and the language arts. It should give the bright pupil the chance to apply practically and at increasingly high levels the knowledge he gains from all branches of the curriculum. And it should help him cultivate skill in human relations.

Develop a love of learning. We know college teachers who have had the courage to interview some of their former students to discover how well college instruction carries over into life. Again and again the results are disappointing. One teacher of English literature found that his best majors were reading nothing more elevating than current magazines and newspapers, and mainly headlines, stock market, and sports news in the papers. A language teacher found his best majors had not read or spoken a word of the language in the years since graduation. A teacher of education visited students who had worked with him in a summer workshop in modern methods, only to find them teaching as they had been taught when they were in school fifteen or more years before. In contrast, the typical graduate keeps his interest in football. He follows professional teams. He journeys long distances at great expense to see his alma mater's team in

43

its big game.   As Frank Ashburn, headmaster of Brooks School, once said, "All we need to do is to make study an extracurricular activity."

We are not decrying the study of literature or language or education, or football, nor are we making a plea for vocational training.   We do urge teachers to evaluate results objectively. Teachers who "teach by the book," limit activities to the curriculum, give inflexible assignments, and mark largely on the basis of final examinations should find out whether they are not in fact teaching their students just to get through so much work and then drop the whole subject.

Inculcate desirable methods of learning, thinking, and sharing.   The bright pupil who is not encouraged to learn more than the curriculum requires is missing both extra knowledge that he might acquire and helpful exercise in learning, thinking, and sharing.   Moreover, because he does not have to work hard or think critically, he has no incentive to improve his method of learning or the logic of his thinking.   And, because he is not acquiring knowledge and skills which he might put to the service of slower classmates, he has less to share even if the desire to share is present.

Encourage initiative.   Initiative, like any other character trait, thrives on exercise and is blighted by disuse.   The initiative typical of the bright child is encouraged when he is given the opportunity to choose ways in which to enrich his program. The standard practice of letting him choose from a list of books for review is a minor but pertinent example.   Experience shows that, though he will sometimes prefer *Lamb's Tales* to the original Shakespeare, he is more likely to pick the hard titles.

Give play to creativity.   One of the tragic shortcomings in the development of bright boys and girls is the extent to which they lose the creativity which is typical of them as young children. Part of the reason is the pressure for conformity exerted by their parents, teachers, and, most of all, their contemporaries.   Part of the loss is due to their being forced to learn techniques of expression in a setting that inhibits expression.   Paradoxically, these children are also increasingly inhibited because they do not know the techniques which they require in order to express what they feel.   In writing, in art, in music, in mechanical invention, the child, or individual of any age, should create rather than imitate.   He must experience the pleasure of producing. But, when he wants to express himself better, he needs help with appropriate techniques and practice in their use.   Take, for illustration, what still happens to some young artists.   Parents and other children expect the young artist to reproduce what they see.   Teachers insist on correct perspective before the child is ready to learn it.   They try to teach it by making him do a pencil copy of a picture of railway tracks disappearing in the distance.   He has no chance in class to create, to express his feelings.   When, independently, he wants to reproduce the blue he sees (or feels) when working at a "green" meadow, he has no knowledge of how to mix his colors.

The teacher who can cultivate or revive creativeness is a creative artist in his own profession.

THE TEACHER'S PLANNING

Much enrichment grows almost casually out of a class discussion.   A teacher writes: "We were studying the Westward Movement.   A boy volunteered, 'My father is reading a book about Lewis and Clark by a man named De Voto.'   I suggested that he read the book and review it before the class.   His report mentioned the dances which the soldiers performed for the Indians.   A musical member of the class pounced upon that and did some research of his own.   Soon he was taking over part of the physical-education period to teach the class some of the authentic old square dances."

Alertness to suggestions of this type, whether they occur in a more or less formal class discussion or in a group planning session, will give you more ideas for enrichment than you can follow up.   The problem is not to find something to do but to select what is best to do. If you know your pupils well enough, you judge the merits of a proposal almost intuitively. Nonetheless, you ought to bear in mind some questions which may help you keep a pupil from wasting time or sacrificing more-desirable activities. Here are some of the points to be considered:

Is the activity a challenge to the pupil but within his powers? Will it satisfy any special needs he may have; for example, will it win him recognition from the group? Will it give him desirable social experience; for example, working with others if he is shy, working independently if he lacks initiative? Will it take time that might better be spent on fundamentals? Is it related to the curriculum? Is it badly out of sequence, that is, will it tempt the pupil to neglect facts and relations which are necessary for a well-rounded knowledge of a subject? Will it serve the general objectives of enrichment: challenge; breadth; depth; increase of skills; love of learning; practice in learning, thinking, and sharing; initiative; and creativity?

You will hardly subject yourself to systematic questioning on all of these points, but merely reading them through this once may increase the critical judgment which you should exercise before approving an enrichment activity. Similar considerations may lead you to suggest activities that will help overcome a weakness in subject matter or personality.

All of the knowledge that you gain in identifying your bright pupils helps you judge what they need and do not need in the way of enrichment. If you are lucky enough to teach in a system with an adequate testing program and good cumulative records, your problem is greatly simplified. For example, the record of a boy in Grade VI shows that in kindergarten, when his age was 5 years and 2 months, he scored in the 90th percentile on the Monroe Reading Aptitude Test. In Grade II, when he was aged 7 years and 7 months, he reached the fourth-grade level on the Durrell-Sullivan Reading Tests. In Grade IV, aged 9 years and 5 months, his grade levels obtained from the Iowa Every-Pupil Test of Basic Skills were 7.1 in reading and 4.7 in arithmetic. In Grade VI, aged 11 years and 7 months, he was given another form of the Iowa Every-Pupil Test. His grade level in reading was beyond the eighth-grade level and in arithmetic his level was 6.2. If this pupil were in your room, you would have to think over these scores in relation to what you knew about him from other sources. The test results certainly suggest that, though he has been keeping his arithmetic up to grade level, it would not be best to let him dash through his mathematics in order to finish a library book.

We do not mean that a bright pupil should develop uniformly in every subject. On the contrary, wise enrichment will give him opportunity to specialize in line with his particular interests and abilities. But you do have to guard against his human tendency to avoid what is difficult in favor of what is easy or overwhelmingly interesting. The pupil who knows he can spend free time as he likes rushes through his regular work as fast as he can. He may neglect to study the assignment thoroughly and may even claim to have finished when he actually has not. His hardest subjects are naturally the ones he neglects most, though they may be fundamental to his interests. The boy who hopes to be a pilot may slight arithmetic in order to work on his model plane, though mathematics is going to be more important to him than skill with tools.

It is not easy to plan enrichment that will help a bright pupil improve a relatively weak subject, especially if he is already beyond the level at which the rest of the class is working. "More of the same" bores him to rebellion. A bright boy said, "I know my tables. I haven't made any mistakes on these problems in multiplication. Why do I have to do more?" But just having him work ahead in his arithmetic book is not always sound enrichment either. If he is merely learning something that he will be required to study again tomorrow or next week, he is anticipating uselessly and just postponing boredom. Ideally you and he will agree on an activity that will interest him though he will have to learn more mathematics to carry it out.

A review of the activities which lead to learning will suggest many opportunities that you can give a student to enrich the required curriculum.   At the risk of being trite, we offer a list.

The use of the senses: vision, hearing, smell, taste, and touch.   Generations of American high-school students have read Wordsworth's lines:

> A primrose by a river's brim
> A yellow primrose was to him,
> And it was nothing more.

Ironically, to most of these students a yellow primrose is nothing more than a name.   When a pupil's ideas of scientific phenomena and geography, as well as poetry, depend largely on verbal descriptions, he needs experiences which endow words with meaning.   Good audio-visual aids, field trips, and firsthand contacts—"learning by doing"—are valuable to all pupils at all levels.

Reading is the customary means which a pupil uses to learn for himself more than his average age mates are learning.   It is, for all of us, the essential tool of independent study and research. And, as Ruth Strang says, "Reading contributes to [gifted children's] personal-social development in many ways.   It builds up self-esteem; it is a satisfying way to use leisure time; it helps them to understand themselves and others." [3]   Helping a student find the books he needs when he needs them is the core of curriculum enrichment.

Experimentation is so regularly associated with science that it is easy to forget how a pupil who deliberately tries new ways of doing things may illuminate for himself the theories and techniques of other subjects.   Word order in prose and verse, rhythm in verse and music, color combinations in art, problem solutions in geometry—the list is endless.   Whenever a student asks himself, "What would happen if . . . ?" proceeds to find out, observes closely, and compares results with past experiences or with expectations, he is learning both facts and methods.

Building (for example, apparatus, scenery, or models) is the concrete expression of abstract thought.   It serves to keep the gifted child in touch with reality and gives him exercise in manual

Reference work. Bright boys and girls quickly learn to use card catalogues and standard reference works. They have a lively curiosity and naturally turn to books to find answers to their questions. They should have ready access to the school and public libraries.

Hearing herself as others hear her. Disk or tape recordings which the pupil can play back to himself are excellent aids in the teaching of music, foreign languages, and correct English. They make the pupil aware of his mistakes. And they are fun!

Unit of work on books around the world. This corner of a classroom in the George Washington School, Cleveland, shows how pupils in Major Work Classes use painting and puppets to illustrate the costumes of the countries about which they are reading.

and technical skills which later will add wealth to his daily and professional life.

Interviewing people who are actually doing the things that heretofore he has only read about is a bridge to reality, and may be a source of inspiration and guidance.

Talking with friends, teachers, parents, and other adults adds breadth to a pupil's knowledge and gives him skill in human relations. He learns that a group is more than a sum of individuals and that a group working together has better ideas and makes fewer mistakes than even a gifted person working alone. Chauncey Brewster Tinker, Yale's great authority on the Age of Johnson, was a stickler for assignments and a daily test on each assignment, but he once told his class that the true benefit of a college education came from the hours spent on the window seat talking with one's friends. And certainly Dr. Johnson was a model.

Creation is the acme of the learning process. It gives purpose to effort and it rewards achievement. Creative writing is to reading as $E=mc^2$ is to arithmetic.

SCHEDULING

The time available for a pupil to work on an "extra" controls your plans. If snippets from the end of periods are the only free time a pupil has, you have to be sure that the books and materials he needs are ready to his hand. Occasionally you will know by tests or otherwise that one or several pupils are so well versed in the regular work that they can be excused from it for a whole period or for a sequence of periods. If you ordinarily teach small groups of pupils of like ability, you can work with these pupils on a group project and later let them continue on their own while you work with the slower groups. You may be able to schedule a period a day, or at least one a week, as an activity period. Units, projects, and "activity programs" are generally designed to promote individual contributions. When

49

these methods are adapted to secondary-school classes, as in the junior-high-school curriculum in New York City schools, one teacher may instruct one class in several subjects and so have the group for more time each day. Both the added time and the chance to integrate subject matter promote enrichment. Junior high schools have for many years scheduled activity periods or club periods once or oftener a week. "Supervised study" allows pupils to work at different levels. High schools have from time immemorial scheduled study periods which superior students have not always used to advantage, and have not really needed for preparing their regular classes. Most high schools also have faculty-supervised clubs as extracurricular activities. Once a student is thoroughly interested in work started under an enrichment program, he will spend many, perhaps too many, out-of-school hours on it. In general, scheduling may be like putting together a picture puzzle. The big pieces show up readily, but you cannot ignore the little ones, and if you work hard you come out with a harmonious whole.

A fifth-grade teacher writes:

The last chapter in our social studies book was on Mexico. The average group took a week and a half reading it orally and discussing it. The bright group read the material in two days and then used the remaining periods for independent projects: the volcanoes of Mexico (complete with maps, diagrams, and a *smoking* model of Popocatepetl); costumes, with colored paintings; the history of Mexico, in far more detail than the book gives it; festival days; and topography, with a plaster-of-Paris model. When the slow group had finished, the bright group gave oral reports to the whole class and explained the construction work. All were given a test based on the text to be sure no one had skipped anything.

BOOKS AND MATERIALS

There is no standard list of the books and materials that you will need to start and carry on an enrichment program. A fairly good room library, a magazine table, a bulletin board, a cupboard stocked with art materials, a record player and records, a science kit (minus explosives), a typewriter, and perhaps a microscope will do wonders in stimulating suggestions for projects. But once an activity is under way it will require an increasing variety of materials specifically connected with it. Some of these will be already available in other rooms in your school or from the school warehouse. In gathering equipment and materials and in planning programs for your pupils, you should, of course, have the help of the school librarian, the reading specialist, the supervisors, and, if he exists, the co-ordinator for the gifted. But you will secure most help from the bright pupils themselves. (Appendix III describes published sources of information about enrichment materials and contains references to reading lists of books adapted to various mental ages.)

PUPIL PLANNING

Curriculum Development in the Elementary Schools, a bulletin issued by the New York City schools, contains detailed descriptions of how teachers at every level from kindergarten up can give pupils experiences in planning.[4] The teacher sees many natural opportunities every day to let children decide on a course of action. In addition, planning sessions are scheduled as part of each day's program. The guide says, "As children plan with their teachers and with each other they learn to make choices, assume responsibility, exercise judgment, evaluate experiences, and respect classmates' points of view. All of these experiences contribute to the children's growth as individuals by giving them valuable experience in the democratic processes."

Good planning, by the teacher, by the individual pupil, by the class, by all together, should provide "who, what, when, and how" and, too often overlooked, an evaluating session on "how well." Regardless of enrichment, your best way to improve your teaching is to plan carefully what you are going to do day by day, and at some regular time each day to judge for yourself how well your plans have worked. The habit of objectively evaluating results serves to discipline the imagination.

Classes which have not had experience with planning may at first waste a great deal of time. Fear of such waste may keep you from giving them the chance to learn how to plan efficiently. There are several ways to overcome the hazard. One is to schedule the planning sessions—so many minutes each morning or each period, or a half period at the beginning of the week. Secondary-school teachers sometimes start a period by announcing what they hope to accomplish that day and asking for comments and suggestions. Then, at the end of the period, the simple question, "Did we do what we planned?" serves to compare objectives and achievement. Asking students at the beginning of the year to write briefly about what they hope to get out of a course gives you a basis for making plans with them and, if you keep the papers, for comparing their long-range plans with what they actually do.

A group or individual project that is to stretch over a considerable period of time should be based on written plans, set down by the pupils and checked by the teacher. These properly include a statement of purpose, a description of how the project fits into the curriculum, lists of books and materials that will be needed and where they can be procured, names of people who may be expected to help and how their help is to be solicited, what form the culmination of the project will take, when it is to be completed, and how the results are to be judged.

You will find that, as pupils grow accustomed to planning with you, giving them a large share of responsibility actually saves you time. The individuals' plans develop a momentum of their own which carries them along from day to day and week to week so that you do not have to think out each day what you should do with each pupil. The bright pupil will show great ingenuity in finding books and materials and in getting help from outside authorities. Much that he suggests and many of the things he procures will be of interest and use to the class as a whole.

The bright pupil's plans for what he will do in his spare

52

time may be based on a vivid wish rather than on probability of action. He is like the author who says, "The best short story in the world is the one I'm going to write tomorrow." If you will see that the pupil compares results with plans, you can generally afford to let him learn for himself to be more realistic. But when he proposes a project that you know is beyond his ability, or one that is sure to cause great inconvenience to the class or to the people he will ask for help, or one that seems to you unrelated to his needs, you should lead him to see your point of view. You will find the pertinent question a better instrument of guidance than the firm direction, because it helps him to apply his own critical judgment.

In working with a bright pupil on his plans, both in the making and in the execution of them, encourage him to keep a notebook of his plans, ideas, experiments, and observations. Encourage him to read Franklin's *Autobiography* and to talk with you about Franklin's system of self-improvement. A librarian may be able to suggest other diaries, commonplace books, or notebooks kept by famous people in whom the pupil might be specially interested. For example, both artists and engineers find Leonardo da Vinci's notebooks fascinating. One other suggestion: ask the bright pupil to write down the questions that he wants help in answering. If he does this, he will save you and anyone whom he consults much time and inconvenience. He will not keep running for help, he will find the answers to many of his own questions, and when he does come for help he will be quite sure of what he wants to know.

Promoting pupil planning, like enrichment as a whole, is as much an attitude as a technique. In all of your contacts with the student you do well to remember that you are trying to teach him to help himself. Your temptation will be to tell him what to do, where to go, what to read, and what he should eventually find out. You may, in effect, encourage him to look in the answer book before he works the problem. But if, in planning with him, you wait for him to suggest, you are in a position to give friendly guidance.

You should lead the pupil to consider his plans with a view

to most of the points which might be used in judging them. He profits from thinking how a project will satisfy his personal needs, both social and scholastic. If he needs to be a better mixer, he will readily see that a group project is more in order than a solitary effort, though he may prefer the latter. If he reads a great deal anyhow and is weak in mathematics, the activity should involve at least some mathematics. And he ought to plan some way of sharing with the class what he learns.

IV

Enrichment: Methods and Content

Formerly, when a bright youngster finished regular classroom work I merely gave him extra work or had him help the slower boys and girls. Sometimes I let him read. Now I have my room set up for all kinds of enrichment activities: in science and art, math, and music, as well as a larger library. And my best students are using their free time for creative writing and research.

—A Teacher.

Your role as teacher does not end when you make pupils responsible for plans and activities. You remain as responsible as ever, and you share in all they do. You help them plan constructively and you veto what is foolish, wasteful, or dangerous. You watch progress, criticize, and when necessary give specific instruction or insist on drill.

NOT DOMINANCE, NOT LAISSEZ-FAIRE, BUT GUIDANCE

Lewin, Lippitt, and White, in a classic experiment, studied the effects of autocratic, laissez-faire, and democratic leadership on boys engaged in club activities.[1] The experimenters were mainly interested in the causes of aggressively hostile behavior. But their results suggest that the students of a democratic teacher would have the best self-discipline and the best attitude toward learning. They found that autocratic methods produced either hostility or apathy. Laissez-faire, letting boys do what they wanted, resulted in their running wild. Brandwein describes an adaptation of the Lewin experiment to the teaching of bright students.[2] Two laboratories, separated by the laboratory assistants' room, were used. In one laboratory, students worked without supervision. In the other, an instructor visited the students at least once each period, required a monthly report, and was always ready to advise. The "free" group were noisy and messy and neglected their work in favor of class assignments. The supervised group did better work, kept their lab clean, and had few disciplinary problems. Experience with tutorial work at Yale and Harvard has also shown that when students are released from some (but not all) classes to work independently, independent work is neglected in favor of required work. If guidance were to be substituted for all class requirements, as Killian has proposed, the results might be different. Certainly the evidence to date favors encouragement of planning and initiative on the pupil's part but regular supervision by the teacher and insistence on a high level of performance.

ADDED SUBJECTS

One relatively sure way of broadening a pupil's knowledge is to arrange for him to have systematic instruction in an extra subject, that is, to add to his curriculum. A great many elementary schools are now giving all children some instruction in subjects not traditionally included. French, Spanish, shop, typing, and cooking are favorites. But in these, as in the regular curriculum, the bright child can learn faster and learn more than his average contemporaries. Moreover he can be expected in the long run to make more practical use of what he learns, particularly in the case of a foreign language.[3] His superior verbal ability gives him power to acquire mastery. He will probably become interested in the peoples who use the language, and will acquire a great deal of general information about one or more foreign countries. He can, if he wishes, qualify for foreign service. The United States needs more and more people gifted with tongues to represent our state department and our industries abroad. But to be of lasting advantage the language study must consist of more than learning to sing "Sur le pont d'Avignon" and writing "Noël" on Christmas cards. Several periods a week and exercise in increasingly difficult reading and speaking are necessary.

If you are an elementary-school teacher who already has a crowded schedule and if you do not know any foreign language well enough to teach it—not to mention not knowing how to type or to run a lathe or to make bouillabaisse—you may think that adding one of these subjects is a sheer impossibility. But teachers and principals have found a variety of solutions. The most usual are for teachers to exchange pupils when one can teach a subject better than the other, to excuse the bright pupil from his regular room to go to the shop or to a higher grade where the subject is taught regularly, to accept the help of a qualified parent either as a volunteer or as a paid worker, and to have peripatetic teachers or superivsors who give instruction in their specialties (just as some schools have special teachers for art, music, and remedial reading). The program has to be explained carefully to parents and pupils. If all the children in a class are given some foreign-language instruction, the other pupils readily understand having groups of gifted pupils working on a language together.

When a typewriter is available, bright students are sometimes given self-instruction manuals and allowed to spend stated periods teaching themselves. Expert teachers of typewriting may disapprove this method, and a person who still types by the hunt-and-peck system might agree. But often the bright child is destined for a straight liberal-arts course and will never learn to type unless he teaches himself. Certainly the ability to type accurately and fast is a skill which should be acquired by any bright pupil who may become a creative worker. He should,

57

too, practice composing on the typewriter. We strongly recommend that bright pupils who have not learned to type in elementary school take typing as an added subject in high school.

Added subjects are much easier to arrange and to schedule in high school than in elementary school. Generally the courses are being offered anyway. In the case of courses more advanced than those usually offered, for example, the calculus or a fourth or fifth year of a foreign language, the appropriate subject-matter specialist is probably qualified and eager to give instruction. A great many bright high-school students are able to take more courses than are required for the diploma or for college entrance. A student who can do both the regular homework and the extra work in less time than that normally allotted for study should be given the opportunity to broaden his knowledge and to qualify for college admission with advanced standing.

The choice of extra courses should be made with a view to both breadth and depth. The Educational Policies Commission, in its pamphlet *Education of the Gifted,* says that every gifted pupil should learn one foreign language to the point of reading mastery, advanced mathematics through the calculus if possible, and more history and social studies than are normally included in the curriculum. The Commission also says that the talented should devote their extra time to work in their special fields.[4]

We have reports of high-school students who seem to have profited greatly from taking extra subjects in their own curriculum (e.g., an extra foreign language in the college curriculum) or in another curriculum (e.g., accounting or typing or shop for the student in the college curriculum). Students in high schools where physics, chemistry, and advanced mathematics are not taught are being excused from school for a period or more a day to be tutored in one of these subjects by a scientist or engineer working in a local industry. Many of the industries which are suffering from a shortage of technical personnel are urging local companies to send qualified employees to the schools to teach either a period or two a day or a regular schedule for a term or two. The inconvenience is more than balanced by the necessity for meeting the future demand for scientists. The president of your local Chamber of Commerce or Manufacturers' Association will be glad to act as a liaison officer.

A student who excels in a foreign language, ancient or modern, should be encouraged to combine his third year with a fourth or a fourth with a fifth. This device is not used nearly as much as it should be. The good student who has finished two years of language in high school, or who has had a thorough grounding in it in elementary school, is equipped to tackle advanced work. The lower course serves to guard against his missing any of the fundamentals or required reading. The higher course challenges him to use his abilities to the full. Putting in two class periods a day and some extra study time on one language has something of the effect of the "concentrated courses" which proved so efficient in language teaching during the war and which are now being given in some colleges and summer schools. (In such courses, the student puts all of his time on one language for six weeks. Research has shown that he acquires and retains greater mastery than one who spreads the same number of hours of instruction and study over three or more years.) One student, who did not take Latin in his first year in high school, took Latin I as a sophomore, Latin II as a junior, and then was allowed to combine Latin III and IV in his senior year. When he went to college in the fall, he took an examination and easily qualified for advanced standing.

HOW TO STUDY

Whatever grade or subject you teach, you should consider enriching your bright pupils' programs with special work in how

59

to study. Bright pupils generally romp through elementary school, and often through high school, with so little hard work that they never experience the need for concentrated intellectual effort. Enrichment is designed to overcome this, but the extra work may be so much in line with a special interest and so well motivated that the student never generalizes his methods of attack. The bright pupil who advances faster than the average needs many study tools before his age mates do and some they never do. For example, bright pupils need to learn the alphabet early because they make early use of dictionaries and encyclopedias. One second-grade teacher says he has found that the brightest four or five pupils in his room profit from practice in using tables of contents, alphabetical indexes, and the school-library card catalogue. They begin to use encyclopedias for finding information related to specific activities.

A young creative writer needs such standard aids for the study of words as Roget's *Thesaurus,* Fowler's *Modern English Usage,* and Walker's *Rhyming Dictionary,* books which even his teachers will seldom use. The bright pupil needs to know the quickest means of locating general information and of pinpointing specific information. He needs practice in skimming and analyzing (shades of Burke's Speech!), so that he uses each type of reading with purpose and discrimination. The ability to do independent work depends on the student's knowledge of the scientific method: hypothesis, collection of data, experimentation, controls, testing, and evaluation by prediction, all essentially study techniques. You can show him how the method applies, advise with him about plans, and help him evaluate results. But independent experience is the great teacher.

A good how-to-study manual, like *Tips,* prepared by the New York State Counselors Association, will help students learn how to attack problems, teach them the most efficient ways of memorizing and note-taking, give them hints about concentration, and discuss the do's and don'ts of when, where, and how.[5] Presumably any pupil with a mental age of 11, and perhaps some with less, could profit from owning and studying *Tips.*

READING AND RESEARCH

The modern classroom resembles very closely the living room of a book-loving family. We know one family that has the *Britannica, The Century Dictionary,* and *The Catholic Encyclopedia* on the shelves nearest the dining table. A meal rarely goes by without someone hopping up to verify a fact or seek support for a point of view. We know a fifth-grade classroom that has both *The Thorndike-Century Junior Dictionary* and the big Merriam-Webster, both *The World Book* and the eleventh edition of *The Encyclopaedia Britannica.* The same room has copies of junior-high-school textbooks in mathematics, science, and history. There is a permanent collection of books for recreational reading and a shifting loan collection from the public library. A rack in one corner holds a collection of current magazines, kept up to date by a room committee. The children in this room make constant use of the books: in free time, in working on projects, and for reference during discussions.

The cardinal principle of all enrichment is, "Let's look it up."

Your selection of books for the permanent collection in your room should certainly give much weight to the needs of your brightest pupils. They will be the ones who use the books most and who will profit most from having at hand books in line with their interests and abilities. What reference books to include, and particularly what encyclopedia, may be the big problem, because of the expense. A book that is too difficult is useless, and one that is too easy may be scorned. Each room should have as wide a range of dictionaries and encyclopedias as possible. If you cannot acquire a copy of an unabridged dictionary for your own room, make arrangements to let your bright pupils use one in the library or in a higher grade. A *Webster's Collegiate Dictionary* ought to be on the reference shelf as early as Grade II. A dictionary is a basal text for a bright pupil, and he ought to have a copy of the *Collegiate* in his desk as soon as he shows he can use it. *The World Almanac* is cheap and useful, and there should be a copy of the current edition in every room. (Keep your old copies, too.) Bright pupils begin to refer to encyclopedias very early. They find one that is alphabetically arranged the most useful. A set of *The World Book* or the *Britannica Junior* is helpful in all grades. *The Columbia Encyclopedia* might be added in Grade V, and the regular *Britannica* in Grade VI. An old edition of a big encyclopedia is not to be despised, especially if you have the *Columbia* to use as a supplement. Few schools supply a big encyclopedia to separate rooms, but parents have been known to pass on an old set when they were buying a new edition. Full-sized, up-to-date atlases are a must, even in the early grades.

One warning is necessary about the bright pupil's use of reference books. He is easily tempted into reading on and on in the dictionary or encyclopedia without regard to the topic he started looking up. This is haphazard enrichment. Teach him that efficient work habits demand the location of information in the most readily available source, in the simplest pertinent form, and in the quickest time. He should not go to the library to consult an unabridged dictionary merely to find out how to spell a word given in his spelling book.

Textbooks from a wide range of grades are usually easy to secure. You do well to have books from at least the two grades above yours, and you should know how to secure even more advanced books quickly. One seventh-grade teacher reports dusting off his old college mathematics books and turning them over to a bright boy.

Bright children are omnivorous readers. The more books of all sorts you can keep in your room, the better your bright pupils will like it. A good principle is to provide classics as well as current books. Your public librarian will be delighted to help you make selections from the lists referred to in Appendix III.

When an individual pupil or a group is working on a project, you will want to help make a list of books that may be needed and of the sources from which they can be borrowed for the time they will be needed. In some cases the books will have to be borrowed in relays, those needed first, first, and so on. Try to include a few surprise volumes in each batch and watch to see if they are discovered and used. This is one way to increase the range of offerings, and it will help you judge next time how high in the range you should go.

Modern school architects regularly provide for a library room in their plans for a school. Almost as regularly, the school becomes overcrowded and the administration converts the library into a classroom. We wish that every school could have a homelike, colorful, but restful library well stocked with books and presided over by a friendly well-trained librarian. And we wish that bright children from the first grade on might be given the run of the library and be trained early in how to use the catalogue. But buildings are crowded and librarians are scarcer than teachers. One makeshift solution is to have central stacks. A great many books can be shelved in a small space like a spare cloak room or along corridor walls (fire laws permitting). If book racks on wheels are provided, all the books necessary for a project can be easily transported to the classroom. Bright pupils can serve as cataloguers and library clerks.

Public libraries regularly circulate more books to children than to adults. In one surburban town, one year's score was 30,000 to 23,000. (We shall pass over the question of why Johnny's father doesn't read.) Librarians are proud of a library's popularity with young readers and do everything they can to increase it and to make the use of the library a lasting habit. They welcome even very young readers, especially when they are bright children. The teacher in the lower grades should know at what age children are allowed to take out library cards and should help bright children secure theirs as soon as possible. Teachers in the upper grades should check to be sure that their bright pupils do have cards. Most librarians schedule a variety of services adapted to children of different ages: story-telling hours for the youngest, instruction in the use of the library for older students, special exhibitions of books in fields that may interest bright pupils, art exhibits, and hobby shows. The Los Angeles public library holds a special semimonthly library class for bright pupils.[6] If your public library publishes a bulletin, be sure to post it where your bright pupils can see it, and call their attention to anything mentioned in the bulletin that you think they might like.

If your class is taking a field trip to the library, try to let the librarian know in advance the names of your bright pupils and the special interests of each. An artful display of books might be perfect bait. And do not forget that the librarian may have identified as bright some quiet readers whom you have missed.

FIELD TRIPS

Field trips are an old and valuable feature of school life. Kindergartners explore the neighborhood of the school and drop in at the nearest fire station. High-school seniors travel to Washington in cherry-blossom time and race each other to the top of the Monument. But analysis of teachers' reports on how they use field trips to enrich bright pupils' programs shows that some classes take very few trips—one school is limited by school-board regulations to one trip a year per class—and that little or no special consideration is given to the bright pupils' part. A teacher of a third grade writes:

In the past, a yearly trip to the science museum as the culmination of our science study was the extent of our making use of community resources. This was partly due to the attitude of the rest of the faculty, but I had not made a survey of possibilities. I find my class can walk to the science museum (and the docents there are glad to have us several times a year), to the botanical garden, to the swamp in the park (it's amazingly full of life!), and to the historical-society collection. When transportation can be arranged, we go to the central public library, the airport, the nature center, the art gallery, and the old harbor fort.

Enrichment: Methods and Content

One principal tells of asking all his teachers to investigate possibilities in the way of excursions. A large number were found that no one had thought of before; for example, a pond for nature study, a small park where dinosaur footprints were preserved, a ravine which showed a series of geological formations, the commercial-art department of a big store, and the wholesale produce market. The teachers found books about state and local history and about the geology of the region that mentioned interesting places none of them had ever thought of going to see. They suggested that the state department of education ought to conduct a state-wide study along the same lines and issue a bulletin.

Bright pupils have much to contribute to planning class excursions and much to gain from them. In brief, they can suggest places to go, help make the advance arrangements, study up on background materials, write reports, and evaluate results. For example, a bright fifth-grader found in his family's library a sixty-year-old volume, *A Century of Our City*. The stilted prose would have discouraged most of his classmates, but he plowed through it. He listed what the book said about various spots near the school and suggested a project on "Then and Now." He undertook to report on the background while others tried to find out how changes had come about. The trips to the various sites were made by small committees in the afternoons after school. Another bright pupil wrote a sort of pageant to serve as a culmination. Asked how the "unit" could be evaluated, the originator said, "We'd better ask the sixth grade to our show and see what they say."

Individual differences can be served by confining some excursions to committees or to individuals who have special interests. If transportation is necessary, one or two parents can usually be found to provide it. (Before you ask a parent to take youngsters on a trip, be sure that you are not violating a school regulation. Be sure, too, that the parent who does the driving is amply covered by insurance.) Often the places to be visited are ones to which pupils can go alone after school. When you know that a pupil regularly gets around the city alone, you can suggest places he might like to visit "for the fun of it." Many bright students in high school and upper elementary grades visit museums and galleries and other places of interest on their own initiative. One high-school senior writes, "About once a month I pay a call on the beautiful people in the art museum."

HOBBIES

You can do many things to make a pupil's hobby more valuable to him. And he can share his hobby with the rest of the class as a means of general enrichment. We do not mean that you should turn a hobby into work—far from it. But anyone who is deeply interested in his hobby welcomes all the help he can get. And he delights in the recognition which comes when he explains what he is doing.

Many bright pupils have hobbies which bear directly or indirectly on subjects of the regular curriculum. A young scientist can well be allowed to work at his hobby during any part of the science period which he doesn't need for learning the day's lesson. He can probably tell you what there is in the textbook that he would like to study, what other books he would like to have in the room, and what apparatus. He may be able to bring in books and a science kit that are beyond your resources. When the class is studying a point on which he has specialized, he can give demonstrations or put on an exhibit. Similarly, many social-studies units can be livened up by the contributions of hobbyists; for example, by an exhibit of Indian arrowheads, a collection of autographs, records of period music, and puppets in period costume.

Hobby clubs, in both elementary and secondary school, have the advantage of cutting across grades and so making it possible for a fair number of enthusiasts to get together. Sometimes, as in forming quartets and chamber-music groups, this may be the only way the needed members may be found.   For all, it means a chance to share, and to give and receive criticism.

Hobby exhibits are perennially popular.   School, state, and national science fairs have monopolized public attention of late, and you will want to sponsor any pupil of yours who wishes to submit an entry.   But you and your class can have a lot of fun, and you will learn much about your pupils' interests and abilities, if you hold an occasional show in your own room.

DEVICES AND ACTIVITIES

Under the following headings we suggest as briefly as possible some types of enrichment activity.   These are in addition to, or growing out of, those already discussed (i.e., added subjects, how to study, reading and research, field trips, and hobbies).   There is obviously much overlapping.

Additional work.   Spelling, arithmetic problems, reading.   (Additional work is not considered enrichment if merely "more of the same."   It should be like that of the bright group that studied Mexican history in more detail than the rest of the class.)

Advanced work.   In own text, in texts from a higher grade, in a higher grade, on problems assigned by the teacher.   High-ability groups working faster than regular groups.   Independent work and research.

Construction work.   Maps, charts, dioramas, transparencies, costumes, puppets, models, apparatus.

Holiday   programs.   Planning,   rehearsing,   conducting.   Hanukkah as well as Christmas.

Dramatics.   Original plays, adaptations of texts, standard plays, and skits.   Culmination of units or projects, assembly programs, holiday programs.   Roles distributed (by pupils or teacher) on basis of difficulty.

Exhibitions.   Art, hobby, creative-writing.   Room, school, and adult hobby clubs.

Creative work. Writing, art, music, mechanics, dancing, devising puzzles. School and room newspapers. A weekly page in local paper. Illustrating own works. Story telling to own class or younger children. Murals.

Debates and panel discussions. English, science, social studies. In home room, in assembly, interscholastic.

Broadcasting. Soloist. Orchestra. Speaker. Actor. School or private broadcasting station.

Camping. For biology and zoology students.

Student days. Social-studies classes take over town offices.

Chores related to subjects. Cataloguing the library, serving as librarian, budgeting materials, collecting milk and bank money, clerking for eye tests in lower grades, teaching lower grade, helping slower classmates.

Demonstrations. Of science experiments, models or costumes, dances. Playing an instrument for the class.

Projects. Class, group, individual. In all subjects, including science and art. Rhythm band.

Reports. Oral to class. Written. Book reviews, research topics, term essays, original plays.

THE SKY IS THE LIMIT

When you set out to help a student learn all that is called for in the curriculum and as much more as he can absorb with profit and without overwork, you and he will think of many inviting ways to achieve your purpose. As one teacher has said, "The sky is the limit." One case shows how far enrichment can go. A bright boy seemed to his fifth-grade teacher to be dawdling a great deal. The teacher could speak French and substituted French lessons for part of his work in language arts. By junior high school, when the social-studies class was writing letters to "pen pals" in Europe, he was able to write his in French. By the end of junior year in high school he had taken all the French and Latin which his school offered. The French teacher arranged for him to go to France as an exchange student in his senior year. When he returned, he entered college with advanced standing and majored in Romance languages.

EXPLAINING ENRICHMENT TO PUPILS

Pupils readily accept an established program but may resent change. The bright pupil who has been drifting, or at least has found smooth sailing, in the regular curriculum can be upset when he finds himself being pushed into a gale of work. The average or slow pupil may ask, "Why can't I do that, too?"

Fairness is the first safeguard. Classroom duties, class positions, team captaincies, and any honor that does not absolutely require superior ability may well be rotated. The experience of co-operating with a leader is as necessary for a bright child as is experience in leadership. Similarly, as many privileges as possible should be open to all, perhaps on the basis of effort or improvement. One teacher used his bright pupils as messengers on the theory that it would not hurt them to lose class time. He had to give up the system when the class complained about the bright pupils' frequent and—perhaps unduly—prolonged absences from the room. But teachers who rotate messenger duties, or use them as rewards for cleanliness or co-operation or improvement in work, have no trouble.

Extra credit for extra work generally does more harm than good. The bright pupil gets an A without it. The slow pupil thinks it unfair. Formal assignments on different levels in the same class, unless groups based on ability meet separately, are also a source of difficulty. The bright say, "Why?" and the slow do not understand.

Class discussion and group planning are the best basis for setting up and maintaining an enrichment program. You can explain your ideas about why and how pupils might go beyond the curriculum, and give the class a chance to criticize and make suggestions. Accept their suggestions whenever you can. If you are proposing a specific project and ask, "Who would be a good person to . . . ?" the class will probably pick the most able candidate. If not, you can easily add to that committee by asking for volunteers or making suggestions of your own. When you talk over interesting individual projects and books for review and give the students free choice, the bright and gifted will probably pick the more challenging. Once the system is under way, even if it means that the bright children spend more time in the library, all the pupils will find that each does his full share of work. And if you cultivate the bright pupils' curiosity and initiative, they will not hold back. A teacher reports:

I have five bright boys in Grade VI. The group does a lot of independent work. They are far ahead of the class, taking up materials that the rest won't get. Their reports stimulate the rest of the class. It's amusing to watch members of the class try to trip up the bright ones with difficult questions. This calls for deeper thinking from them all, and provides many pleasure-full moments in my teaching.

EVALUATION OF ENRICHMENT

Ralph Tyler, a great authority on evaluation, once said, "If you know clearly what you wish to accomplish and will examine your results objectively and honestly, you can usually find some means of telling how well you have succeeded." He cited a typical objective of teachers of English literature, one which many think is promoted by enrichment, namely, "To induce a love of good literature." You can tell if you have succeeded, Tyler said, if you will find out what your students read voluntarily after completing your course. Just an examination of their library cards might be illuminating.

Good evaluation of an enrichment activity requires a joint effort by pupil and teacher. Each step in an activity should be evaluated by itself and as a means to an end. First you talk over the proposal in general terms. Is it worth doing? Really interesting? What purpose will it serve? Then you consider how best to schedule available time and to obtain needed books and materials. You agree on a tentative date for completion. At this stage it is wise to ask, "How shall we judge how well you have done?" and arrange for some concrete product, for example, a report or a demonstration. There should be periodic evaluation of progress with a view to meeting the time set for completion. When the product is finished, the pupil should rate it for himself. Is it the best he can do? Is it satisfactory?

The pupil should also make a report to the class, and they should not only discuss it but evaluate it. Theodore Hall, in his little book about Cleveland's Major Work Classes, *Gifted Children: The Cleveland Story*,[7] describes a group from Grades II–III–IV which was rating an oral report. On the board was a list of questions. Do we have: 1. Poise? 2. Worth-while facts? 3. Visual aids? 4. Distinct speech? 5. Good English? 6. Careful preparation? 7. Correct length? 8. Interesting topic? 9. Notes in outline? The class discussed the report in the light of each question, and agreed on a mark for the report as a whole. The children had learned to take criticism as constructive and to profit from it.

Your own evaluation of what a pupil is doing and of his final product should question his initiative, persistence, and originality. If in your estimation he falls short in any of these, talk it over with him. He may not improve on this project, but next time he will probably be sure he is really interested before he undertakes an activity.

You will also want to be positive that the time and effort a pupil puts into enrichment do not keep him from making regular progress in all of the subjects of the curriculum. He should certainly be expected to take all tests and examinations which the class takes. If you have doubts about his learning of the fundamentals, give him informal tests on these from time to time. The purpose of enrichment is not to replace the curriculum but to add to it.

V

Utilizing Community Resources

We have a very active lay committee on the gifted.
It has surveyed our community to find men and women
to act as "resource people" and maintains a file of
names and special interests.   When we need a person
to consult on a project, the secretary of the committee
is glad to help the pupils make arrangements.   The
committee was instrumental in securing advanced
science instruction for some of our high-school stu-
dents.   It started a scholarship fund that now helps
two bright students go to college each year.
—A Teacher.

Few schools, or even whole school systems, have available
all the people and all the materials which bright pupils need to
round out their learning experiences.   And pupils in even the
best-equipped schools profit from contacts with successful adults,
from direct observation of many phases of the life and work of
the community, and from direct participation in some of these.

THE USE OF COMMUNITY RESOURCES

A parallel exists between the use of audio-visual aids to instruction and the use of community resources in teaching the
bright and gifted.   When each teacher has to find out for himself
what films and slides are available, write for them, collect money
to pay for them, borrow a projector, arrange for darkening his

room or using another—not many visual aids are employed. But when there is a director of visual education who keeps himself and the teachers posted on materials and who attends to all details, films and other aids are a regular and popular feature of classroom work. Similarly, in school systems which have a supervisor for the education of the bright and gifted and in communities which have active committees, community resources are likely to be well known and fully utilized. Many of the ideas we shall discuss in this chapter you can follow up on your own or with the help of a service club or other community group. But you will probably do more and do it more efficiently if you have organized backing.

The Palo Alto, California, Unified School District has both a co-ordinator of work for the gifted and a teacher committee on gifted children. The District issues a booklet, *The Gifted Child*, which tells teachers where they can get help in carrying out all phases of an enrichment program. The central office maintains a file listing the names of all resource persons in Palo Alto who have shown themselves willing to assist in the school, directions for reaching these people, the limits of their availability, and the nature of any displays or exhibits they may possess.[1]

Stamford, Connecticut, has a committee on the gifted appointed by the Citizens' School League. This is a lay committee with professional consultants. It keeps a file of people in industry and the professions who are willing to serve as resource persons.

BENEFITS OF AN ORGANIZED PROGRAM

Programs like those in Palo Alto and Stamford do more than help teachers supplement instruction. They introduce bright youngsters from all sorts of backgrounds to the people in the locality who value intellectual pursuits. The boys and girls come to realize something of the rewards of learning and to see that these rewards can be both spiritual and material. They feel they have older friends to whom they can turn for advice and, if necessary, for help in securing employment. The adults have their attention focused on the promise of youth. They keep track of the bright and talented pupils whom they meet, and later enlist them in community service. The interest of the adults actually engaged in the program spreads through the community, which becomes more aware of its responsibility to the bright and gifted and more willing to provide the schools with the wherewithal to do a good job of education.

Bright children from underprivileged homes stand to gain immeasurably from a well-developed community program, and the community stands to gain by helping them because they are our least-utilized source of the brain power which we desperately need. Widened contacts with exemplary adults inspire underprivileged but bright youngsters to aim high in life. In some cases, a pupil is handicapped because he cannot afford the special lessons or the books and materials which he needs to develop his talent. But if your community has a committee whose members share the point of view that *all* bright children are important, you have a ready means of obtaining help.

STARTING A COMMITTEE

Committees on the bright and gifted have started in various ways, though the recent origin of most of them reflects the current national interest in the shortage of scientists and other professionally trained people. A local superintendent, with the approval of his board of education, may set up a committee composed of teachers or of laymen or of both. The superintendent may have been prompted to take action by his own reading, by a state-department official, by parents of bright children, or by a teacher or group of teachers. Some committees are branches of state, regional, or national committees or societies. In a few cases parents of bright children have taken the initiative and organized themselves into committees to work for better school provisions and better community contacts. These parent groups, like those of parents of the severely retarded, have secured excellent results.

If your town has no committee on the gifted, you and your colleagues who are interested in bright children may well be the means of starting one. You will know the best approach: discussion with your principal and the teachers in your own school, a motion made in a teachers-association meeting, or a friendly talk with the superintendent. You may find yourself, like one teacher with initiative, a member of local, state, regional, national, and international committees. He has had a lot of interesting work—and a lot of fun.

One of the best committees we know consists of twenty people, fourteen laymen and six teachers, appointed by the school superintendent with the full approval of the board of education. The committee spent several months studying the education of the bright, gifted, and talented. Each member read the latest books, which were then discussed in committee meetings. The committee paid a nationally known specialist to advise with them and to talk at an open meeting of teachers and parents. They asked the local supervisors of special subjects to give them information about the best means of educating children with special talents. Representatives of the committee met with similar committees in neighboring communities and served on the state committee. Three members, including one teacher, attended a national educational convention where teaching the bright and gifted was a topic. When the committee reached the point of making some tentative recommendations, they asked the superintendent and the board of education to review these. As a result of this committee's work, the following projects have been completed or are continuing:

A series of small group meetings with teachers in schools which have many children with high IQ's.

A survey to help teachers pool their experience in the best methods of teaching bright pupils.

Arrangements for teachers to visit the Hunter College Elementary School and other special classes for bright children.

Articles on the bright and gifted in the local newspapers.

A speakers' bureau to arrange for talks at meetings of all kinds of local groups.

A TV broadcast by the chairman of the committee.

A survey of the bright pupils in the system, as identified by the teachers and by psychological examinations.

An institute on the bright and gifted conducted by a state teachers college, in co-operation with the state committee.

An extension course for teachers on teaching the bright and gifted.

A central file of resource persons.

Clerical assistance from parent volunteers.

Transportation for field trips.

A special class for bright children in one elementary school. This is described as "a pilot project in ability grouping."

HELP FROM LOCAL ORGANIZATIONS

All of the service clubs and many other organizations have traditions of helping youngsters. A large number of community projects that are sponsored by community organizations are described by Robert J. Havighurst, Eugene Stivers, and Robert F. DeHaan in *A Survey of the Education of Gifted Children.*[2] Music and art predominate in the activities, but there are also projects for creative writing, dramatics, science, nature study, foreign languages, and photography. Special mention is due the Indianapolis Junior League and the Indianapolis Foundation, which have provided scholarships for teachers to study the education of gifted children.

Practically every community, no matter how small, has some clubs that can be led to help bright and talented children individually or in groups. Racial and religious groups are also often glad to help their bright young members. A small town might have a paint-and-clay club whose members give talented young artists free lessons, a French club which conducts a volunteer French class for children one afternoon a week, a poetry club which admits high-school students to membership, and a scholarship association. New Canaan, Connecticut, a town of 8,000, has an art group which exhibits young artists' pictures, a Town Players' Club which gives parts to young actors, and a Junior Audubon Society.

If you have no committee on the gifted, perhaps you could get the P.T.A. to survey the organizations in your town which might help bright children. Such a survey will be aided by the fact that a large number of organizations will be represented in the P.T.A. membership. Similarly, a teachers-association committee or just the faculty of your school will have a wide firsthand knowledge of the organized groups in the community, their major interests, and how best to approach them.

You yourself probably belong to one or more clubs which you might interest in bright boys and girls. When your turn comes to give a talk or to arrange a program, take as your topic "Teaching the Bright and Gifted." Suggest that your club appoint a committee to see what it can do to help. Do not expect immediate results. Your fellow members will certainly want to study the possibilities and they may have prior obligations. But if you have an idea which you think your club should support, tactfully remind the members of it from time to time.

Knowledge that it has helped youngsters to real achievement serves to keep an organization's interest alive. One of the reasons that children's orchestras and choirs are so generously supported is that their sponsors can attend the public performances. The adults have a feeling of personal pride in what the youngsters do. They shine with reflected glory. If you are responsible for securing an organization's help for bright youngsters, try to see that the youngsters reciprocate. The College Club likes to have a scholarship holder come to a meeting and tell his experiences. A student whose singing lessons are paid for by the Sons of Apollo should give a program at their annual banquet. When young artists exhibit their work in the public library, the sponsoring club's name should be in the biggest letters.

HELP FROM COLLEGES AND UNIVERSITIES

Colleges and universities have been very generous in promoting special activities for children. For example, the University of Kansas, through its Department of Art, conducts voluntary classes in drawing, painting, clay modeling, woodcraft, weaving, block printing, metal work, carving, puppet work, and paper craft. Some of the classes meet in the art museum and some in city schoolrooms.[3]

The Peabody Museum of Yale University has a School Service Department. Trained docents arrange visits, tell stories, and teach lessons in all phases of natural history. Bright children are given special encouragement. They draw books from the museum's library and are allowed use of the museum exhibits. We shall quote in a later chapter a seven-year-old's story inspired by a visit to the museum; a picture of the hero, the dinosaur Monoclonius, is one of our illustrations.

In Norfolk, Connecticut, a town of 1,500, the Ellen Battell Stoeckel Trust maintains the Norfolk Music School of Yale University. As part of its program, this school offers local children instruction in painting, drawing, and the modern dance. Each public-school teacher is allowed to nominate pupils for membership. Classes are held two mornings a week in August. At the end of the season an exhibition of the children's work is open to the public. An official account of one season starts with quotations from Herbert Read's *Education for Peace*: "Self-expression is self-improvement," and, "The grace we can acquire by means of music, poetry, and the plastic arts is not a superficial acquirement but the key to all knowledge and all noble behavior."

HELP FROM INDUSTRY

There seems to be every reason why industry should support projects for bright children. There is a precedent in the support which 4-H Clubs receive from companies that depend directly or indirectly on farming. National Dairy Products, Swift and Company, and the Union Bag and Paper Corporation are a few of the big corporations which help the 4-H by supplying consultants, giving materials, and sponsoring contests.

David Sarnoff, Chairman of the Radio Corporation of America, has proposed that industrial technologists be released to teach science and mathematics in high schools which have been unable to secure teachers in these fields. The American Cyanamid Corporation has an arrangement whereby bright students observe and assist in the company's laboratories. The Stamford committee on the gifted canvassed the local industries and found 125 companies willing to appoint educational representatives who would provide speakers for classrooms and arrange for students to visit the plants. The companies set up exhibits of materials and processes to be loaned to classes studying related topics. They agreed to instruct both teachers and students in the newest techniques. In several states in its territory, the Southern New England Telephone Company sends special teams into both elementary and secondary schools, and invites teachers to bring their classes to visit telephone plants. Industrial co-operation of this type brings to small schools enrichment that otherwise might be beyond their means.

You can make a start in securing help from big companies by studying the *Educators Guide to Free Films*.[4] If you find some that fit in with a project which your students have under way, write for them. Then, if your bright students want more information, they can correspond with the companies. If your town has a Chamber of Commerce or a Manufacturers' Association, talk with the secretary about inducing the local companies to follow Stamford's example.

RESOURCE PERSONS

If the parents in your community co-operate like those in the pamphlet *Fifty Teachers to a Classroom*,[5] you and your pupils have no trouble in locating people to help you when you need firsthand information. And the more ample the program of enrichment in your classroom—the larger the number of projects and the greater the depth and breadth of the knowledge that your bright pupils pursue—the more help you do need. Neither you by yourself nor the books your pupils read can give the pupils all the facts they want to know.

Moreover, when people with special knowledge come into the classroom or allow themselves to be interviewed at their offices or homes, they teach in more ways than one. Most pupils, even those from superior homes, have rather limited contacts with adults. Just meeting people of varied intellectual interests stimulates a bright pupil. He sees that there is a world of the mind and that he may win a place in it.

Almost always the pupils who are working on a project can themselves think of someone, or find out from their parents about someone, who will gladly help. But if you and your fellow teachers (and your lay committee on the gifted) systematically explore the local possibilities, you can increase both the number of consultants and the kinds of help which they may offer. One mathematics and science department in a small city has a list of eighty consultants, who among them have an amazing variety of special interests and special equipment. One suburban town has an alphabetical file that begins, "actor, actress, architect," and ends with "weaver." The possibilities are so nearly limitless and differ so from town to town that a classification of the kinds of help to be sought from resource people is perhaps more suggestive than one by occupations. There is a good deal of overlapping in the following classification, and no doubt there are many omissions. No list is a good substitute for the attitude which prompts you and your pupils to ask, "Is there anyone who could add in any way to what we can do for ourselves?"

Help with specific units and projects. Examples: a farmer for a unit on milk; a public-utility official for a unit on power; a lawyer for a debate on forms of city government.

Illustrations and exhibits to illustrate units, projects, or the regular curriculum. Examples: a tourist with color photographs; an industrialist with a collection of the tools used in the early days of his industry; a music lover with a collection of appropriate records.

Practical applications of any type of study. Examples: an accountant on the use of arithmetic or on mechanical computers; a newspaper reporter on his work; a chemist on industrial chemistry.

Supplementary instructors in a regular subject. Examples: one or more natives of France to accustom students of French to differing habits of speech (intonation, speed, accent); a writer to criticize advanced compositions; a musician to play; a painter to paint; a cartoonist to draw; a poet or actor to read poetry.

Instruction in a subject, or at a level, not available in the regular curriculum. Examples: people skilled in a foreign language, the dance, mathematics, physics.

Coaching in extracurricular activities. Examples: an actor for dramatics; an athlete in a sport; a newspaper editor for the school paper; a poet for the poetry club.

Educational guidance. Examples: college graduates on their colleges; a doctor on the kind of training doctors must have.

Vocational guidance. Examples: a lawyer to talk with an individual student or to a group on the law; an elected official to discuss politics and government service.

If a list arranged by occupations seems more practical to you than this, you can use the Yellow Pages of your telephone book as a guide to both what kind of help is available and who can give it. Do not forget, though, to add categories like collectors, hobbyists, and travelers.

You need to know who can give what kind of help, when and how often each person is willing to come to school or have students visit him, and how effective each person is with pupils at different levels of achievement. You will want this information readily available in your school, but, because excellent resource people may be drawn from a wide territory and because teachers in other districts may discover some you would not, a master file in a central office is desirable. If clerical help is available, perhaps by arrangement with a committee or with the P.T.A., the master file can be duplicated. If not, you will find it profitable to make a visit to the office and take some notes for your own use.

Experience suggests some courtesies and some precautions in making arrangements with resource persons. There should be definite agreement as to time and place, and as to how long a visit or interview is to last. If possible, the school should offer to arrange transportation for anyone coming to the school, particularly if he is bringing any considerable amount of materials with him. In the latter case he might be grateful for pupils' help in loading and unloading. People generally like an invitation written by the pupils themselves, but, when pupils have made arrangements, you should check with the adult and perhaps remind him of his appointment. Try not to impose on one person too frequently.

Not all specialists are good teachers. If one asks your advice, stress the desirability of pictures and collections—of audiovisual aids, though a layman might not understand the term. Suggest that he encourage students to ask questions, but that when they ask something which they should be able to find out for themselves he might well reply with a guiding question. When students are to interview an individual in his home or office, try to have two or three go together.   They profit from exchanging notes.   And when two youngsters are together there is practically no chance that an immoral adult will try to take advantage of them.

Few volunteers have the time and surplus energy to undertake anything like regular instruction.   For example, a volunteer should not be urged to undertake the responsibility of coaching a whole play.   When regular instruction is required, if only for a period a day or for a few weeks, some arrangement should be made to pay the individual.   If school funds are not available, the regular employer may be willing to let an individual work with the school on company time as a public service.   In several towns, citizens of a common racial background are paying the salaries of part-time elementary- and secondary-school instructors in their traditional language.

Materials and equipment for a special project are often loaned to a school by individuals and by business firms, as well as by public libraries and museums.   And sometimes the P.T.A. or another organization will give a school musical instruments, a microscope, a tape recorder, or encylopedias that have not been provided for in the regular school budget.   Your resource persons often volunteer to secure materials and equipment for you. If they do not volunteer, you probably should not beg.   But we have known a tactful, "How I wish we had . . .," to produce results.

COMMUNITY CLASSES AND CLUBS

Museums, libraries, the Scouts, church groups, community houses, hobby clubs, summer camps, local foundations, and recreation agencies, as well as private teachers, offer a large variety of out-of-school lessons and cultural activities in which bright youngsters can take part.   You should be familiar with all of the opportunities in your neighborhood so you can steer youngsters into those suited to their interests and talents.

When you know a pupil is taking out-of-school lessons or, for example, is playing in a community orchestra, try to talk with his teacher or director about the "size" of the child's talent and about ways in which you can foster it. Often you can arrange for a talented child to devote considerable school time to his specialty and to use it in contributing to school projects. The recognition which he gains in this way will help him resist the pressure to slight his talent in order to be more like the rest of the gang. You should also consider the desirability of releasing a talented young person from part of his scheduled work in school. If he can take special lessons in school hours, he will still have time for valuable after-school association with other children. New York State makes formal provision for "released-time" lessons and sets up regulations to govern them.

If some type of instruction is notably missing from your school's curriculum and is not offered by any out-of-school group, think what club in your community specializes in a related activity and might sponsor a course.

The diversity of special training that may be available is suggested by the sixty merit badges which Boy Scouts can earn. Scouts do much of their studying for a badge on their own—and this is a virtue in many out-of-school activities—but the Scoutmaster also arranges for them to have special instruction from experts. An Eagle Scout has to qualify for twenty-one badges. Explorer Scouts go even further. When an Explorer was being chosen to accompany the United States geophysical-year expedition to the antarctic, the seven final candidates all had special accomplishments which would have been useful to the expedition. For example, one was a skilled radio technician, another a geologist. These young men were only freshmen in college, but were already virtually professionals in their fields.

SUMMER CLASSES

Bright students, following the example of their teachers, should use at least part of the long summer vacation for self-improvement. Unfortunately the connotations of the word "vacation" seem to have caused most summer programs to forgo anything that smacks of books and study. Recreational and camp programs may include arts and crafts and music, though they are mainly given over to athletics. Only the library provides a rendezvous for the youngster with literary inclinations, and, between staff shortages and vacations, the library may not be able to do much more than circulate books. The eager young scientist, if he is to carry his work forward, may be driven to solitary effort.

If your community has a summer recreation program, draw the director's attention to this situation. Ask your public librarian about summer hours and whether or not the library has summer meetings for discussing books and for creative writing which you might suggest to bright students. Try to see that nature study is included in playground programs and in the programs of day camps.

CONTESTS, AWARDS, AND EXHIBITS

Fifty-six awards and prizes were distributed at the graduating exercises of one high-school class of 259 students. Scarcely a week goes by that your newspaper does not carry the announcement of an essay contest, a spelling bee, or an oratorical contest. Some of these are local, and the prize is all of $5. Some are national, and the winner may receive a college scholarship worth $2,000 a year for four years. Lenny Ross, aged 10 years, height 4 feet, 4 inches, won $100,000 on N.B.C.'s program *The Big Surprise* by answering a series of questions on the stock market. Taxes took $67,000 of his $100,000, but the New York Stock Exchange gave him a bonus of $2,500 in stock and $40 a month for five years to invest in a monthly investment plan. And the *Wall Street Journal* presented him with a free subscription.

Occasionally a very bright student wins a batch of prizes. One senior won a Freedoms Foundation Award, his school newspaper's award for excellence in journalism, a service-club award for excellence in creative writing, and the local advertising club's essay contest, and Yale gave him a full scholarship.

Winners of the Westinghouse Science Talent Search not only receive scholarships but also a great deal of honor. The National Merit Scholarships recognize the high esteem in which winners will be held and therefore award the title of winner and a token prize to students who qualify but who do not need financial assistance.

Encourage a student who wants to try for the Latin Club's prize book, the *Atlantic's* award for writing, the State Science Fair, *The $64,000 Question,* or any similar contest. Regardless of the size of the award, competing for a prize is a powerful stimulus to learning. And because the majority of the contestants must lose, prize contests afford lessons in sportsmanship. They also teach a student to rate himself against other bright youngsters. He sees that persistent effort and high standards are essential to accomplishment. The prolonged effort entailed by some competitions may help a student judge whether or not his major interest lies in the given field. If he continues to the end and, win or lose, values what he has learned, he may have proved to himself what he wants to do in life.

If you find you are being swamped by requests to stage contests and to help your pupils who enter, you have the right to insist that the contests meet certain conditions. Their subjects should be related to the curriculum. The work a student does should be of value to him as an individual and not merely as a gamble for a prize. Writing an essay on history is one thing, collecting bottle tops another. If you are to serve as a preliminary judge, i,e., to select the best essay from your class to forward to the final judges, the work involved ought to be a true substitute for work you would do anyway; for example, contest essays might be selected from term essays regularly required. You have not only the right but the obligation to refuse extra duties that would materially interfere with your teaching of your whole class. Finally, try to see that adult organizations do not exploit the winner for their own ends and to his disadvantage.

STUDENT DAY IN CITY GOVERNMENT

All over the United States, usually during American Education Week, students take over municipal governments for a day. The custom serves to teach the student officials and their contemporaries more about the management of the various departments of their city. It gives recognition to student leaders. It may provide a lasting interest in holding political office. The whole student body and many parents follow the newspaper stories of the event and may become more intelligent observers of governmental procedures. And the need to set a good example to the students may reinforce the actual officeholders' ideals of honest and efficient conduct of civil affairs.

If your community does not have such a government day, suggest that the student council take it up with the mayor. In most cities the Junior Chamber of Commerce is glad to assist.

Students in Broward County, Florida, sat in for the county school board and school officials for one day in American Education Week in 1956. In a discussion of policies, the fourteen youngsters agreed: "All the glory is being showered on football players when it rightfully should go to outstanding students." They recommended a scholarship program for honor students in each of the county's six high schools. They also endorsed an $18,500,000 bond issue for building classrooms, which was later actually approved by the voters in a regular election. They suggested the establishment of a vocational high school to attract students who now leave school before they graduate, a study of possible changes in the school curriculum, and more recreational facilities.

STUDENTS SERVE THE COMMUNITY

One of the common goals of education is to teach students to serve their fellow human beings and the state. Bright youngsters, as we have said, typically have the will to serve and an insight which lets them see where they can be of help. If their services are utilized, the students grow in sympathy and in vision. Teachers, student councils, and the boards of service organizations should be alert to ways in which students can help. More organizations should follow the example of the American Red Cross and set up a junior division.

Elementary- as well as secondary-school students can help in Community Chest campaigns, Red Cross drives, clean-up campaigns, and safety drives. Other opportunities for service are offered in selling Christmas Seals and Easter Seals, in the March of Dimes, and in a host of fund-raising campaigns. In Rochester, New York, two 11-year-old girls had the idea of spending their Saturday mornings working at the Humane Society's Shelter for Animals. Now the Society has five hundred volunteers on its rolls. In another community, sixth-graders who were members of the Junior Red Cross made a crateful of toys for distribution to children in Displaced Persons' Camps overseas.

The opportunities for community service, like the opportunities for all kinds of enrichment, are limited only by the time available for capitalizing on them. Bright students, because they can finish their regular work in less than normal time, very generally have a surplus. They should put it to good use.

VI

Special Groups

I am trying to persuade my principal to have one division of bright children who will go through junior high school together.   If this plan is impossible, I am going to try to organize a group of bright children from Grades VII and VIII to meet with me once a week for one hour.   This can easily be arranged in our departmental setup.

—A Teacher.

Teachers are inclined to think of ability grouping primarily as a matter of administrative policy.   But grouping may concern you very directly.   If your system has anything like a democratic administration, you can have a hand in determining what the policies will be.   If ability grouping is already the practice of your system, you will want to know the best methods of picking students to recommend for the special groups.   You may want to teach a special group yourself.   At least you will want to know how methods that have been found useful with special groups might help you to teach your bright pupils.   Finally, and far from least, you will have to explain to parents the provision your school makes for bright children—or why it does not make such provision.

Whatever your school does for bright children, formally or informally or as an exception to the rules, you are the person best able to advise with the principal, the parents, and the child. You will want to know about the many possibilities so that you can recommend the one which, in the light of your knowledge of the individual and of the situation, seems right to you.

THE CASE FOR SPECIAL GROUPS

Some forms of special grouping are almost universally used at one grade level or another, and always have been. Regulations governing age of entrance to kindergarten really reflect ability grouping on the basis of probable social maturity, for example, the ability to get along away from mother and to button up. Six years was set as the age of entrance to first grade because of studies that showed the average child was able to learn to read then. Reading groups based on ability are common practice in primary grades. Retardation of a slow learner is ability grouping. The college course in high school is almost always restricted to students whose grades average something more than passing. Those who qualify for college are a select group, and advanced degrees have traditionally been restricted to very superior students. Adults normally flock with those of similar ability and interests, like birds of a feather.

No two students have identical abilities in all subjects, but the more alike the members of a group are in ability and interests, the more efficiently it functions. Whenever the range of knowledge in a specific subject is so great that the pupils cannot work together, the teacher has to spread himself very thin. There is not only the question of the time which must be spent with individuals while the others fend for themselves, but there is also all the labor of making separate plans and of providing varied materials.

Every teacher who has taught classes of bright children is enthusiastic about the relative ease of discipline. Visitors to Cleveland's Major Work Classes are always struck by the orderly, purposeful behavior of the children. Dorothy Norris, supervisor of the classes, says that the pupil who acts as group leader is responsible for discipline, which she defines as "seeing that the ordinary rules of courtesy are observed." [1] The principal of a consolidated high school reports, "Our teachers have concluded

they would rather handle larger groups in the top group than in
the others, because of attention span, desire to co-operate and
learn, easier motivation, independent work level, and more pleasant relationships." And teachers who continue to teach regular
grades after a reorganization of classes according to ability, report that their discipline problems have diminished. "Now,"
writes one teacher, "it's much easier to keep all my students
interested and busy." George V. Sheviakov and Fritz Redl, in
Discipline, say, "The mere mixture of . . . too heterogeneous
elements . . . may in itself constitute a constant producer of
discipline problem behavior without anything else being wrong." [2]

Bright students who work together stimulate each other to
greater intellectual activity than is ordinarily found in a regular
class. They give and take criticism, exchange ideas, and share
research in a way that is hardly possible between pupils of unlike
abilities. And, because all are able to do a great deal of work
and are expected to do it, there is no feeling of discrimination.
A bright elementary-school group can be taught French without
any pupils' being left out. And, incidentally, when a whole
group is capable of profiting from an extra subject or from some
alteration in the standard curriculum, scheduling is infinitely
more convenient.

Periodic surveys have been made of the graduates of Cleveland's Major Work Classes. Walter B. Barbe reports the results
of one survey: the majority of the respondents approved of the
program with enthusiasm, some approved with reservations, and
only 7.9 per cent disapproved. Suggestions for improvement included better-trained teachers, more mixing with other pupils,
more acceleration, more vocational guidance, and more work in
shop and commercial subjects. The men listed the features they
liked best in the following order: opportunity to express individuality, differences from regular curriculum, freedom from regi-
mentation, stimulation and challenge, classmates, foreign language, student-teacher relationships, and small classes. The
women mentioned all of these but listed foreign language at the

top and "individuality" third. Sixty-one per cent of the men and 74 per cent of the women reported that they thought the special classes had helped them make a good adjustment.[3]

OBJECTIONS AND SAFEGUARDS

Critics of ability grouping have several objections to it. These are all worth considering, and the dangers cited should certainly be guarded against in every way possible. Many teachers hesitate to nominate pupils for special classes for fear of making mistakes by passing over some who are qualified. They also fear they might assign some who are not qualified to a fast class, where they would be fish out of water. The methods of identification described in Chapter II will, if systematically used, minimize the chance for mistakes. In addition, it is wise for the teachers of special classes to be alert to recognize any pupil who is having difficulty and, if necessary, to transfer him to another class. A good system, in use in several schools, is to have a formal "reshuffle" at the end of the first six weeks. Teachers of all sections discuss the pupils they think might profit from a transfer. There are enough changes in both directions to keep the pupils from feeling singled out. Baltimore's Robert E. Lee Junior High School draws bright students from all over the city. It also has several sections of average students. A student who finds a special class too difficult has his choice of remaining in Lee or returning to his old school.

Conceit is said by some to be a likely result of ability grouping. Experience indicates that the opposite is nearer the truth. The bright pupils in a regular class very soon find that they are superior to the other children. They pride themselves on A's that they do not have to work for. In a class with their intellectual peers they are subject to competition and criticism from equals. They learn that they have to work for praise and that they can work hard and do no better than someone else. They learn how much there is to learn and, instead of having a know-it-all attitude, they, like Socrates, realize that they know nothing.

Today, most special groups are scheduled to share some classes and activities with other students. The bright pupil who takes shop or typing or plays basketball with youngsters who may be as good or better than he is in these activities is protected from conceit. A program of this sort also answers the objection that special grouping has a flavor of aristocracy, that it is undemocratic.

Some administrators object to special classes because they fear these would entail extra expense. Actually the expense need be no greater than that for regular classes. The classes for bright pupils can be as large as the regular classes. Some extra equipment is desirable, but not essential. The fast groups in high school really need nothing that is not regularly available in the school laboratories and library.

THE BASES OF GROUPING

The selection of pupils for high-ability groups should involve all the techniques of identification. Nomination by the classroom teacher is of prime importance. You are the one who knows best whether the pupil has both the ability and the willingness to work which a special class requires. Only if you fear that you are prejudiced against ability grouping or against a particular pupil should you minimize your role in selection. The pupil's school record is important because it reflects the judgment of successive teachers as to ability and attitude to school. When special classes are organized for individual subjects or when a whole program is planned for students with a particular talent, high interest is essential. In older students this interest might well be vocational in nature. At least, the area of specialization should be related to the student's present vocational plans, though it should not make a change impossible. Standardized tests of both intelligence and achievement, and, if possible, individual psychological examinations, should be given to all pupils.

It is unwise to set an arbitrary lower limit unless there are so many candidates whose IQ's and achievement scores are above this limit that final selection can be made on other grounds. When there are a great many candidates, competitive examinations help in selection. These are used in the selection of students for New York City's specialized high schools. They are widely used in Europe to select students for college, and in this country for appointment to Annapolis and the other Service academies.

A conference of a pupil's teachers, past and present, together with the teacher of the special group and the responsible administrator is advisable. It guards against mistakes, protects the classroom teacher from criticism, and enlists his future co-operation. It helps the special-group teacher to understand the pupil and to start him well.

The wishes of the pupil himself and his parents should always be consulted. In secondary schools this may just be a routine matter of election of the college course with the advice and approval of the home-room teacher and the guidance counselor. If it is more than this, if it involves an honors group or independent study or unusual concentration in one field, both the home-room teacher and the special-class teacher should talk with the student and be sure he understands the amount of independent work he will have to do and the extent to which he will be responsible. If the student objects to associating with "brains" or "eggheads" but is obviously of high caliber, an effort may well be made to help him change his point of view. Have him talk with students already in the class or with those who expect to enter; they may help him make up his mind. The final decision should be approved by the parent.

In elementary schools, especially when joining a special group means transfer to another school, the parent should be seen personally by the teacher in charge of the special class or by the supervisor of special classes, if there is one. A visit to the class is recommended for both parent and pupil. The parent's questions should be answered as fully as possible (except that it is unwise to discuss the exact IQ's of the candidate or of the other children), and the decision should not be rushed. The parent may wish to know the names of other families in the neighborhood who have or have had children in the class.

SOME ESTABLISHED ELEMENTARY-SCHOOL PROGRAMS

We have found it difficult to make a choice of three or four outstanding examples of special classes to describe, not because of a lack of such classes but because there are so many. And the number in the top rank grows with each semester.

Cleveland's Major Work Classes have been in existence for more than thirty-five years. They are under the direction of a special supervisor. Surveys of "graduates" and close co-operation of the teachers with each other and with the parents of their pupils lead to constant improvement of the program. The classes are located in regular elementary schools chosen for convenience of situation. Each class draws from several grades; for example, children from Grades II, III, and IV may be in the same room. There are about a thousand elementary-school pupils in the program. (Because the secondary schools have other opportunities for meeting individual needs, there are only about 250 junior-high-school pupils in Major Work Classes and the same number from senior high school.) Selection for the classes is based on appraisal by the regular class teacher with the help of the supervisor, and with special reference to good adjustment, high achievement, and physical fitness. Information about preschool development is obtained in a conference with parents. A minimum IQ of 125 on an individual Stanford-Binet test is required. The city-wide group-intelligence-test program serves as a screening device. Parents of successful candidates are interviewed by the supervisor to be sure the purpose of the program is understood. Parents are responsible for transporting the child to and from school.

Each special class is an integral part of the school in which it is located. The pupils participate in all school activities, share instruction by specialists, and have the same report cards. The curriculum is enriched in art, music, and foreign language and by field trips. Classroom methods emphasize discussion and research. Units of work are used.

The Cleveland program has been described in many magazine articles; for example, "Tailor-Made for High IQs," by Norris.[4] Two books about it are Merle R. Sumption's *Three Hundred Gifted Children*[5] and Hall's *Gifted Children: The Cleveland Story*. Hall's book charmingly describes actual classes, and contains a valuable "Guide for Developing Classes for Gifted Children" by Norris.[6]

The Colfax School, Pittsburgh, Pennsylvania, is an elementary school, with a kindergarten and Grades I-VI. The principal, Hedwig O. Pregler, has recounted the growing pains of "The Colfax Plan."[7] At first, children in Grades V and VI who had achievement-test scores two years above grade level were brought together for two hours a week to work on a special project under a special teacher. This produced conflicts of interest, and some of the pupils tried to avoid work by playing one class against the other. Some of the pupils who had high achievement but not necessarily high IQ's found the double responsibility too hard. Scheduling was difficult. The next year all the pupils in Grades IV–VI were scheduled for a two-hour program, the regular pupils in clubs and the bright pupils in an enrichment class. The bright pupils rebelled. They preferred the clubs. In the meantime, the librarian had been offering special guidance to the bright group, and that had been very successful. This suggested the organization of bright pupils (this time chosen on the basis of both achievement and IQ) into an academic workshop. There are now three workshops (Grades I and II, III and IV, V and VI), which meet at the same time scheduled for academic work for all classes. This amounts to half a day. The other half day is spent in a regular home room for art, music, and physical education. Each workshop contains as many pupils as a regular class, so the program has not required an extra teacher. The workshops use the Pittsburgh course of study. This was carefully devised to provide for individual differences. It suggests many enrichment activities. In addition, the workshop pupils take Spanish and typing. The workshop teachers emphasize both individual and group projects and the laboratory, or experimental, approach. Even first-graders, Pregler says, are fascinated by experiments to prove a truth or try out a hypothesis "to see what it will do." Each child must learn to think quickly, analytically, logically, critically, and reflectively. He must know how to find facts and to express results clearly. Pregler says, "Thus the Colfax plan through its workshop provides mentally superior children with three essential experiences: group activities both with their social and mental peers; individual activities through projects; and drill in the mental skills."

The University City, Missouri, public schools include eight elementary schools. Special enrichment classes for gifted pupils meet for forty to fifty minutes twice a week in each school. The maximum number in a class is ten. Most of the classes are confined to pupils of a single grade level. The pupils are chosen on the basis of classwork, school marks, and over-all performance as shown by the permanent record. Most of them have IQ's of 140 and above. A special "enrichment-class teacher" conducts the classes. In general, each class works on a project not included in the regular curriculum. The classes are provided as an integral part of the regular program, like speech classes or band instruction. No special publicity is given to them. The success of the program is described in an article by James M. Dunlap, "Gifted Children in an Enriched Program." [8] In three years the program grew from 50 to 275 pupils. Only 25 pupils have failed to adjust satisfactorily to the program. Of 23 "graduates" in junior high school, 14 made the honor roll. This is three and one-half times the number of honor-roll students from a matched control group.

Reading about what others are doing and, even better, visiting a class of bright children help you select the best methods of teaching your bright pupils. Stimulating accounts of other special groups for bright children are available in Gertrude

97

Hildreth's *Educating Gifted Children at Hunter College Elementary School*,[9] Havighurst, Stivers, and DeHaan's *A Survey of the Education of Gifted Children*,[10] Helen Roberts' *Current Trends in the Education of the Gifted*,[11] and many articles in educational magazines.

When a special group must contain as many pupils as a regular class, there is no reason why the required number cannot be made up from children at two or three grade levels, as in Cleveland and in the Colfax School. Sharing nonacademic activities with other pupils lets each age group have a wide range of ordinary associations with their age mates. Flexible requirements for admission to the special group facilitate enrolling the desired number of pupils.

Sometimes a small special group can be scheduled for a single subject, like French. Clubs that cut across classes can be organized on the basis of ability as well as interest. There has been some experimentation with a special teacher for gifted children who, like a remedial-reading teacher, works with individuals an hour or two a week. The work may be on a project, or the special teacher may act as a guidance counselor. A successful experiment with the counseling plan in Bedford, Ohio, is described by Paul H. Holcomb; the Bedford program enrolled sixty children from Grades I–XII, and though the program was voluntary, only one pupil withdrew.[12]

SECONDARY-SCHOOL PROGRAMS

New York City has a number of specialized high schools, including two for science, one for music and art, one for the performing arts, and one for science and technology. In each of these, the course of study is planned for pupils who intend to go to college. It requires the usual college-entrance courses in English, social studies, and foreign language, but provides an opportunity to major in mathematics and science (or art or music) and to do honors work in these subjects. The provisions for general education permit a student to change his mind about his specialty. One graduate of Stuyvesant High School, which offers specialized training in mathematics and science, majored in French at Yale and entered law school. He was a member of Phi Beta Kappa. J. Wayne Wrightstone, in an article, "The Career High School," describes New York City's specialized schools and its terminal vocational schools. He points out that the combination of common interest and a common purpose motivates the students in each of these schools.[13]

Many high schools, including some in small cities and in rural districts, now have honors or seminar classes in addition to the college-preparatory curriculum. These classes are open to limited numbers of students who have done unusually good work and have shown a deep interest in a subject. James Hobson, psychologist of the Brookline, Massachusetts, schools, says that their high school offers a course in creative writing to thirty juniors and thirty seniors in four classes of fifteen each, taught by Mr. Francis W. Newsom, the author of *Writer's Technique.* The students have won prize after prize in national contests and been able to obtain advanced standing in college English. Brandwein, in *The Gifted Student as Future Scientist*, describes the science program in Forest Hills High School, a general four-year high school in a suburban community of greater New York City. Forest Hills students have had notable success in the Westinghouse National Science Talent Search.[14]

High-school teachers often help individual students and clubs do volunteer work of a high caliber in their special subjects. One English teacher, appointed official censor of a school magazine, was soon helping the editors improve their writing. A teacher of botany invited two outstanding students to share his walks in search of specimens and then taught them how to identify and classify what they had found. An art teacher sponsored a student's admission to the local paint-and-clay-club life classes and regularly helped him with his technique. A chemistry teacher, who was official sponsor of the photography club, added extra meetings for those who wished to study the chemistry of making and developing films. Efforts like these involve overtime work, but, like all close association with bright pupils, they add zest to life.

THE TEACHER OF SPECIAL GROUPS

The choice of the best teacher for a class of bright children is a problem for both teachers and administrators. Choices based on seniority or convenience may or may not work out. Several schools which have had long experience with ability grouping have published their conclusions. This section amalgamates our own observations with what Norris, Pregler, and Brandwein have said.

The teacher must have the standard attributes of good teachers everywhere. He must like youngsters of the age he is to teach. He must have great vitality, which generally means good health. A sense of humor is a priceless asset. He must be a well-adjusted person, able to accept his own feelings without undue worry and the children's feelings without undue antagonism.

The teacher of a special class should be eager to teach the class, not as a matter of prestige, but because he believes that ability grouping of the type which his school uses offers the best means of serving the pupils and through them the community. But he must not have false ideas of the superiority of the bright and gifted. Rather he has to like them for the same reasons he likes other children. He has to have a mind open to new methods, and he must be willing to experiment and to improvise in order to satisfy individual differences and needs. He must recognize that an individualized program requires more work, if perhaps less strain, than teaching a basal text. He must believe in democratic methods in the classroom, and particularly in pupils' sharing responsibility for planning. He should habitually speak and write excellent English. He should have a broad cultural background. He must be willing to learn with his pupils, but if he is teaching a special subject he must be a specialist in it and have great enthusiasm for it.

Our notes on one successful teacher of a gifted group read: "She is the supreme example of a good teacher—friendly, open-minded, interested in each individual and constantly seeking clues to each one's problems of learning and adjustment. She sets the stage for progress in line with ability and is critical of less than full achievement but ever ready to encourage effort and progress. She is alert to extend help in crises, but patient in leaving alone. She is of herself a good example."

VII

Acceleration

*Acceleration I never did favor too strongly . . .
mostly because it took the child away from his age
group, which I felt might upset his social adjustment.
Now I have a better understanding of the factors involved and see the advantages that can be derived if
proper enrichment is provided also.*
                                                    —A Teacher.

The great majority of school systems in the United States
set a minimum age for entrance to first grade.   The minimum
varies within narrow limits.   A few systems say that the child
must be 6 years old as of September 1 of the year he enters.
Others admit children to first grade if they are 5 years and 6
months old on September 1.   Where there are one-year kinder-
gartens, the age for entrance to kindergarten is set as one year
younger than that for Grade I.

When a barrier date, let's say age 6 on or before December
31 of the year of admission, is firmly held, a child born on December 31 will always be admitted and one born on January 1 always refused.   The former, if he progresses through school at the
normal rate, will graduate from high school when he is 17 years
and 6 months old and from college when he is 21 years and 6
months old.   The child born a day later will be 18 years and 6
months and 22 years and 6 months respectively.   The average
age for graduation from high school would thus be 18 years and
from college 22 years.   Studies have shown that the average
graduation ages tend to be slightly higher.   The class of Yale
1956 averaged 22 years and 10 months in June, 1956.

Acceleration

Acceleration is defined as any procedure which enables a student to complete his education a year or more earlier than the norm for his age. The common procedures are early admission to kindergarten, skipping a grade, "rapid progress," e.g., doing three years' work in two, early admission to college (by skipping one or two years of high school), and college admission with advanced standing.

THE CASE FOR ACCELERATION

"The major problem in my future," writes a bright eighth-grader, "is TIME. H.S.: 4 yrs. College: 4 yrs. Medical School: 4 yrs. Interne: 3 yrs. Getting myself set up: 3 yrs. Earning myself a reputation: 2 yrs. By the time I am a full-fledged doctor I will be an old man."

Add two years in the Army to the above schedule, and perhaps a year or two to the estimate for earning a reputation, and you realize that youngsters looking forward to professional careers are bound to the wheel of time. And when you consider the superior creativeness of the years before 35, you realize that, if education can be speeded up, both the individual and society have much to gain. But many teachers and administrators oppose any acceleration because they feel that pupils a year or more younger than the majority of their classmates are at a disadvantage socially. This opposition is often based on personal experience. A good many of today's teachers were accelerated when they were in school because they early showed the ability and intellectual interest which eventually led them to choose teaching as a career. Any of these who felt at all out of things in college, either because they really were immature or because of any other reason, are inclined to lay the blame on their having been "too young." Of course, no one who has been accelerated can tell what might have happened or how he would have felt if he had not been. It is worthy of remark that acceleration is one of the changes suggested by graduates of Cleveland's Major Work Classes, in which acceleration is not practiced.

Terman devotes a whole chapter of *The Gifted Child Grows Up* to "The Problem of School Acceleration." He compares his subjects who graduated from high school before the age of 16 years and 6 months (i.e., accelerated by at least a full year) with those 16 years and 6 months or older at graduation. Though many of the subjects thought acceleration had disadvantages, the actual achievements of those who had been accelerated surpassed the achievements of those who had not been accelerated. More of the young than of the older subjects graduated from college, the young group had higher average grades, more of them took honors, and more entered graduate school. As a group, the younger subjects have had greater vocational success, and they have adjusted to adult life at least as well emotionally and socially as the older group. Terman concludes that, whatever the disadvantages of acceleration may be, they are usually temporary and would be even fewer if more bright young people advanced more rapidly through school.[1]

Several other research studies confirm Terman's conclusions, notably one by Noel Keys, "The Underage Student in High School and College," [2] and one by Sidney L. Pressey, *Educational Acceleration: Appraisal and Basic Problems*.[3] We have tabulated the ages of the members of Phi Beta Kappa in the class of 1956 at Yale. The median age of the forty members was 21 years and 8 months at graduation, or more than a year less than the average age of the class. The oldest student elected to Phi Beta Kappa was 22 years and 4 months at graduation, the youngest, 19 years and 11 months. Yale seniors regard election to Phi Beta Kappa as a top college honor. These students had a goodly share of nonacademic honors as well.

The adjustment which an accelerated pupil makes in school and college depends on his ability, physique, and personality, upon the amount by which he is accelerated, and upon when and how he is accelerated. The last factor, the type of acceleration, to some extent controls time and amount.

EARLY ADMISSION
TO KINDERGARTEN OR FIRST GRADE

A school superintendent tells of answering the telephone one September evening. A mother was on the wire. She understood that the age for admission to kindergarten was set as "5 years old on or before October 31." A child who had been born on November 1 was not eligible. Was this correct? The superintendent said yes, that some definite date had to be fixed and that, looking forward to first grade and beyond, the child would benefit by waiting a year. "But," said the mother, "he was born at 12.02 A.M." "Sorry," said the superintendent, "but we've found if we make one exception we must make twenty." "Oh well," the mother concluded, "I kept telling that doctor to hurry up."

An experiment with early admission to first grade was begun in 1922 in the New Haven, Connecticut, public schools. At one time, New Haven had admitted children to first grade in September if they had reached their fifth birthday. Principals and teachers had felt that the majority of these children were not able to do first-grade work, and the age for admission to first grade was raised to 5 years and 8 months as of the date of opening of school in September. Children continued to be admitted to the kindergarten at the age of 4 but stayed in kindergarten two years until they reached the required age for first grade. A number of these children seemed ready for first grade. In October, 1922, eight were recommended for study by the school psychologist. They had been 5 years and 6 or 7 months old when school opened. Their mental ages ranged from 7 years and 2 months down to 5 years and 8 months, the IQ's from 128 down to 101. All were assigned to first grade. All completed the work satisfactorily and continued to be among the best pupils in their class in Grades II and III. The plan grew rapidly until a hundred and more children were tested each year and about half admitted to Grade I. When a child was not admitted, because of a mental age below 5 years and 8 months or marked signs of immaturity, instability, lack of motor co-ordination, or poor health, the parents were interviewed. The parents proved co-operative. The bright children admitted early to first grade were followed closely through the grades and through high school. The great majority ranked high in their classes and showed superior adjustment in every way.

A large number of other studies show the wisdom of early admission of exceptional children to kindergarten or Grade I when proper precautions have been taken to be sure that the child is mentally and socially as mature as most of his classmates. The evidence is summarized by D. A. Worcester in his book *The Education of Children of Above-Average Mentality.* He concludes that bright students as much as 8 months younger than the regular age for admission to kindergarten did in every way as well as or better than their age mates who started a year later. Those admitted early, he says, "gained a year of school life without loss of social adjustment." [4]

Hobson has for many years been following children admitted to kindergarten in Brookline when they were as much as 9 months younger than the regular age (4 years and 9 months on October 1) but had mental ages of 5 or more and were correspondingly mature in other ways. He has written us that ten classes with these younger pupils have now graduated from high school (1946–1955) and that the younger pupils "have continued to exceed the other pupils scholastically . . . and to almost as great an extent in activity participation."

Some administrators have had difficulty over early admission by special test because of parental misunderstanding. Misunderstanding can be avoided if the purpose of the program and the requirements for early admission are carefully explained to the parents before a child is tested. The results of the test should also be discussed with the parents. Jack W. Birch, director of special education in the Pittsburgh public schools, reports that in the three years 1951–1953 the Pittsburgh schools accepted forty-three children for early admission to first grade. The examining psychologists recommended against early admission in about 400 other cases, but, because the parents had been warned that the chances were against acceptance and because the psychologists discussed the implications of the test results with each child's parents, there were few difficulties.[5]

When a kindergarten teacher notices a child who seems unusually bright and mature, a transfer to Grade I should be considered. If no psychologist is available, the first-grade teacher might give the child a reading-readiness test. If his score is one that, according to the manual, indicates that he is ready to read, he should be considered for Grade I. A kindergarten child who can already read should certainly be a candidate for transfer. Sometimes the ability to read escapes the kindergarten teacher's notice. One teacher of a two-year kindergarten recommended that a girl who was finishing the first year be admitted to Grade I the following fall. The psychologist who studied the child discovered she could already read "almost anything." The kindergarten teacher had noticed that the child sometimes seemed to know a word, but had not tried her out with actual reading.

UNGRADED PRIMARY GROUPS

One good way to solve the problems of early admission is to avoid formal classification by grades in the first years of school. Under this system, grouping remains flexible. A child soon after admission may work and play with children who are chronologically older than he is. If the teachers' observations and whatever test results are available suggest that he is ready to read, he can join the other beginners. Sooner or later he moves on with the group in which he fits best on the basis of physical and social development and school achievement.

107

Acceleration

Ungraded groups may be planned to span two or more years. The first two years may be thought of as kindergarten and reading readiness, or as reading readiness and beginning reading. In systems which cannot afford a kindergarten and have set the age for admission at about 5 years and 6 months, the primary group will contain some children who are being readied for reading and some who have been reading for a year or more. The bright child may, in any case, spend one year instead of two (or two instead of three) in the primary group. But when he is "promoted" he goes on to the new grade with children whom he already knows. He and his teachers feel confident of his ability to hold his own.

COMBINATION GRADES

Economy or lack of space may force the assignment to one room of children from two different grades. A frequent practice has been to put, say, the brightest fifteen children from Grade III with the slowest fifteen from Grade IV. We suggest that a better combination may result when the brightest from both grades are placed together. Because the brightest are likely to be also the youngest, and the slowest the oldest, putting the bright together tends to reduce the age spread. Moreover, bright children of different ages work better together than do bright and slow children, regardless of age. Cleveland's Major Work Classes combine bright children from three grades as a matter of policy, and teachers in other school systems have found similar combinations easy to teach.

When a combination grade is necessary, the teacher can adjust his intraclass groups on the basis of ability and achievement rather than technical grade level. When a pupil from the lower grade fits well with those from the upper grade, he may, when the combination is broken up, be promoted with them. The pupil gains a year but, as in the case of primary grouping, he goes ahead with children whom he already knows.

Acceleration

SKIPPING

"Skipping" is the traditional means of acceleration. As one principal writes, "To us acceleration means skipping." It is widely practiced. A 1955 survey of 24 California cities shows that 11 may skip a pupil in elementary school, 7 in junior high school, and 5 in senior high school.[6]

The advantages and the dangers of skipping are clear-cut. The bright pupil who jumps ahead a year has the advantage of associating with classmates who are more nearly his equals in mental age. He profits from keener intellectual competition and from having more associates who can share his interests. He finishes his education sooner, starts earning sooner, and is equipped to profit from his creative years. But there are dangers if he is immature physically and socially compared with the pupils in the grade to which he skips. The older students may exclude him from games and other nonacademic activities. Or he may be allowed to compete but, discovering that he can never win, be unwilling to continue trying—which is quite likely to happen, because the bright student is accustomed to learn easily. When he finds he is not good at a sport, he is impatient with the effort improvement requires and may give up before he acquires any skill. Then he may fall back on his academic ability as the main means of gaining recognition and become a bookworm. Sometimes he cannot even hold his own academically because he has skipped fundamental processes necessary for understanding the work of the upper grade.

Under these circumstances the wise administrator studies the child and the situation and acts accordingly. Here are two cases from the same school.

Betsy was tested at the request of her mother, who wanted to see her moved from reading-readiness room to Grade I in December. Betsy has a good IQ but she was just beginning to read and still showing some reversals. Her conversation during the examination showed deep concern as to whether she could read well enough to go on to first grade, which would indicate a good deal of parental pressure on the child herself. She was not an especially large girl. So she was kept with her group to move along with them at the end of the year.

Calvin was in Grade I but reading second- and third-grade books. His sister had taught him to read when he was in kindergarten and she in Grade III. He was large for his age and seemed well adjusted. He wanted to move on to Grade II. When the move was first made he was a little upset because he missed his first-grade teacher, whom he liked very much. After only a day, however, he seemed happy with the second-grade group, and has since gotten along very well.

When a bright pupil's achievement is well ahead of the grade in which he is placed, the teacher may feel unable to provide the challenge he needs. One teacher writes:

Perry transferred into my Grade III from a town in the West. At first he got along very well, but was soon in trouble. He was obviously a good student, but group work bored him and if I gave him charge of a group he would waste time by fooling with them. Then I tried him on an advanced reader. This helped, but was too easy for him. So I asked the psychologist to see him. It turned out that Perry had an IQ of 140 and was two or three grades advanced in language, social studies, and arithmetic. I felt I was doing all I could—there were 39 in my class, and a number of behavior problems were ever ready to ply their art. But I was his only challenge and certainly it was an adult challenge unfair to a child. Perry needed to work with children who could share his interests and compete with him. After long study by the principal and psychologist and the upper-grade teacher, we decided in January to put Perry ahead a grade. He did superior work in that grade and is now leading his fifth grade. He still doesn't have much competition and we're arranging for him to take a scholarship examination in hopes he can attend a big private day school near his home.

A child who is large and heavy for his age meets older children more nearly as an equal. But many bright children who inherit small stature are nonetheless physically developed beyond their chronological ages. The index which specialists use to determine degree of advancement relates to the development of the wristbone. This can be determined by X-ray, but few schools are equipped to study a child by this method. The classroom teacher's judgment of development is, therefore, of special importance in the case of the undersized but bright child who is a candidate for skipping. If he has good health and physical toughness and the spirit that lets him hold his own in athletics and rough-and-tumble play, he certainly should not be kept back just because he is small. If he is socially mature and at ease with older children but not athletic, perhaps even physically weak, the decision is more difficult. If he has older friends, he should probably be allowed to skip. But if he is socially immature, prefers to play with younger children, and is "picked on" by his present classmates, he should not skip.

The adjustment of a pupil who skips depends not only on his abilities and development but also upon the make-up of the new class. Before a final decision is made, the ranges of achievement and of age in the upper class should be ascertained. The skipper's achievement in all subjects should at least equal the median achievement of the upper class, or he may be driven too hard in an attempt to keep up. His achievement in one or two subjects should be above average so that his self-confidence will not be undermined. Estimates of achievement should be confirmed by standardized tests.

If the upper class happens to contain a large majority of youngsters who are old for their grade, especially if many of these are repeaters who dislike school, the skipper's difficulties in making a good adjustment are increased.

Much depends on the attitude of the teacher of the upper class. Is he interested in bright children? Does he believe in acceleration? Does he try to provide for individual differences? If not, he might make the lot of a young newcomer hard. A bright pupil who is ready to skip could well wait a year to avoid a teacher who would not receive him gladly. In the meantime, he will need to have his abilities challenged to the full.

Experience indicates that a pupil should not be skipped

more than once in elementary school. An exception might be made for a very bright pupil who is old for his grade because he started school late or because of some other reason. In any case, a pupil should not skip when he will be more than a year younger than the normal lower limit for the upper grade. For example, the majority of children in Grade III would be from 7 years and 8 months to 8 years and 8 months old in September if the official age for entering kindergarten had been 4 years and 8 months or older as of September 1. A pupil who skips into this grade should be at least 6 years and 8 months old in September. In general, the sooner a pupil skips, the more easily he will adjust. Early skipping avoids the danger of placing a preadolescent among adolescents.

In secondary school, some pupils who have already skipped a grade in elementary school may be so advanced in achievement and so mature physically and socially that they should skip another grade. But they might find "rapid progress" more satisfactory.

RAPID PROGRESS

The term "rapid progress" is customarily used to describe methods by which pupils cover the whole curriculum in less than normal time. It is distinguished from "skipping," which means omitting part of the curriculum. One method of rapid progress is to group bright pupils in classes which cover the curriculum rapidly. For example, rapid-progress classes in Baltimore's Robert E. Lee Junior High School do three years' work in two,[7] and the University of Chicago Laboratory School covers the eight elementary-school years in seven.[8] Another method is to let students attend summer school. Attendance at three six-week summer sessions saves half a year. A third method permits students to take extra courses and thus accumulate extra credits toward graduation. Harvard, since the days of President Eliot, has allowed good students to take an extra course each year. If

School choristers preparing for a Christmas program. Boys and girls who are talented in music often receive their first formal musical instruction in school. The recognition which is given them by their schoolmates and by the public encourages them to cultivate their talent.

The dinosaur who wrote with his horn. This may not be the dinosaur that one imaginative boy said went to school and learned to write with his horn (see page 120). But Monoclonius and his fellows in Yale's Peabody Museum fascinate the thousands of bright youngsters who visit the museum each year.

The swamp is full of life. Field trips are a regular part of the curriculum for many bright boys and girls. A science class which visits a neighborhood swamp will bring back enough material to stock a whole aquarium.

they also attend summer school, they can do four years' work in three. Walter Gifford, former president of the American Telephone and Telegraph Company, is one of Harvard's many distinguished three-year graduates.

A small secondary school may not have enough pupils to justify setting up rapid-progress classes or a summer school. But if its program is flexible enough to permit a bright student to take an extra course each year, it can arrange for him to secure additional credits by independent study and special examination. He can then save a year in completing the requirements for graduation. One high-school student took extra courses in freshman and sophomore years. During the summer following his sophomore year, he worked as a camp counselor and studied each afternoon during the compulsory quiet period. He covered all of his next year's work in both English and German. In the fall he received high marks in special examinations in each subject and received credit for a year's work in each. He was admitted to the senior class, and by taking an extra course that year qualified for graduation in June.

EARLY ADMISSION TO COLLEGE

The drive for educated manpower has centered interest on early admission to college and on early graduation. Experiments in various methods to help qualified young people graduate earlier have been financed by the Fund for the Advancement of Education, which was established by the Ford Foundation. College scholarships have been awarded to superior young students, and the colleges have been given extra grants to arrange for guidance and to study the results.

The first Ford Scholars were chosen on the basis of academic promise and personal maturity. The essential conditions were that they be able to satisfy all the entrance requirements of the co-operating college which they were to attend and that they be ready to enter before they reached the age of 16 years and 6 months.   Under the plan, 420 boys and girls entered college in the fall of 1951.   Of these, 37 had completed Grade XII, 209 Grade XI, and 174 Grade X.[9]   The follow-up studies which have been made show that most of these young people did well in college.   They adjusted best at places, like Chicago and Columbia, which have always admitted young scholars of exceptional merit and so were able to treat the Ford Scholars like any other freshmen.   They did least well at Yale, which had put them in a special dormitory group and in other ways had placed them in the limelight.   But even at Yale the majority of the boys did well both scholastically and socially.[10]

Quentin Anderson, adviser to early-admissions students at Columbia, has reported to the Fund for the Advancement of Education that Columbia is enthusiastic about the program. Only 8 of the 51 students in the first group, which graduated in 1955, dropped out.   Some of these were too immature, some became emotionally upset, and others had to leave because of conditions at home.   Those who dropped out came mainly from small high schools and had trouble adjusting to life in a big city. The 43 who graduated averaged a year younger than the class as a whole (16 years and 4 months at entrance, against 17 years and 6 months).   Nine were elected to Phi Beta Kappa, twice the proportion of the class as a whole.   Almost three quarters of them entered graduate work in the fall of 1955.

Most of the participating colleges plan to continue to accept some very young students who are scholastically qualified and personally mature, and other colleges are following suit.   A high-school sophomore or junior who thinks he would profit by early admission to college should certainly inquire about the possibility.

ADMISSION WITH ADVANCED STANDING

More and more colleges are admitting students with advanced standing.   This is partly the result of various studies of articulation between school and college, which found that, when bright college freshmen had to repeat work they had already covered, they lost interest in the academic side of college life. Obviously a young man or woman who had done well in four years of French would prefer an advanced class in college to one with fellow freshmen who had had only two years. But too often no advanced course was offered to freshmen and no provisions were made for the exceptional student.

The "Kenyon Plan" has popularized the system of opening advanced classes to freshmen who can show they are qualified. The plan was organized by the late Gordon Chalmers when he was president of Kenyon College and was financed by the Fund for the Advancement of Education. In 1955 the College Entrance Examination Board took over the administration of the plan. It is now called the "Advanced Placement Program."

Entering college with advanced standing makes it easier for a student to finish college in three years and to combine undergraduate with graduate work. Because of the advantages to the student who is admitted to college with advanced standing, several secondary schools, including some not formally associated with the plan, have instituted honors sections, seminars, and rapid-progress groups for bright students. Many educators feel that it may be better for most bright students to enter at the normal age but with advanced standing than to enter early. Students who enter with advanced standing may choose to spend a full four years in college, and use their advanced standing as a means to taking more courses. Regardless of acceleration, the plan has breathed new life into schools old and new.

SHORTER FORMAL EDUCATION

Whether you teach in kindergarten or graduate school or at some point between, you might well put your mind on the desirability of shortening the traditional period of formal education. Is there any real reason why bright students should be kept in college until they are 22 or older? Their less bright contemporaries regularly go to work at 17 or 18. A boy of 17, with his family's permission, can enlist in the Navy. Young men of 18 are subject to the draft. History shows that bright teen-agers who have been encouraged to study and learn are capable of doing intellectual work at any level. The results of standardized achievement tests prove that bright pupils have the ability to do the 12 years of preparatory work now required (Grades I–XII) in 9 years or less.

If all bright children were to enter college at 15 or 16, there would be no question of social maladjustment in college. The young person who graduated from college at 19 or 20 would be ready either to start work or to enter graduate school. Those who studied for the professions would be ready to start practice near the beginning of their most creative period.

A shorter period of formal education would mean enormous savings in teacher personnel and in building space. The money saved in this way would facilitate the payment of adequate salaries to teachers. It would help provide scholarships to more bright boys and girls.

VIII

The Fundamentals

The moquito's (check this) *messenger on his horse-fly floo* (flew) *into the Spider's web. A Peace* (piece) *of the web fell over his mowth* (mouth): *but he got out by Takeing* (taking) *his canteen and wetting the web so It* (it) *wood* (would. Fred, THIS was a spelling word!!) *get sogey* (soggy).

> —From "The War of the Mosquitoes and the Ants," by Fred, age 7 years and 9 months, IQ 140, Grade II, with his teacher's corrections in parentheses.

Until a bright pupil learns the fundamentals of a subject thoroughly, he remains under a handicap in it. As time goes on, he begins to say, "I never was any good at math"—or drawing or French or music. But if a skillful teacher discovers the root of his trouble and can help him make a fresh start, the pupil may renew his interest in the subject and become really expert. At least he will be able to use it as a tool. A typical case is reported by one third-grade teacher:

Very few of the bright children with whom I work are lacking in basic fundamentals. But one girl, with an IQ of 145, hated arithmetic. I discovered that some of this dislike came from lack of understanding of the basic materials and skills. She didn't like the subject because she couldn't do well in it. So I took her back to arithmetic beginnings: basic counting, handling of numbers of objects, adding to and taking away from a group of objects, etc.

117

Gradually, as she saw and felt the quantity in these objects, she was able to transfer to abstract numbers. We used an abacus, number cards, flash cards, counted everything in sight, played all sorts of arithmetic games, used toy money, made temperature charts, etc. I had an equally bright boy work with her when I couldn't be free, and soon she was helping slower children. I think this was the most effective part of the program. After developing a basic comprehension of number, she spent all her free time using arithmetic flash cards with the slow group and so drilled herself. I put the answers on the back of the card to be sure she didn't just practice mistakes.

OFF TO A BAD START

A not unusual course of events may cause a bright child to fall further and further behind and eventually to fail a subject. He is impatient with routine and so dislikes drill. His interest in ideas and his general ability make it possible for him to grasp the main point of what a teacher says or of a paragraph he reads, though he misses details and could not himself make the same point correctly. For example, a bright student may get the general idea of what his French teacher says in French, though he himself cannot conjugate a French verb. Then, when he finds he cannot command the basic techniques to communicate his ideas in French, he loses interest in learning the language. The same process may inhibit interest and progress in any field. One counselor describes the case of a boy in Grade IX:

This boy has an IQ of 130. The record shows he got into considerable disciplinary difficulty in Grade II. He was large for his age and perhaps should have skipped a class. His record has the following comment from his teacher in Grade V: "He answers social-studies questions without reading the book. He seems to see the answers in a flash." In other words, he probably never really had to read to find information. At any rate, he now reads badly and feels jittery when faced with a difficult text. But he still gets a B average.

118

The Fundamentals

Our reports show that many secondary-school students do badly in mathematics because they are not at home in the fundamental processes of arithmetic. One home-room teacher writes: "Al has an IQ of 126. His father is an engineer, and Al lists science and mathematics as his favorite subjects. But last marking period he flunked math. I talked with him about it and was not surprised that he likes the more difficult parts of the subject but dislikes drill work. He apparently grasps theories and enjoys thinking about them but can't work the problems." Others in Al's situation fail to share his liking for the subject, and drop it as soon as they can.

The theory that there are many factors in intelligence, that a person's verbal ability and mathematical ability may differ in degree, does not excuse the bright pupil from mastering the fundamentals of all the subjects which he takes. His general ability is almost surely great enough for such mastery. Even the pupil untalented in fields like music and art can learn the basic techniques which are necessary for understanding and appreciation.

SEQUENTIAL STANDARDS

In principle, a child should not be forced to learn a skill before he is physically and mentally ready to learn, but he should have techniques available when he needs them. He should have the knowledge necessary for progress, but he should not have to learn anything he is not going to use with fair regularity. Practically, and especially in the case of the bright child, it may be very difficult to decide questions of readiness and of need. A story like Fred's about the mosquitoes and the ants requires the use of many words not on any spelling list for Grade II. Should Fred be made to drill on these words? Is there more danger of his losing in creativity from not being able to spell the words he uses or from disliking to be corrected and drilled?

Fred's teacher, in this dilemma, is holding him to the

119

standard for his grade. *"This* was a spelling word." The teacher also has Fred and the other students circulate their best stories through the room library. A story that is to be circulated must be copied in correct form. Fred made a fair copy of the thirty pages of "The War," and it was a favorite with his classmates. Samples of later stories show much improvement in spelling and no diminution in invention. In a paper on dinosaurs he explains that Triceratops' horn was originally a thorn that got stuck in his nose when he was playing in a "pricker bush." No one could get it out. "When he went to school he found he could write with his horn. He began to like it." (Fred has confused three-horned Triceratops with single-horned Monoclonius—but he has arrived at a concept of natural selection.)

There is no doubt that a bright pupil should at least keep pace with his class as it learns the fundamentals. Have him take the tests the other pupils take, and, if he falls down on a fundamental process, drill him on it. But just keeping up is not enough, because he will not be able to do the advanced work he needs as a challenge unless he is well ahead of the average in his command of the fundamentals. A rough rule of thumb is that his command of the fundamentals of the regular subjects of the curriculum should be about as far ahead of his chronological age-grade level as is his mental age. When he asks how to do something, help him learn. If, in your opinion, the process is one he will need regularly, tell him so and arrange for him to practice it. If he has a continuing interest, he will presumably progress rapidly in mastering the pertinent fundamentals. But he should not let his mastery of the fundamentals in other subjects lag too far behind.

Regular progress in the fundamentals of English is especially important to the bright pupil. His success in living up to his ability may very well depend on the way he speaks and writes. If he does not habitually speak and write correctly, he will feel inferior, he will *be inferior,* when he associates with able people who have set high standards for themselves. One third-grade teacher of children with poor backgrounds is determined that his bright pupils are not to be handicapped by bad English. He writes:

They and their parents regularly use forms like, "Me and my sister," "broked," "cou'n't" for "couldn't," and "dint" for "didn't." I assigned the bright group the job of printing the correct forms and making up sentences for correct usage. Then they painted a large snow man. Every time a child used "Me and," he had to give the snow man a black eye—a round piece of black construction paper. When a third black eye appeared, the class had extra language homework. Group pressure very soon worked to correct the individual offenders.

The NEA pamphlets on reading, spelling, writing, and arithmetic include brief and helpful standards of progress. These pamphlets are in the series *What Research Says to the Teacher*.[1] Basal texts, especially a series of basal texts planned by one editor, present the fundamentals of their subjects in logical sequence. When your pupils are doing most of their work on projects, you can check their progress in fundamentals by occasionally having them do a lesson or two, including all written exercises, in a basal text. The results of standardized achievement tests give you an excellent idea of a pupil's knowledge of the fundamentals of the subjects tested. But because the bright pupil may do well on a test by virtue of a wide range of general knowledge, you should analyze the test to see which questions deal with which fundamentals and then study his answers in the light of your analysis. You may discover wide gaps in his knowledge.

DISCOVERING DEFICIENCIES

A bright student's deficiencies may escape detection, even by himself. He is likely to be glib in his use of words and to give the impression, even to himself, that he knows more than he does. Deficiencies in reading are especially likely to go undetected. The bright student who is a poor reader may pay careful attention in class and pick up so much knowledge that it is hard to believe he is not studying his textbooks efficiently. Or he may be spending twice the time he should have to spend in preparing an assignment. Ralph C. Preston tested the reading skills of the twenty-two juniors eligible for Phi Beta Kappa at the College for Women, University of Pennsylvania. Eight of the twenty-two were very slow readers. One was reading at the rate of only 157 words per minute, that is, at about the third-grade level. Six of the eight knew they were slow readers and would have welcomed instruction in college to help them develop speed.[2]

The earlier a deficiency is discovered, the more easily it can be corrected, partly because the student does not feel too advanced to go back to beginnings and partly because bad habits have not become so thoroughly established. Our emphasis on early discovery of deficiencies or, better still, correct learning from the start is not meant as criticism of the elementary-school teacher. Retrogressive blame—the graduate school blames the college, the college the high school, the high school the elementary school, the elementary school the parents—gets us nowhere. Every teacher at every level should be alert to the possibility that a student does not have adequate knowledge of the fundamentals of one or several subjects. And the teacher should be ready to discuss the problem with the student and to show him what he can do to help himself.

The experienced teacher sets out at once to gauge a new pupil's level of knowledge. Even if there are good cumulative records, the teacher gives a new class written work and corrects it carefully. When a pupil transfers from another school, the teacher talks with him and questions him in much the fashion in which oral examinations for college entrance were given a century ago. The procedure is quick and valuable at all levels in all subjects. If you ask a pupil to read aloud to you or to translate a passage from French or to work a mathematics prob-

lem orally, you secure a quick and fairly accurate impression of
his accomplishment.

When a class has been taking up new subject matter, there
is no perfect substitute for the old-fashioned written examination
which you yourself set. You are the only one who knows just
what your students are supposed to have learned and how you
hope they will be able to employ their knowledge. And the
old-fashioned method of meticulous correction in red ink of
each mistake has much merit, particularly if you and the pupil
review together what you have written on his paper, for then
both of you can see what kind of mistake he is making. When
talking over his paper with him, you can ask him to explain an
answer or to do a problem orally. One teacher writes: "I was
very puzzled when Molly did every one of her multiplication examples wrong. She was the brightest girl in the class and knew
her tables well. I asked her to sit beside me and do an example
aloud. Her first words explained the trouble. She was multiplying from left to right."

You may also want to give the pupil a written diagnostic
test. You can use one issued by a publisher or make one of
your own. The names of some diagnostic tests which teachers
have found useful are given in the list of published tests in Appendix II. Specialized books on teaching a subject generally
contain sections on diagnosis. Glenn Myers Blair's valuable
book *Diagnostic and Remedial Teaching* deals with methods of
discovering and correcting deficiencies. Part I takes up reading
at all levels through senior high school. Part II takes up arithmetic, spelling, handwriting, and the fundamentals of English.
Emphasis is on what the classroom teacher himself can do to
discover, diagnose, and correct deficiencies.[3]

Bright pupils profit from collecting their own mistakes.
They are good enough scientists, especially if you explain how
scientific the method is, to treat a collection of mistakes as pertinent data and to try to find the common element—the cause
of the mistake. And just seeing how many times they make the

same mistake can have a stimulating effect.   One Latin teacher has his students put dots in the margins of their dictionaries next to the words which they look up.   When a student finds five dots next to *onus* he does not need a scholar's word count to convince him that he should learn it.

Bright pupils may be more aware of their specific shortcomings than you are.   Try asking the class to rate themselves on the use of a specific fundamental.   At the least, self-rating impresses the individual with the importance of correctness and helps make him responsible for his own improvement.

A NOTE ON ARITHMETIC

Arithmetic is mentioned more than all other subjects combined in our reports from teachers on their bright pupils who are having trouble with fundamentals.   This is partly due to the amount of written work ordinarily done in arithmetic—the obviousness of a wrong answer makes a lack of knowledge easy to discover.   But there are reasons to believe that deficiencies are more common in arithmetic than in other subjects.

We asked 633 bright pupils to tell us which subject they liked best, which least, and which made them work hardest. Mathematics ranked at the top of the answers to each question. One hundred and fifty-two (23 per cent) said they liked math best, 185 (26 per cent) liked math least, and 236 (35 per cent) said math made them work hardest.   Twenty-five of the pupils said that mathematics made them work hardest and that they liked it best.   This last combination reflects the bright student's reaction to challenge.[4]

It seems to us that the bright students who dislike mathematics are also reacting in a typical fashion.   They are used to learning quickly, and may dislike work which must be done slowly and accurately.   When a pupil's interest is not aroused, he may fail to see why he should work hard at math, and may neglect it as much as he is allowed.   He will drop behind and not be ready to take up new work with the class. This leads to more trouble and more neglect of the subject.

In 1956, the Educational Testing Service surveyed the teaching of mathematics. The report of the survey lays the blame for the neglect of mathematics partly on an out-of-date curriculum and partly on the attitude of most teachers to mathematics. The teachers themselves, having found mathematics difficult in school, dropped it as soon as they could. Their attitude spreads to their pupils and aggravates an already bad situation. One remedy proposed in the report is a refresher course for the teacher to "nourish him on the why's and how's of mathematical phenomena and to liberate him from the confinements of the text book so that he may enjoy a lively appreciation of the thousands of important uses that mathematics has in the modern world." [5] We heartily approve of refresher courses, but we must say that the teachers from whom we have reports seem to us to be working hard and intelligently to interest their pupils in mathematics and to hold all their students up to a high standard.

DRILL

Drill is actually enjoyed by most bright pupils *if* they see its necessity and *if* it is skillfully managed. Here are some comments from teachers at different grade levels:

Drill goes on all year for my first-grade children, constantly adding new families or syllables to their vocabulary. The gifted child enjoys it very much as he realizes this drill enables him to recognize new words.

Billy, Grade V, age 9, IQ 149, Stanford Achievement Test grade level about 7.9, becomes very annoyed when he doesn't do a good job. He had a great deal of difficulty reducing fractions. After a week I gave him an oral test on his tables. I found he knew them only as long as they were in order. I drilled him on the tables backwards and forwards and all ways. He learned them very quickly, and our next step was drill work in reducing, finding the

125

least common denominator, and canceling. He saw how the drill helped him recognize relationships and carried on with it until he was doing a good job.

Carl, a very bright boy in Grade VIII, had trouble picking out subject and verb. After ordinary drill on nouns and verbs he still stumbled. So I started him on diagraming. He was much interested and came to my room several times in his free periods. I explained more about diagrams and what had to be found to draw one correctly. We went over many sentences and he realized that the noun subject was not too hard to find. After using diagrams for drill, Carl had no trouble with sentence parts.

The danger in giving bright pupils drill work is that they may already know the materials thoroughly. In that case it is a waste of time and dull, and it may give the pupil a distaste for school and for study. When you are sure that a pupil has already learned a fact or a technique, or when a pretest (e.g., on the spelling words or the French vocabulary for the coming week) reveals that he does not need drill, he should be given the time for some enrichment activity.

If you are bored by drill work, you can be sure that your pupils will be, too. But if you are convinced that it is necessary and put your heart into making it interesting, your students will enjoy it and profit from it. No matter how well you know your educational psychology, you should occasionally check your methods of drilling to be sure that they meet the conditions necessary for learning.

Effective drill presupposes four conditions: desire for improvement, understanding, continuing effort, and satisfaction with progress. Mere repetition does not result in learning. Pupils who are punished by being made to copy a sentence five hundred times will copy it five hundred times correctly and the next day will misspell the words it contained.

Bright pupils are quick to see how knowledge of a subject will help them immediately in their schoolwork and ultimately in their lifework. Again and again our reports from teachers describe cases like the following: "Abe, Grade II, IQ 143, was reading on the fourth-grade level. But arithmetic in any form didn't interest him at all. He couldn't do it and didn't care. He said he wanted to be a scientist, so I explained to him how much he'd need his arithmetic. After this he drilled hard and managed to catch up with the class. He skipped Grade III. At the start of Grade IV his reading level was 7.8 and arithmetic 4.3."

Though bright pupils have superior reasoning power, you cannot presume on understanding. Billy did not grasp the number relationships in tables he could repeat by rote. Carl drilled on nouns and verbs without understanding their functions in a sentence. When a pupil is not learning a fundamental process as he should, or when he is failing to apply what you think he knows, there is no satisfactory substitute for a conference about the difficulty. Get him to tell you why he thinks you are insisting on that particular drill. Then take it up "backwards and forwards and all ways" to see if he understands the principle involved.

You can ensure effort by making the drill interesting. Games, puzzles, and competitions, all enlist bright pupils' energies and make them work with an intensity that promotes learning. The main principle is to keep the individual or the class alert and eager. One third-grade teacher writes: "I rattle off an example such as $2 + 5 + 4 - 8 + 6 - 2 + 5 - 4 \times 3$ and the children write the answer. They love this. Sometimes I let a child give the examples and I take his place in the group. They try hard to 'stick' the teacher. We play casino, and '21.' Lately we've been having team competitions, and we have challenged another third grade to an 'arithmetic bee' next Friday."

Novelty adds interest and appeal. One teacher writes: "The tape recorder used in reading, speech, and music helps the child to hear and correct his own mistakes. It's surprising how quickly he corrects them." Mental arithmetic drill is more exciting when one child works the problems on a calculating machine as a gauge of speed and a check on accuracy.

Workbooks are one means of letting a student see what progress he is making. They are easily and quickly checked. You should from time to time go over what the pupil has done, not only to be sure that the work is correct but also to give him the encouragement of your personal interest. The bright pupil can also profit from studying the NEA pamphlets on reading, spelling, handwriting, and arithmetic, and by checking himself against the standards proposed there. It is most important that he devise or adopt some method of measuring his own progress, week by week and month by month. His own graph of number of mistakes compared with number of correct responses will impress and stimulate him more than general praise from you, as necessary and effective as this is.

Teachers generally find that one of the best methods of drilling a bright pupil is to make him responsible for drilling someone else. Occasionally two bright pupils who are working on the same level drill each other and compete to see which can catch the other out. More usually the bright pupil drills a slower pupil and learns at the same time. This is a particularly good way to ensure the overlearning that makes knowledge long-lasting, because it avoids the dullness of mere repetition.

Knowing that he is going to be responsible for using knowledge accurately is a great stimulus to a pupil's learning. One seventh-grade teacher reports:

One of my brighter pupils came from out of state last fall. He had a record of good marks, but his spelling was poor and his speech slipshod. I had him work orally with me before class and in his free periods. I'd point out his mistakes and he'd try to correct them. The class would also correct him when he made a mistake in grammar. As the weeks progressed he improved somewhat, but the real progress came when the class asked him to write up some short articles on sports for the class's weekly newspaper. He was so interested that he voluntarily used the dictionary and double checked his spelling. Being intelligent, he put speech and spelling together and soon found out that some words can be sounded out and others have to be recognized.

Finding time to give individual drill to a bright pupil may be a big problem. Some of our reports from teachers mention using periods when the class is studying materials that the bright pupil already knows. For example, "Sandy is a very good speller and almost always has his pretest perfect. So when the rest of the class are working on their spelling words, he and I drill on arithmetic." Other reports tell of meeting with the pupil before or after school, of having him come to the teacher when they both have a free period, of putting him with a group that needs the same kind of drill, and of showing his parents how to help him at home. Once you are sure that a bright pupil wants to improve his knowledge of fundamentals, you can profitably shift a good deal of the responsibility to him.

REMEDIAL WORK

So far we have been discussing methods of teaching the fundamentals and of helping a student make up deficiencies on the assumption that "he could if he would." There are, of course, cases, and these the most severe and the most difficult to help, where the trouble is due to no lack in effort to learn on the pupil's part, and to no lack in skill on the part of his successive teachers. When a child fails to respond to your efforts to help him improve, and especially when a bright child fails to make rapid progress once you have located and explained the kind of mistake he is making, you should consider the possibility that some cause other than lack of study is operating.

If possible, a child with a stubborn deficiency should be referred to a school psychologist for study. Large numbers of children who have been studied by psychologists have been found to be suffering from physical or emotional handicaps. A case that turned out well reads:

Cy was referred for study because his teachers had been unable to rouse in him any interest in schoolwork. Despite his parents' willingness to co-operate, nothing that parents or teachers had tried had proved successful. He was 8 years and 7 months old. A Stanford-Binet test indicated a mental age of 10-4 and IQ of 120. He showed unusual reasoning ability. His vocabulary and memory were excellent. But when Cy started a reading test, he was intensely nervous and sat twisting his hair. His reading measured below first-grade level. He had a decided tendency to reversals of letters and words. The psychologist then tested him for handedness and found he was left-handed and left-eyed, though he had been trained from early childhood to use his right hand. He showed signs of being emotionally upset. His sense of personal worth was low. He felt he was often unjustly punished, and that he never got a square deal. He walked and talked in his sleep. He was constantly tired, though the physical examination disclosed no defects. He was placed under a remedial teacher, who encouraged him to use his left hand. Within the year he was sleeping well, feeling self-confident, and making good progress in his regular grade.

Remedial teachers are not trained to study a child to the extent that psychologists do, but they are experts in cause-and-effect relationships in their special subjects. They can give you good advice not only about the kind of help a particular child needs with a specific problem but also about how to avoid aggravating any emotional difficulty there may be.

If you do not have access to either psychological or remedial-teaching services, you will have to do the best you can without them. We take up the common reasons for bright pupils' underachievement in the next chapter, and some of their emotional difficulties in the chapter after that.

IX

Motivating the Underachievers

George had a reputation for being a nonworker. He would sit and daydream, chew pencils and rulers, cut up paper, get down on the floor and study the cracks or dig out the dirt, lie over the desk top—anything but put his name on a paper. He was pushed through Grades I and II by the hounding of his mother and the thankfulness of his teachers. But in Grade III, in early October, when I gave the Weekly Reader *reading test, he had 59 out of 60 answers correct.*
—*A Teacher.*

Pete's teachers agree that he is bright but lazy. He never finishes his work in class, and hands in incomplete assignments. I talked with his father, who is highly disturbed by the boy's lack of drive. When the father talks with him about his report card, Pete just says, "I passed, didn't I?"
—*A High-School Counselor.*

We know of nothing more provoking than to have a very able student who refuses to do good work. The teachers from whom we have reports on underachievers apparently share our feelings. A typical account ends, "And now I'm at the end of my rope." And parents come to us in despair, saying, "What can we do? Walter is bright, but he's getting all C's and D's and will never get into Harvard."

131

CAUSES OF UNDERACHIEVEMENT

Several scholars have compared bright and gifted students who did good work in school and college with equally bright students who did poor work or failed. Strang has discussed their findings very helpfully.[1] Notable studies are those by Terman,[2] Robert J. Dowd,[3] Jesse A. Bond,[4] and J. C. Gowan.[5] We ourselves have analyzed our teachers' reports on pupils who are weak in fundamentals or who are underachievers in relation to their ability. We have also studied the educational records of underachievers in college.

All observers agree on one main fact about underachievers: boys greatly outnumber girls. Otherwise there seems to be no common denominator. No one cause and no pattern of causes appears in all cases. But certain types of difficulty do occur more or less frequently.

Many underachievers come from broken homes or homes where there is considerable strife and strain. Teachers often say that the parents of an underachiever either do not discipline him effectively or disagree over discipline. Children from homes like these may be emotionally upset and fail to adjust to school. We shall discuss these topics in the next chapter.

Poor physical health, many moves from school to school, and marked immaturity are occasionally said to cause underachievement. It must be remembered that many well-adjusted high-achievers have overcome these specific handicaps. But the safe first step in working with an underachiever is to arrange for a thorough physical examination, including checks on vision, hearing, and metabolism. Sometimes the only trouble with a boy is that he is using all his energy in physical growth—he's "shooting up."

Many underachievers describe themselves and are described by their teachers as lazy, as lacking in persistence when faced with a dull, routine, or hard task, and as given to preferring pleasure to work. They are prone to subordinate study to extracurricular activities of all kinds, though Gowan found the underachievers whom he studied "self-sufficient and unsociable."

Study habits are notoriously bad among underachievers. Many such pupils find it next to impossible to settle down to work. When they are supposed to be studying they sit and watch TV, listen to records, or daydream. They do not know how to distribute their time. They will spend every available minute on a subject they like and leave their other books unopened. They ignore the recommendations of the study manuals about schedules, quiet, note-taking, and review. Their reading habits are poor, and they do not know when—or how— to locate information or to skim, or when—or how—to read closely. They lack power of concentration.

Bad study habits or the absence of the habit of study seem to be of long standing with many underachievers. Terman's gifted subjects who flunked out of college commonly explained that "in high school they had made high marks without doing any serious work and that in college they underestimated the amount of work necessary to secure passing grades." [6] Similarly, some high-school students fail because they never had to work in elementary school and did not learn how. The high standards of their secondary schools and the competition of other students of superior ability who are good workers prove too much for them.

Dowd found that most of his college-level underachievers had had poor high-school records and were weak in the fundamentals, especially in the mechanics of English and in reading skills. And high-school teachers frequently complain that the lower schools send on pupils who do not know basic facts and processes. One Latin teacher says, "I have to begin by teaching my classes the alphabet so that they can use the dictionary."

High-achievers are not stereotyped any more than are underachievers. But comparison of the two groups reveals three possible generalizations, which have implications for motivation and thus are important to anyone trying to help the underachiever.

First, the high-achiever is more likely than the under-achiever to have made a definite choice of a career. He is working toward a known goal. Moreover, his chosen career is in line with his interests and aptitudes. Not only is the under-achiever less likely to have picked a career, but, if he has made a decision, it is often the result of parental pressure and is out of line with his interests and aptitudes. He is either drifting or sailing against the wind.

Second, the high-achiever is more likely to be accelerated by a year or two than is the underachiever. Acceleration seems to motivate achievement in several ways. Principally, we think, it marks an individual in his own mind and in the minds of his classmates as bright. He has a reputation to live up to. And the pupil who is accelerated is more consistently challenged. He learns to use his mind by using it.

Third, the parents of high-achievers are more likely than are the parents of underachievers to be studious people. They read more books. They are often engaged in a profession which demands continuing study. They like to go to museums and galleries and they take their children with them. In brief, they set an example of intellectual activity which provides their children with a good model. The children do not think "brains" and "eggheads" are queer.

CONFERENCES WITH A PUPIL

If you can talk intimately with a bright underachiever from time to time, you have excellent opportunities to discover what his difficulties are and to help him overcome them. As one teacher writes, "Occasionally during the noon hour or after school a child becomes confidential and tells a great deal about himself; his troubles and worries, his interests and his hobbies, his aims and his ideals." Moreover, as you and the pupil come to know each other better, the mutual antagonism which so often exists between the underachiever and the teacher tends to evaporate.   You and the pupil begin to like each other.   You want to help him.   He wants to work for you.

Unless you are fortunate enough to have a schedule that permits periodic private conferences with all of your pupils, you will probably have to ask the underachiever to come in early or to stay after school so that he can talk with you about his work. Teachers, counselors, and principals all agree that a conference of this kind succeeds best when there has been careful advance preparation.

Preparation does not take many minutes and in the long run it saves much time and makes the time spent worth while. Take a look at the pupil's cumulative record to refresh your mind on the evidence of his ability.   Note any interests listed.   See if there is any clue to what may be causing his difficulties.   Keep in mind the main causes we have discussed: trouble in the home, poor physical health, poor study habits, lack of purpose, and lack of challenge.   You will not be able to check on all of these in one conference, but you should be alert to anything the pupil says which will give you specific information about any of them.

Try to plan the conference for a place and time when you are assured of privacy and freedom from interruption.   Too many of our reports on conferences tell of taking a pupil into the hall or of taking him to one side of the room during class period. These reports show that hall and "aside" conferences usually last longer than the teacher expected, that the pupil is embarrassed and silent, that the class gets restless and curious, and that the results are rarely favorable.   Of course, you frequently stop by a pupil's desk or call him to yours to help him with his work, and in the process you gain valuable insights into his problems.   But when you want to have a real talk, pick a time when neither of you has conflicting responsibilities.

An experienced principal writes: "A conference progresses more harmoniously for all concerned if there is a relaxed atmosphere and if everyone is at his ease to discuss the problem. A friendly manner and an open mind go a long way to ironing out the difficulties for all concerned."   You can achieve both a friendly manner and an open mind if you determine ahead of time not to scold and not to preach. Tell yourself that you want to help the pupil help himself and that scolding and preaching will only make matters worse. Ask yourself, "How can I convince John that my real purpose is to help him?" The best answer is generally, "By not offering advice until he asks for it."

The effectiveness of letting the pupil do most of the talking cannot be overemphasized. It is amazing the way a person of any age who talks to a sympathetic listener gains an objective view of himself. Putting his thoughts in words gets them out where he can take a look at them apart from his feelings. He sees what is foolish. Sooner or later he hears himself saying what he knows he ought to do. This "nondirecting counseling" is particularly effective with a bright student. His insight helps him realize a situation and discover the path he should follow. He begins to direct himself instead of halfheartedly following directions.

There are a few stock questions and comments which help you guide the conversation, if you think you are not getting anywhere. The record may give you a lead on some of these. A question about a brother or sister, particularly one who is so much older or younger that there is no suspicion of invidious comparisons, may elicit information about home life. "Who are your best friends?" leads to disclosures about social adjustment. Reference to some past illness or absence opens up the matter of health. "Where do you study at home?" "What do you like most to do out of school?" "Have you any idea what you will be?" "What's your favorite subject?" are questions of obvious import, but nonetheless useful. Remember that you cannot expect to learn everything in one session.

Try to find out how the student rates his own ability. If necessary, ask him, "How much better do you think you could do if you tried?" Then, without telling him his IQ or using technical terms, talk with him about any evidence you have that he is really bright. A student who is convinced that he has the ability to lead his class has a standard to live up to. It is much better to show him he could be at the top than to scold him because he is not doing as well as he might.

The conference should close with an agreement for a later meeting. Because the pupil knows he will talk with you again soon, he keeps thinking about his proposals for improvement and tries to earn your approval. The later meeting can be very brief. A minute or two before class is enough for him to tell you how he is getting along and for you to let him know he is improving. If he is not improving or if you think you need more information or that he needs support, make a definite date for another full-fledged conference.

One high-school teacher writes:

Irv wasn't doing nearly as well for me in American History as he had done two years before in World History, and I remembered that even then I'd thought he wasn't working anywhere near up to his ability. In the present course he had failed several weekly tests in succession. I asked him to drop in after school. Before he came I went to the counselor's office and had a look at his record: IQ 122 (Otis), but reading only average, and vocabulary and spelling both below average. When Irv came in I asked him how he explained his failures. He replied he didn't know. I asked him where he studied at home. He said he didn't, not much. He got by, by listening carefully in class, but he guessed he'd have to study some for me. Then I went over his achievement-test scores with him, and suggested that he set up a daily routine that would include special exercises to increase his vocabulary and improve his spelling. I arranged to schedule him for a special remedial period three times a week during his regular study-hall period and for him to spend the time with me. He resented this at first. Gradually, however, he began to add words from his history reading to his vocabulary, and his comprehension improved. He was encouraged and his interest perked up. He didn't become a miraculous scholar but he did pass my course.

GROUP CONFERENCES

Sometimes the best approach to an underachiever is through a class or group discussion. When he realizes that others in the group have problems like his own and hears what they are doing to overcome them, he feels that he might do likewise. Moreover he may listen to what the group says and adopt suggestions which they make much more readily than he will heed you. The group discussion is probably more effective if you refrain from mentioning the individual. If he is bright, he will know that the shoe fits.

Our reports of group discussions of desirable behavior and attitudes are mainly concerned with matters of order. But there are enough on topics like efficient study, scientific thinking, standards of promotion, the practical uses of Latin, and the proper place of extracurricular activities to show how effectively a free exchange of opinion establishes high standards and builds good morale. When a group as a group decides that the class should be on its good behavior to help a substitute teacher or that everyone should hand his assignments in on time, the previously non-co-operative pupil usually falls in line. If he does not, talk with him privately.

Bright pupils should take turns as discussion leaders. An underachiever who finds he is to be in charge of a meeting on how to study has a pressing reason to learn how.

Group conferences require extra-careful preparation. J. Jeffery Auer and Henry Lee Ewbank, in their *Handbook for Discussion Leaders,* say that most unsuccessful group meetings are the result, not of what happens at the meeting, but of what did not happen before. Auer and Ewbank offer much practical help, and you and your older students should study the *Handbook.*[7]

A high-school teacher reports:

We devote one home-room period a week (45 minutes) to discussion. Students take turns as leaders, and I am just another member of the group, but I am an active one. Topics have included smoking regulations, need for study, how to study, need to support extracurricular organizations, and need to have fathers attend Parents' Nights. The students really do grow in responsibility when they have a chance to reason out their attitudes. It's a sort of "group therapy."

MOTIVE POWER

Robert S. Woodworth, in his *Psychology,* presents the formula, ability $\times$ motivation $=$ achievement.[8] Instead of this we might say, IQ $\times$ motivation $=$ achievement. If you put this into figures and vary motivation on a scale of 100, you see what an enormous difference strong motivation makes. $125 \times 100 = 12,500$. $125 \times 0 = 0$.

Of course there is no living creature without some motivation. If we did not respond to hunger and thirst, the zero results in the way of food and water would end in death. And there is probably no such thing as perfect motivation, if only because there are so many motives that they are sure to conflict sooner or later. We may want very much to finish a detective story, but if we are very hungry we cannot continue to concentrate on it.

The net strength of a given set of motives, balancing out the pluses and minuses, varies from individual to individual and from situation to situation. The art of pedagogy is the art of discerning how best to motivate your pupils to achieve the objectives you think worthy. But you are limited in many ways. The psychologist in the laboratory can make a chimpanzee strive desperately to solve the problem of how to get at a dish of food. All the psychologist has to do is to withhold other food so that the animal has to starve until it succeeds. You can hardly keep a pupil hungry until he learns his lessons. When you work from the other direction, when you try to increase the reward, you are up against the fact that most of your pupils are already to some extent satisfied or have other means of gaining satisfaction. A student who craves recognition may be getting more by misbehaving than he could by working hard. Moreover, the rewards of learning are more or less remote. It may be very hard for even a bright student, particularly if he is young, to see how doing his lessons will have a result he will like.

Individual differences in motivation still puzzle psychologists.   Why do two people with the same intelligence and similar backgrounds differ in what they wish to accomplish or, if they agree on a goal, in the effort and persistence they show in trying to gain it?   And why do girls very generally try to finish their assignments when many boys refuse to take the same assignments seriously?   How can teachers discover and mobilize a student's existing motives?   Can a teacher instill a new motive?

So far no one has answered these questions in a way that gives the classroom teacher rules to follow.   Psychologists are working hard on the problem and may sometime be able to offer specific guides.   In the meantime, the best you can do is to be aware of some of the common motives which experience has proved are powerful, and to adapt your methods so as to enlist these.

CURIOSITY, MANIPULATION, MASTERY

Put a mechanical puzzle on the table where a bright child can see it, and he is practically sure to start playing with it. Even if there are no directions, he will turn it this way and that until he thinks he can see what he is supposed to do.   Then he will keep trying until he succeeds.   Note that you do not have to assign the puzzle as a task or teach the right method of attack or grade the result.

A great deal of the world's progress has resulted from human curiosity and the human being's tendency to handle—manipulate—objects until he understands—masters—them. Teachers can utilize the motive which underlies this trial-and-error type of learning to induce their pupils to acquire more knowledge and to work harder.   One elementary teacher writes: "I set my room up to appeal to the students' curiosity.   There is a science table, an art cupboard, a library table, a bulletin board. I change the materials from time to time, and the children bring in appropriate materials of their own.   Whenever a pupil has free time, he's at liberty to investigate.   Sooner rather than later he'll settle on some topic he wants to know all about." A high-school history teacher says, "I've learned to distinguish between the casual 'why' and what I call 'the hot-and-bothered why.' When a student is disturbed to the point where he feels he has to find out something, I know he has a good topic for his term paper. And what an incredible amount of work he'll do!"

Many underachievers begin to want to learn when they manipulate objects. The teacher of beginning arithmetic employs blocks—or apples. The teacher of spherical trigonometry has a sphere that comes apart. The student who "plays" with blocks or a dismembered sphere begins to get concepts of number and space. When a pupil is given an opportunity to design and to build—to use tools, clay, Erector sets, science kits—the teacher has an opportunity to put matter in a subject, to show the pupil how study serves a practical end.

Curiosity is easily stirred, but it can be killed off just as easily. The most lethal method is by smothering with meaningless detail. There is a high mortality in foreign-language courses which start by requiring the students to memorize words, forms, and derivations apart from meaningful prose. But students who first meet a language in a passage whose meaning is already familiar, for example the Lord's Prayer, begin to ask what each word means, how the analogous English word came to its present form, and why the word order is different. They are eager to learn.

The problem approach stimulates both curiosity and the desire for mastery. If the solution of the problem involves "manipulation," e.g., building a model to demonstrate a point or performing an experiment to test an hypothesis, so much the better. But the problem must be one that appeals to the pupil. There is all the difference in the world between the first-grader's experiment with germinating seeds that he means to plant in a garden and the high-school senior's going through the motions of performing a chemistry experiment when he knows he can read about it in his text. The lab course is extremely interesting to the science major, who knows he must become an expert technician and wants to practice "measuring and mixing." But the student who is not working up to his ability in science because he expects to be a writer needs a different challenge. If he can be led to read Fabre's essays and can see how good writers and good experimental scientists share a passion for accurate observation and the recording of specific detail, he may then want to test his own powers by repeating, say, an experiment to prove Pascal's Law: "Pressure applied to a confined fluid at any point is transmitted undiminished through the fluid in all directions. . . ." We know one wise science teacher who catches the interest of his underachievers by having them read accounts of the practical applications of principles. He gives them descriptions of four-wheel brakes first and Pascal's Law second, and, if they don't want to experiment, he is content to let matters rest.

BUILDING ON INTERESTS

Experienced teachers have found that the most successful way of getting an underachiever to work harder is to build on some established interest. The case of George, the nonworking third-grader who is described at the opening of this chapter, is one of our favorites. His teacher tells how, encouraged by the discovery that George was a good reader, he managed to change the boy's attitude toward school.

I live in the neighborhood in which I teach. There's a fishing pier across the street from my house, and I often saw George there along with his mother, father, and grandparents. Soon after school opened he brought me a present of two three-inch fish. I asked the librarian for all available material on fishing and marine life and collected everything other teachers in the building could lend me. I just seemingly carelessly left some of this lying around. George began to nibble at the bait and in a few days was hooked hard. I asked him if he wanted to plan his year's work about fishing. His mother came to school and we had a three-way conference about the fundamentals of fishing and about fishing and the fundamentals. The reading was easy. An upper grade had lent us an encyclopedia and he spent much of his time reading it and the books from the library. His research led him into science, social studies, and art. Each week he was required to report to the class. He kept his studies secret so as to surprise them. When they were studying Maine he reported on lobster fishing. They enjoyed his reports, which enriched their own work. He kept a notebook and illustrated it with beautiful detailed drawings. His family took him to the Mystic Marine Museum, and he came back thrilled at having been on a real whaler.

Arithmetic posed a problem. He kept records of the time he spent fishing (and separate records for each other member of the family) and of what was caught, total weight, and market value. He went to the wholesale market to find out about this. He wrote fish stories involving the fisherman's habit of multiplying his catch. Before the end of the year he was drilling cheerfully with the class, even though there wasn't a fish in sight.

George had some guppies at home and we splurged with class funds and bought an aquarium, which he stocked. We all watched them multiply.

He began a shell and rock collection and made it a good one.

Even in music—he found some old sea chanties, which we all enjoyed learning.

I have never had so much fish in one year, but it did help turn a real nonachiever into an achiever. George is in Grade IV now and still working, though his teacher thinks not quite to capacity. After all, one can take just so much fish.

Luckily, most bright pupils do have special interests, which are easily discovered. As we pointed out when discussing the relation of hobbies to enrichment, all you have to do is to give a pupil a chance to talk, or assign the class a paper on the topic, "What I most like to do out of school." But you should not regard an interest as fixed for all time. You can overdo a good thing to the point where you and the child are both tired of it. We have even known fishermen who liked to play ball for a change. And you may feel that a particular interest, valuable though it may be as a hobby, is not challenging a pupil to use his full abilities. You will want to do what you can to help underachievers discover and develop new interests, particularly an interest in a school subject.

The genesis and growth of an individual's special interest

in a particular subject are often puzzling. Natural aptitude plays a part. Everyone likes to do what he can do well, whether this is arithmetic or painting. An interest thrives on success. A child with aptitude for mathematical reasoning likes arithmetic if he feels he is making progress in it and if he is praised for his accomplishments. If he is made to feel that he is doing badly, interest dies. Similarly, interest in an enrichment activity or a hobby grows as a child progresses in ability to grasp concepts or techniques and apply them. Your job as a teacher is to see that he explores many fields of knowledge and that, if his interest is caught, he has an opportunity to try himself out, is challenged to improve, and recognizes the improvement which he makes.

The pupil's direct experience with subjects and skills which might become special interests is necessarily limited. But vicarious experience is almost unlimited, both in breadth and depth. Any activity which the child sees admired adults engage in, either in real life or on TV, may appeal to him as something he would like to try. And, because adults have perfected their skills, the child has a model to copy and a standard to achieve. Books, both those he studies in his courses and those he reads for pleasure, are a main source of vicarious experience, and the accomplishments of people whom he meets in books may kindle his imagination. Many an underachiever has been reformed when a teacher gave him a good nontechnical biography of a pioneer in the teacher's subject.

Teachers use various methods to capitalize an underachiever's special interest. The most common is to talk to him about how knowledge of one or more subjects will help him become expert in his favored field. (It would be better still to let him talk himself into realizing this.) A project centering on an interest can be expanded to show the relation of different branches of knowledge, though few teachers can stand as much fish as George's did. When the class is studying a topic which involves an underachiever's interest even remotely, he can be asked to give the class a special report on it. In this case he

Story hour at the museum. The modern museum has skilled storytellers, who make the world of nature come alive for children too young to read. Teachers and parents of bright children should be familiar with the summer and winter programs of museums within reach of their community.

The dance. Youngsters who are interested and talented in ballet may have to seek private instruction. This group is enrolled in Miss Merle Marsicano's class at the Norfolk Summer Art School, Norfolk, Conn.

Landscape painting. Study of painting heightens every bright youngster's appreciation of art. He may, like Winston Churchill and Dwight Eisenhower, find painting an absorbing recreation, and he may discover a talent which justifies a professional career.

almost has to explain the connection to the class, and so will see it clearly himself. And the experience of working hard both for his own sake and out of pride in his hobby may be what he needs to convince him that careful preparation has values in itself. If the class receives his report well, he gains a status that he will want to keep. The able but lazy student can be energized by giving him a role which requires skill and effort, as in the case of the boy who learned to spell and punctuate when he began to write articles for the class paper. Sometimes a bright underachiever who is assigned to tutor a slower pupil reacts, like other beginning teachers, by preparing himself thoroughly. One seventh-grade teacher reports: "Lou was very good at math and worked hard in math period, but was lazy and inattentive in every other period. I placed his seat next to that of Giff, a very nice but not very bright boy. I asked Lou to help Giff with his math. Rather to my surprise he soon made himself responsible for helping Giff in all his subjects, and began to pay attention in class and study hard out of class to be sure he was right."

COMPETITION

A teacher of typewriting reports: "I have no problem with motivation. Students like to see their progress. Class charts and individual charts are posted. Timed tests for accuracy and speed are given regularly, but entries are placed on the charts only when the scores are better than the preceding scores. Thus the student competes with himself as well as with his classmates. And the class as a whole strives to better its average."

Educators have been known to argue fiercely about competition. We think it is possible to see where the danger lies and where the merit and to avoid the former while taking advantage of the latter.

The danger in competition between school children is that some are almost doomed to failure and the evils of frustration while others win success with little effort. Moreover, the fruits of victory, even though temporary, are sweet. Children can become excessive in their striving and overstrain themselves or resort to questionable methods to assure success. As Viktor Lowenfeld points out in *Creative and Mental Growth,* they may sacrifice originality and suppress self-expression in order to imitate the standards by which they expect to be judged.[9]

The merit of competition is that it does reflect a usual condition of adult life. There always have been and presumably always will be positions open only to those who have proved both ability and stamina by competition. True, the competition is rarely formal, and failure rarely final, but the element of comparison is there, in business as in sport. And the idea of proving oneself against strenuous competition certainly induces individuals to exert great and prolonged effort.

The evidence seems to indicate that the bright child who does not compete at least informally with other bright children tends to underachieve when he comes face to face with a difficult task. He fails to "measure up"—up to the job and up to his ability. He suffers from overrating himself and overconfidence. And when he sees others succeed where he has failed, he does not know how to take his disappointment. He may, in life and in games, become a bad sport, one who does not know how to win generously or lose gracefully.

Conant, in *The Citadel of Learning,* says:

> The spirit of competition is not, to my mind, something to be deplored. If kept in bounds by a spirit of "fair play," it is a healthy aspect of our tremendous emphasis on sports. There is no reason why the same type of motivation could not be utilized in the study of mathematics and foreign languages, provided, as in athletics, selection of the naturally talented is accepted as a matter of course; and provided that public opinion becomes convinced of the importance of the undertaking.[10]

Competition implies rewards and recognition—Conant is thinking of advanced standing in college and of college scholarships—but you can kindle the spirit of competition in an underachiever without resort to any formal contest or to the giving of prizes. One way is to be sure he realizes that he must do as well as his peers if he is to be grouped with them. One fifth-grade teacher reports: "Otto was about the brightest boy in the class but he wasn't concentrating on his drill in arithmetic and was actually holding back the top group. I said nothing but just transferred him to the middle group. When he found they were solving problems faster than he could, he very soon got down to work."

Whenever a subject offers possibilities for quantitative checks on achievement similar to those on speed and accuracy in typing, you can encourage students to compete with their own records and with other students. Teachers report this kind of competition in spelling, arithmetic computation, reading speed, vocabulary building (especially in foreign languages), and reading the books on a list. The list may relate to any subject where extra reading is desirable. In this type of situation the pupil recognizes that by extra effort he can surpass the average and perhaps prove himself superior to his classmates. Note that no promise of extra credit is necessary. The hope of achieving what the ordinary person does not do is enough.

A challenge in and of itself serves to stimulate the high-achiever. The motive is that which prompts men to scale mountains. When asked why he wanted to climb Mt. Everest, Mallory answered, "Because it's there." But the bright underachiever, confronted by a challenge, may just daydream of what he will do. He sets his "level of aspiration" unrealistically high for one of his past performance. Do not belittle him, but try to get him to make a start. Set him a task you know he can finish in the week, encourage him from day to day, and see that his record for the week (if he is successful) is duly acknowledged. Then he may set out to do better in the next week. Once he begins trying to surpass himself, the battle is won. And in the meantime he will have learned not to fool himself.

REWARDS

The desire for recognition, to be known as a person in one's own right, is one of the strongest of human motives. Most psychologists consider it a universal need. It can be satisfied in many ways. The individual wants the other members of the group to recognize as valuable the contributions which he makes. When he achieves this, his satisfaction is reinforced by the feeling of security which he gains. But if the group does not value a constructive effort, the individual makes himself conspicuous in other ways, perhaps by going to extremes in some particular, for example, in not working. Similarly, a child wants the expressed approval of his parents and his teacher. If he cannot earn approval he will at least compel attention, probably by misbehaving.

One of the strong arguments for grouping bright pupils together is that to do so increases the chances that the group will honor intellectual effort and achievement, whereas a regular class may not be able to appreciate these. In the regular class a bright pupil may study hard only when he cannot gain distinction in any other way—he would rather be an egghead than a nobody. Acceleration, too, places the mark of recognition on brightness. The student continues to strive for high achievement because it is his claim to fame.

Teachers have always used rewards to stimulate learning. Quintilian, the master of Rome's first public school, wrote nineteen hundred years ago, "The young pupil must be questioned and praised and taught to rejoice when he has done well. . . . At times also he must be engaged in competition and should be allowed to believe himself successful more often than not, while he should be encouraged to do his best by such rewards as may appeal to his tender years." In 1956, one first-grade teacher wrote, "When a child completes a library book, he brings it to school, receives a star, and has the opportunity to tell the story." Critics of marking systems, honor rolls, and contest prizes—

148

what Havighurst calls "extrinsic motivation"—say that the student too often works merely for the prize and so fails to develop any permanent interest in a subject, that as soon as he has seen his A for the year recorded, he thinks he has finished with what he has learned and rapidly forgets most of it. There is undoubtedly truth in this, and the effect is doubly bad in the case of the bright student who gets his A without trying. But, though gold stars are generally out of fashion, most teachers would cheerfully award a galaxy if they thought the bright underachiever would work harder. The trouble is that too usually he will not. He either does not care or rejects the reward as not worth the effort. He distinguishes himself from his bright fellows by making a cult of laziness.

If you have a student like this, your best chance of rousing him is to help him realize that working hard enough to earn an A now may be the only way he can achieve a goal which he thinks desirable. A boy whose main interest is swimming may be neglecting his schoolwork and getting poor marks. If he can be shown that his best hope of becoming an Olympic star is to go to Yale or Michigan or another college with an excellent swimming coach, he may begin to study harder in order to gain admission. A boy who already wishes to go to college can be shown that the probability of being admitted to the college of his choice will increase if he raises his average. Call a materialistic youngster's attention to the comparative lifetime earnings of high-school and college graduates: $165,000 for the former, $268,000 for the latter.

We must confess that all kinds of rewards seem to carry more weight with young people who are good students anyway than with the underachiever. The good students gather in the honors in stride. They may try a little harder to be sure of making Phi Beta Kappa, but they try hard anyway. We do not mean that there is no worth in honor societies, the New York State Regents' Gold Seal Diploma, the annual dinner tendered to senior-high-school honor pupils by the Woonsocket, R. I., board of education, and other devices for giving public recognition for good work. These may not change the attitude of the habitual underachiever but they do affect the large body of students. If good work is known to be honorable and honored, more bright students will do their best from the beginning.

PUNISHMENT

Parents of a stubborn underachiever often resort to punishment in the effort to get him to work. Favorite punishments are to forbid extracurricular activities, watching TV, or going to parties; extra tasks may be imposed or an allowance reduced. School authorities take similar action when they appropriately can. The denial of a privilege to a student who has not earned it is just and reasonable. It often forces a failing student to work hard enough to pass. Occasionally it wakes an underachiever up to his own foolish shortsightedness. But punishment is more effective in teaching a child what not to do than it is in stimulating study. If a boy who is punished for not working is not to hate the very idea of study, his teachers must maintain friendly relations with him and convince him that they are willing to work as hard to help him as they expect him to work for his own benefit. The cessation of punishment when the required standard is achieved may make a child try to maintain that standard. But if he is to rise above it he must have a positive goal which he wishes to reach.

GOALS, IMMEDIATE AND REMOTE

There is no discernible common denominator in underachievement, but high achievement is always accompanied by *purpose*. As Wrightstone said, "Purpose is the motive power of the learning process."

The ability to fix upon a distant goal and plan how to reach it and persist in efforts to reach it is an attribute of maturity.

And the more distant the goal, the more mature a person must be to see it clearly. Gordon W. Allport, in his book *Becoming,* writes, "The possession of long-range goals, regarded as central to one's personal existence, distinguishes the human being from the animal, the adult from the child, and in many cases the healthy personality from the sick." [11] Just as you do not expect a younger child to have a long span of interest, you do not expect him to look far ahead. But every time you help him plan how to do one thing in order to achieve another you are building his sense of purpose. Consider the difference in learning to spell words because they are the lesson for the day and learning to spell in order to write a correct letter.

To have one central purpose is valuable, but there should also be both minor purposes and intermediate purposes. The minor purposes need not necessarily be related to the major purpose. A student profits when he is trying to fill out a series in his stamp collection, even though his true ambition is to be an engineer. When the major goal is a relatively distant one, the steps toward it must be recognizable. Plans for a project in the elementary school should provide both for a culminating report and also for intermediate reports which, fairly complete in themselves, will become parts of the grand finale. The older student who is planning to become a doctor takes courage as he completes each step in his education.

The underachiever may think rather vaguely, "I'd like to know more about aviation," or even say, "I want to be an aviator." But he is not serious enough about either to make plans or to survive a difficulty. Give him a book about flying and he will drop it when he meets a sentence or a mathematical formula which he cannot understand.

If you have an underachiever with an infant ambition, nourish it carefully. Talk with him about it. Ask his family to arrange trips connected with it. Ask the librarian to give him an exciting book about it. Have him do a term paper on it or make a special report to the class. Praise him for any sincere effort he makes and for any evidence he gives of special

151

knowledge. Do not worry over whether or not his goal is one worthy of a lifetime interest. Changes in purpose do no harm. The virtue, at least in the case of the underachiever, is in the effort. The work is its own reward.

There are underachievers who suddenly find themselves and see where they want to go and how to get there. Some acquire a new and abiding interest apparently by chance. They make new friends or stumble on a new hobby or read a biography, and know, "This is it." The youngster's conviction is as irrational as love at first sight. But you must arrange for the pupil to catch a glimpse of the possibility—propinquity is Cupid's weapon. You can do your part by being sure that an underachiever has the opportunity to read biographies of leaders in different fields, to make interesting friends, and to share these friends' hobbies. Not a few underachievers wake up when a teacher takes time to be nice to them. They like the teacher and begin to realize that school need not be as dull as they had thought. They may take the teacher as a model and become academic-minded.

X

Mental Hygiene

On the playground, he wanders off by himself, finds a place to sit, and stays there. He never engages in games unless forced to. When he tires of staying by himself he picks up a bug and frightens the girls. Or he goes to the boys' game and kicks the ball. When I ask why, he replies, "I don't know."

—A Teacher.

Often my friends refer to me as "Shortie," and this hurts me a great deal. I suppose such a problem cannot be helped since it is up to the individual to help himself. Yet, why can't some people have regard for the feelings of others? I have tried to combat my inferiority complex, but the lack of consideration shown by some of my friends only increases my unhappiness. I have never written about this or told anyone how I feel. Maybe now someone will understand my problem and perhaps sympathize with me.

—A High-School Senior, writing on "My Major Problem."

All authorities agree that, on the average, the mental health of bright individuals is somewhat better than that of the population as a whole. *As a group* they have fewer breakdowns, are less likely to be hospitalized for mental illness, and have a lower suicide rate. Moreover, those who do become seriously maladjusted or mentally ill have a higher rate of recovery than less bright people who have suffered similarly.

153

MENTAL ILLNESS AND MENTAL HYGIENE

Unfortunately the average incidence of mental illness in our general population is so high that a group which is merely "better than average" is far from immune. At present it is estimated that as many as 12 per cent of the total population may expect hospitalization for mental illness for a longer or shorter period. There are many more who will be maladjusted to the point where they are extremely difficult to work with and to live with. It is estimated that as many as 20 per cent of the total population are maladjusted to this extent.

The effects of mental illness or serious maladjustment are tragic wherever they occur. They are particularly tragic in the case of a bright individual with high potentialities. The loss is not only his and his family's, but the world's. Consider that, if as few as 5 per cent of the top 10 per cent in intelligence of our population aged 20–60 suffer from mental illness, we are losing the services of 410,000 superior people. Probably at least another 820,000 are too maladjusted to fulfill their potentialities. If all of these people were functioning at capacity there would be smaller shortages of scientists, engineers, teachers, doctors, and other professional workers. Furthermore, there are only a few hundred people alive in the United States today who have IQ's of 180 or more. If their mental health is only slightly better than average, some of them will be disabled, at least temporarily, by mental illness, and some will be maladjusted to a point where they function at much less than capacity. One of these might have been another Shakespeare.

Depressing as are the statistics on mental illness, there is hope in the large and increasing proportion of individuals who regain health and fill positions of responsibility. Terman reported that by 1945 about 5 per cent of his gifted subjects (then aged 25–44) had suffered from serious maladjustment at one time or another, but more than half of these had materially improved under treatment. He concluded, "Superior intelligence does not appear to be a causal factor in mental disorder as found in this group but seems, rather, to have helped those affected to overcome their difficulties. The insight and intelligent co-operation shown by those who became mental patients has almost certainly contributed to the improvement noted in several of the cases." [1]   And since 1945 there have been notable advances in the treatment of mental patients.

The same high intelligence which helps bright individuals overcome mental illness helps bright children solve problems that, if not solved, might have serious effects.   Observers and the young people themselves agree that brightness often entails difficulties in adjustment and that these troubles grow lighter as the children grow older.   Hollingworth, in an article, "The Child of Very Superior Intelligence as a Special Problem in Social Adjustment," says, "Apparently these superior organisms tolerate well the strains put upon them by reason of their deviation from the average.   However, that an organism stands strain well is no reason for putting or leaving strain unnecessarily upon it." [2]   In an article, "Hazards of the High I.Q.," a psychiatrist, Douglas A. Thom, and his collaborator, Nancy Newell, though agreeing with Hollingworth, have commented, "Nevertheless . . . early environmental experiences leave their mark in conditioned reactions which, by repetition, become permanent traits." [3]   The moral is that you should not leave the bright pupil to solve his emotional problems by himself any more than you should let him take care of himself in academic matters.

A WORD OF CAUTION

You will probably be both happier and more efficient if, in your attempts to help your bright pupils make a good adjustment, you think of yourself as a teacher, "first, foremost, and all the time."   As a teacher, you work constructively to help all children, including your bright children, *learn and grow*.   You correct mistakes so that the child will realize for himself what is expected of him and will strive to achieve the highest standard of learning and of human relations possible for him. The psychiatrist or therapist, on the other hand, is concerned with diagnosis and treatment of maladjustment and mental illness.

Much that you do as a good teacher gives to the normal child strength to resist strain and to the maladjusted child strength to overcome the results of strains that have been too great. But if you trespass on the province of the psychiatrist, not only are you being unethical—because you do not have the requisite knowledge and training—but also you are making trouble for yourself and your class. One psychiatric team, after years of work with classroom teachers, pointed out that the therapist must accept and permit the expression of infantile demands and drives, while the teacher must work for the socially acceptable control of these, and that the therapist, working with an individual, does not need to restrain behavior that might be contagious and disrupt a classroom. The team concluded that "understanding the child does not entail giving up the control functions" and that "mental hygiene's contribution is to help teachers become more effective teachers, not part-time therapists." [4]

THE ROLE OF THE TEACHER

We do not mean that you should not be well grounded in the psychology of mental illness and mental hygiene. On the contrary, sound knowledge lets you play an important part in prevention. There is increasing evidence that many signs of impending maladjustment appear in quite young children. Teachers are the only agents of the community who have the opportunity to observe children under conditions which disclose such behavior. If you are aware of the symptoms and recognize them in a child, you can mobilize the resources of your community and your state to assist him and his family.

Moreover, whether you wish to or not, you influence the

emotional and social development of every child you teach. If you know something about the causes of maladjustment you can make a special effort to help a child who has a bad background. Studies of well-adjusted children from bad environments show that the saving factor has often been a teacher who took time to be interested and to help. When you cannot act constructively you can at least try to avoid any action that might aggravate the causes of difficulty.

CRACKED AND BROKEN HOMES

Research into the background of disturbed children has shown that from 35 per cent to 50 per cent of them come from homes where strong emotional tension is evident. A 13-year-old girl writes:

I don't consider my problem very major because many girls have the same one. My mother and father were divorced when I was three. Last year my father remarried and my mother followed suit. It's a little difficult loving two mothers and two fathers at the same time. When I visit my father and come home and tell my mother what fun I had she tries to contradict me. She and my stepfather are very jealous of my real father and vice versa. Sometimes I hardly think about it but at others it seems it's unbearable. Sometimes I dream my father is killed or something awful is happening.

The importance of home conditions in the cases of maladjusted bright children is reflected in the article by Thom and Newell cited earlier. It reports a follow-up study of 43 children with IQ's of 130–166 who had been referred to Massachusetts child-guidance clinics between 1927 and 1934. The interval between first contact and follow-up averaged eleven years. By the time of the follow-up, 21 of the children had made a successful adjustment. The other 22 "had achieved only mediocre success or were definitely maladjusted or unhappy." Of the less successful group, 12 had come from homes where there was domestic conflict, and "only one child had had security, harmony, and good training." The homes from which the successful group came "were predominantly good or had improved during the interval between first and second contacts." But (and this is important to remember) in 7 of the successful cases "early training had been lax and inconsistent, or there had been antagonism and friction in the home." These 7 children, "with increasing independence of family influences, were able to make a successful adaptation." [5] Another Massachusetts study shows that of a group of 57 antisocial children, of whom 20 were superior, only 9 came from "a cohesive family group." [6]

Frequently homes are broken or cracked because the parents are themselves maladjusted. In such cases there is little or nothing you can do directly with the home. You are not a marriage counselor any more than you are a therapist. And experience has shown that maladjusted parents rarely co-operate well, if at all, with a teacher. They break all kinds of promises and very generally refuse to take a child to a guidance clinic. But there are helpful measures you can employ in school when you know or suspect there is trouble in the home.

When the parents are divorced or when parental relations are strained the child feels very insecure. You can help him by taking time to give him some individual attention. Do everything you can to make him feel he is somebody in his own right, that he can win your respect and liking. Give him things to do for you, and express your thanks. If he talks to you about conditions at home, reassure him as to his own future. If he thinks a divorce is pending, explain that he will surely be taken care of. Get him to discuss his own vocational plans, and show him how he can still carry them out.

FAULTY HOME DISCIPLINE

The bright child is very quick to see how he can take advantage of a parent who spoils him or whose discipline is inconsistent. He is equally quick to play one parent against the other when they disagree about what should be done. And the child may not be above trying to play the home against the school. One teacher writes:

Sid is in Grade VI. He has an IQ of 139. His parents are both very bright. They've read a lot of psychology and psychiatry and have decided that complete permissiveness is the best policy in child rearing. Sid never finishes an assignment. Anything he sees in the classroom, for example a science kit, he regards as his own, whether he is using it or not. He lies about school to the parents and they believe anything he says. One of his tricks in school is to sit, pencil in hand but doing nothing, until the first child finishes his work. Then Sid drops his pencil and says, "Mother says I'm to work only till the first pupil finishes."

Another teacher writes:

Hal gets anything and everything he wants. His mother tries to drive him hard; his father, pleasant and good-natured, begs her to let up. Smiling, affable Hal sits back and lets the squabbles roll over him. He just can't be bothered with anything unpleasant, least of all work, in home or in school.

Thom and Newell, in the article cited earlier, say that, on first referral to the clinic, 22 of the 43 children "were being handled with inconsistent methods." The discipline improved under the clinic's guidance of the parents, and behavior problems had practically disappeared by the time of the follow-up. "In general," Thom and Newell say, "the early misbehavior may be attributed to the aggressiveness and the self-assertion of the brilliant child who is testing his wit and will against the forces of his environment." [7]

Luckily, most bright children are as quick to respect firm consistent discipline as they are to challenge that which is lax and inconsistent. When they see that misbehavior always results in a penalty, they know that good behavior is the part of wisdom. Their reasoning powers enable them to recognize the justice of the punishment that fits the crime. One teacher writes: "Yates came to school the first day armed with a water pistol and doused another boy. I promptly took the pistol away. The next day he didn't finish his arithmetic, though I'd told him once or twice to get to work. I helped him after school until he had done all the examples and had them correct. Since then, there's been no trouble. His parents say they can't control him at home, but he's good as gold in school."

Bright children who misbehave at home often seem to welcome the stricter discipline of the school. Their insight lets them know that continued misbehavior is foolish, but if they have started misbehaving they find it hard to stop. They are grateful for the support of your firm hand in the effort to control themselves. The occasional bright child who, despite your efforts, persists in aggressive misbehavior in school is probably deeply disturbed. His best hope lies in treatment at a good child-guidance clinic.

SIBLING RIVALRY

The extent to which jealousy of a brother or sister may upset bright children shows how subject they are to strains which affect all children.[8] And in some situations brightness may aggravate sibling rivalry.

When the first-born child is bright, he attracts not only the attention and admiration of his parents but also of their friends. He early becomes a companion of his parents on a level that is out of the reach of a slower child. If there is no new baby in the family until he is five or six or older, he becomes quite used to depending on his parents for company and entertainment. Then, when a new baby comes and his parents devote a great deal of time to the new arrival, he feels that he is being willfully neglected. The following is a severe but typical case.

Ivan, Grade III, age 7 years and 8 months, IQ 134, had a splendid record through second grade. His achievement in all subjects was well advanced. His social adjustment was good, though his teachers commented on the fact that his manners were those of an adult rather than a child's and he seemed to use rather stilted words and phrases. Nonetheless, the other children liked him and he played well with them. In Grade III he went all to pieces. His work, especially his handwriting, deteriorated badly. He was rude to the teacher and constantly fought other children. The school social worker visited the home and found that Ivan had acquired a new baby brother during the summer. His mother reported that when she was in the room Ivan was extremely solicitous for the baby's comfort, but that once, when she had left him alone with the baby, she came back to find him slapping it. And he began to be cruel to his dog. Ivan was given an emergency referral to the child-guidance clinic. After some weeks, during which the psychiatrist saw Ivan and his mother regularly, the boy began to return to normal. His work and his behavior improved. There were no more incidents of cruelty.

When a bright child has a brother or sister who is still brighter, or who does better work in school, he can hardly escape comparisons. Not seldom both his parents and his teachers ask, "Why don't you work as hard as Matty?" The result may be sullen rebellion and refusal to work at all. A psychologist writes:

Linc's high-school home-room teacher called me one night and asked if I could make time to test him. She had had his older brother, a brilliant student, and wondered why Linc didn't do as well. She was almost sure he wasn't stupid, but forcing him had so far done no good. When Linc came into the office for the test he looked cross. He didn't respond to my attempts at friendliness, and I decided to start the test right away and began to shoot questions at him. Almost in spite of himself he got interested and did very well. I didn't calculate his IQ, because I was short of time. He was clearly superior and I thought I'd better have a talk with him. I explained that he was bright and asked why he didn't do better work. Little by little it came out that he thought no one liked him, that all they did was to compare him with his brother. I said, "Now look, a home-room teacher doesn't go to the trouble of calling me up after hours and arranging a special test unless she's interested in a student and wants to help him." It was a new idea to him that he could be worth special attention, and it was the turning point in his high-school career.

A youngster who feels that he is at least as bright as his brother or sister but that he is being deprived of a college education because of being the oldest or youngest or the wrong sex, may be very forlorn. A high-school senior writes: "My parents as of now are planning to send me to college if I can win a scholarship. But if I can't, I can't go, because my younger brother is the main one who needs to go to college."

When you have a student whose sibling you know, try not to compare the two in any way, directly or by implication. Praise your present student for things he does well. Praise him particularly for things he may do better than his brother or sister, but without a hint that you are comparing them. In this way you can give a jealous pupil a sense of his own worth and a degree of self-confidence. Both are necessary for high achievement.

When a parent, in consulting you about a student's poor work, happens to compare it with superior work done by a sibling, you can discuss the need of self-confidence and the danger in comparisons. A mother writes:

We have two bright daughters: Dotty, quick and impulsive, and Betty, slow and methodical. In talking together, Betty's teacher and I discovered that we were both putting pressure on the child to hurry up. The result was that she was doing very little and was manifestly unhappy. We decided that we'd be careful never to compare the two girls' work, and that we'd praise Betty for the meticulously perfect work she did when she was given time. She cheered up immediately, and her teacher thinks that later this year some work with the reading consultant can be arranged which may help Betty learn some short cuts.

WHEN BOTH PARENTS WORK

Parents who recognize that their child is bright are tempted to make as much money as they can to provide for his higher education. They sometimes feel that they are sacrificing themselves for the good of the child, when there is more than a possibility that they are sacrificing the child. We are not saying that mothers should not work, even when there is no stark necessity for it. But great care ought to be taken to keep the child from feeling neglected or rejected.   A 13-year-old girl in Grade VIII writes:

> My major problem is that my mother and father both work and home just isn't what it used to be.   We used to sit home evenings and talk together and enjoy our home.   Now Mom is working she doesn't get much sleep and is irritable and impatient and hollers more.   I've asked her to quit but she says they need the money for me and I'm old enough to take care of myself.   I'd rather have my mother home and not go to college.   I broke down and cried 2 or 3 times.   I just don't know what's going to happen.   We would all have a better home life if she quit working.

> Stuart [writes his teacher] came into my eighth-grade home room with a somewhat bad reputation.   His work had never been good.   We give standardized tests in eighth grade as a help in guidance, but not until then.   I was surprised to see Stuart's scores: IQ 127, achievement all at least up to grade level, and mathematics ninth-grade level.   One afternoon when he'd done everything but work I asked him to stay and talk with me.   This is the conversation as I remember it:
>
> "Stuart, this wasn't one of your good days.   What's the trouble?"
>
> "Went home this noon.   Had a tuna-fish sandwich.   No one at home.   Came back here.   You weren't here, either."
>
> "Would you like someone at home at noon?"
>
> "Yeah, but my mother works.   My brothers work and they've got girls.   They are not interested in me.   No one is."
>
> "Would you like me to talk with your mother?"
>
> "Yeah, but it won't do any good.   She says I'm old enough to take care of myself."
>
> "Would you like to come and visit with me at noontime after you've had lunch?"
>
> "Yeah, I guess so."
>
> I went to see his family at once.   It took some time to convince them that Stuart deserved more attention.   But his mother did give up her job and gave Stuart a hot lunch every noon.   An older brother volunteered to help him with his homework.   His father is spending some time with him and has taken him to New York to the Natural History Museum.   Stuart's attitude to school has changed.   His classwork has improved by leaps and bounds, he's making friends, and he gave the class an enthusiastic account of his trip to New York.   He's not back at noontime to visit with me now,

but he frequently stops after school to see if he can help me—and to talk!

Not all cases turn out as well as Stuart's. But even one success makes a teacher's life worth living.

SHYNESS AND WITHDRAWAL IN SCHOOL

From the bright child's own point of view his principal problem in school is that of making friends. The bright adolescent may suffer from a more-than-typical shyness. A 13-year-old girl writes: "I am self-conscious, so I am afraid to meet new people. I am afraid they may look at me continually and I feel funny. I'm even afraid to stand up and recite for my classmates." And again and again both girls and boys describe themselves as "unable to find anything to say when I meet strangers, particularly of the opposite sex."

Exaggerated shyness in a bright child is sometimes a result of being younger or smaller than the other children in the class. Sometimes it seems both the result and the cause of an undue amount of solitary activity. The child finds reading more pleasant than group play and so does not have much experience in give-and-take with other children. When he discovers that he does not know how to get along with them, even though he may be eager to, he withdraws into a world of his own.

Quiet children often escape their teachers' notice. Thom and Newell say of their group that "the more retiring students had often been overlooked and, from the clinical point of view, had lacked guidance in utilizing their abilities and in making personal adjustments." [9]

Elementary teachers should endeavor to see that all bright children do make many friends, share fully in group activities, and learn to stand up before the class. Secondary-school teachers can help by holding home-room discussions on etiquette and on making and keeping friends. Senior high schools which have conducted short courses in etiquette during activity period or after school have found them extremely popular.

When a pupil at any level fails to overcome his shyness quickly, when he constantly withdraws from contacts with other pupils, and especially if he seems to be daydreaming to excess, he needs careful handling. Rapid forcing of contacts with many pupils or of activities like speaking before the class may aggravate matters. The safer course is to arrange for the pupil to do a considerable amount of work with two or three other pupils. The group can be established on the basis of mutual interests or of a sociogram.

Classes willingly write answers to questions of the type on which sociograms are based, such as, "Whom would you like to have on your team?—in your reading group?—to play with you at recess?" The answers help you locate the bright child who is isolated by his classmates. Then, even though no one has chosen him, you can assign him to work and play with some of the children he has chosen. Be careful to change the composition of the groups from time to time and for different activities. Be careful, too, not to force him constantly on any one popular pupil, because that might cause the star to resent him.

Move slowly in accustoming the self-conscious pupil to oral reports. Let him report several times to small committees before you ask him to stand on his feet before the class.

You can expect the shy pupil to take some time while he gains confidence. He may have occasional relapses to a tongue-tied state and may be inclined to treat these as a sign that he can never speak before the class. Do not accept a failure as final. Join his group on occasion and draw him out on topics you know he has studied. If he responds well, ask him then and there (so he does not have time to worry) to give the same explanation to a somewhat larger group.

The habitually shy pupil, the one who continues to withdraw from contacts with others despite your cautious and continued efforts to help him, may be in great need of skilled psychological assistance. Excessive withdrawal is often a symptom of incipient mental illness. The sooner an expert determines whether or not the pupil is in danger, the better.

Usually the bright pupil shows insight into the problem of

165

his own shyness and applies himself to overcome it. A high-school boy writes:

My major problem is in making friends easily. Shyness can be used as an excuse but it probably [crossed out] isn't that at all. I know the solution is to stop thinking about yourself and being sorry you don't have more friends. The only way to have friends is to be sincerely interested in them. Of course you also have to decide what you want in friends: a flock of casual acquaintances or a few good friends whose friendship will deepen in later years. The main thing to remember is not to forget to be friendly and interested in everyone, especially in high school, and that is what I am going to do.

MATURITY AND IMMATURITY

The bright child is exposed to confusion and strain when he develops at different rates physically, intellectually, socially, and emotionally. He may be big for his chronological age but small for his mental age. His social development tends to be ahead of his chronological age, especially if he has associated much with adults or older children. He probably reads adult books, and so has an intellectual acquaintance with situations and problems which are far beyond his experience. He has little means of judging whether the problems are universal or not, and he cannot know that hosts of people in real life survive situations by which people in books are overcome. And confusion is confounded when his friends are either behind him in intellectual development or ahead of him in physical development. Parents who fail to understand the gap between their child's chronological age and mental age increase his difficulties when they treat him like a baby.

Moral problems depress some bright teen-agers. They struggle with questions like "Why does God permit evil in the world?" "Is God personal or merely a Force?" "If our religion is true, why should we tolerate unbelievers?" "Why are people so prejudiced?" and "Why can't everyone have enough to eat?"

More concretely, they are upset when they see their contemporaries smoke or drink or pet. They decry cliques in their schools. They hate to see classmates join outlawed secret societies.

You can help young people face these problems by having general class discussions of them. You can also encourage the pupils who consult you to join an active church group. When they find other people have the same doubts and worries and are struggling to act constructively, they feel less alone. Do all you yourself can to confirm your pupils in high ideals. Show them that a person can follow an ideal without judging other people and that if he desires to be of service he should not start by throwing stones.

Dating may pose problems for bright girls rather earlier than for most of their contemporaries. All girls tend to mature earlier than boys, and bright girls earlier still. While 12-year-old boys in Grade VII are complaining that their 14-year-old friends prefer dating to baseball, the 12-year-old girls in the same grade can be beset by conflicts with their families and triangles in their love affairs. One writes: "The problem I have in friendship is I like two boys at one time. One of the girls at school liked one of the boys who liked me. He came to me and wanted me to choose, but I didn't say anything because the other boy would get mad. Besides I'm too young to get serious about one boy." Another writes: "If my mother finds my boy friend in the house, she calls me and tells me to get him out of the house. Last night he was just playing cards and Mother told me if he came in the house again I couldn't have him even in the yard. I think Mother is mean, don't you? I will try to overcome this problem although my sister can have Boys in the house, I don't see why I can't."

It seems cruel to laugh at young people's growing pains, but luckily bright youngsters can usually laugh at their own. If they do not make fun of themselves at the moment, they will next month or next year. And time and one's own laughter are marvelous therapeutic agents.

PRESSURE

Between home and school, bright boys and girls can be subjected to great pressure to do many different things.

Younger children commonly have more free time than older, unless their parents are insisting on long hours of practice on a musical instrument. If the child concerned is not really talented and is not interested in music, he can be filled with unhealthy resentment. We confess to sympathy with the child who wrote: "My mother makes me take violin lessons, which I hate. I think I should have more time to play with the other children."

Teen-agers, at a time of life when they need enormous amounts of energy just for growing, sometimes do so many things that they suffer constantly from fatigue. A high-school junior writes: "My major problem is how to be able to keep the few friends I have and do my schoolwork and help my mother and take part in extracurricular activities and find time for my painting and still not be so tired as to fight with my family." Another says, "Homework, chores, a part-time job, my girl—each demands some time each day. I have to keep my marks up so as to get into college, and that means never slight homework. But the teachers always pile it on together. Why can't they synchronize and spread it out a bit?"

Communities which have Parent-Teacher-Student Councils have done a good deal to "synchronize." The Council reaches agreement on a desirable schedule and suggests standards. Parents agree not to demand more than a certain number of hours of chores each week. Students agree not to go out on weekday nights. Teachers agree on maximum amounts of homework and arrange to distribute this evenly over the week.

A simple bit of arithmetic will convince you that homework can make unreasonable demands on even the bright student. If he is taking 5 subjects in a 5-hour schoolday and each teacher gives him homework that requires an hour of study, he will put in a 10-hour day on schoolwork alone. Overwork is one of the strains that can result in maladjustment. We hope that, when parents and teachers are co-ordinating their demands on young people, they will provide an hour or two a day for sheer loafing and one morning a week to "sleep in."

EXPLOITATION

The talented or gifted youngster who gives public performances at an early age may benefit or may suffer. Much depends on how talented he really is. If his performance is worthy of attention on its merits and not just because it is unusual from one so young, he deserves to be heard. And his audiences profit too. It would have been foolish to deprive the world of Menuhin's music until he was 21. Moreover, public appearances, whether on the concert stage, the theatrical stage, or on TV, stimulate high endeavor.

The danger in early exhibition comes when it serves adult cravings for money or fame at the expense of the child's sound development. Parents, and sometimes teachers, may exaggerate and sensationalize a child's unusual abilities. He then learns to look on himself, not as an honest performer earning a career through the use of his talent, but as an infant prodigy. When his years overtake his achievement, as they inevitably will, he finds he has little to offer. In the meantime he has become accustomed to easy success. He is as handicapped as a badly spoiled child.

One principal describes how a child can be exploited within the school. He writes: "We foolishly let out the news that one boy in our school had an IQ of 184 on a Stanford-Binet test. We quoted Symonds to the effect that an IQ as high as this occurred only once in three million children. The newspapers sent a reporter and a photographer to interview the child, and a teachers college wanted him to come talk to a class. It wasn't the right sort of attention, and his parents and I stopped it short." One teacher's quick realization of danger and real regret over an episode also illuminate the possible ill effects of misusing a child's abilities: "Alex could already read when he entered my first grade. He had an IQ of 142. He was still very babyish-looking but got on well with the others. The sixth-grade teacher asked to have him read to her children. She did it, I'm afraid, to show them up and to make fun of their poor work. I felt it was an unhealthy situation for my boy and for her children, too. I never allowed that again."

It seems hardly necessary to say that the students who appear on school programs over local broadcasting stations or hold a panel discussion for the Men's Club are not being exploited. They represent the school. The attention stimulates them and is a reward for good work. But it is wise in nominating a pupil for this type of performance, and in coaching him for it, to make sure that he understands he will be serving the school as well as himself. It is also wise not to use the same individuals over and over again. One talented young pianist writes: "I always have to play for assemblies and at dances. I'd like to dance, too."

LIABILITIES AND ASSETS

Of the 5-year-old Jim who is devoted to dinosaurs, his kindergarten teacher says: "He exceeds most of his contemporaries in imagination and knowledge. Consequently his ideas of fun are somewhat removed from theirs. When he suggests hunting for fossils or dinosaur remains, they don't know what he is talking about. So he tells them what they should do."

The bright pupil cannot help but feel different from his average age mates. He *is* different. He knows and uses words which they cannot understand. He is interested in events and problems with which the other children have no concern. He thinks ahead and sees possible results which make him want to persist in a game or a project when they want to quit. Equally, he sees dangers where they blithely rush in. If he has no companions who are as bright as he is, he begins to feel apart from the group and alone.

One result is a tendency to solitary pursuits, to reading, collecting, and scientific experimentation. The occupations are themselves desirable and satisfying, and therein lies much of their danger. They reward the bright child who devotes himself to them, and so solitariness may be conditioned as a character trait.

The solitary child misses out on group games and especially on rough-and-tumble play. He falls behind in physical skills, and when, by chance, he finds himself in a baseball game, he feels awkward and inadequate. As we have seen, a bright pupil, because in nonphysical activities he is accustomed to easy success, is very likely to exaggerate any weakness at sports and to avoid them.

But the typical bright youngster has assets which give him specific help in facing these situations and adjusting to them. His insight lets him know how other children feel. His breadth of interest lets him enjoy a wide range of activities. His superior physical development makes it possible for him to hold his own even with somewhat older children if he will only try and practice. He is capable of applying his intelligence to human relations and of analyzing and solving his problems. But if he is not to suffer strain in the process, he needs assistance from you.

THE PROPER STUDY OF THE TEACHER IS THE CHILD

Just as systematic observation of each pupil in your room contributes much to your identification of bright children, so also it lets you know which children need most help in adjusting. Run over your class list, thinking about each child as you go. Is he too much alone? A daydreamer? Overaggressive? Does he play for attention? Does he follow you around as though he felt a special need for affection and support? Does he have unusually frequent or severe bursts of temper? Does he take part in group sports and games?

Remember that children change, and that conditions in the home and group also change, sometimes with great rapidity. So be alert to any unusual behavior on the part of a child, and check through your class list once a month or so.

Some more formal methods of exploring the adjustment of your pupils supplement your judgment, the way standardized tests supplement your opinions of intelligence. The sociogram and other sociometric devices are popular with teachers and are useful instruments.[10] Pupils' essays on topics like, "My Major Problem at School," or, "—at Home," can be very revealing. And papers on more general topics, like "Friendship," say much between the lines.

When you think a pupil is not adjusting as well as he might, you should consider the possible sources of difficulty. You will find outlines for a case study in Blair's *Diagnostic and Remedial Teaching* [11] and in our *Practical School Discipline and Mental Hygiene*.[12] Points to keep in mind include: the child's health history, with special reference to birth injuries, brain injuries, and encephalitis; the emotional tone of the home; attitudes toward brothers and sisters; sources of prolonged strain or worry, e.g., over the health of a parent or over the family's economic condition; and any violently distressing incident that may continue to prey on the child's mind. And, as we have said so many times, you must be sure that the bright child is being challenged by his schoolwork.

HELP FROM EXPERTS

If you discover a pupil whose behavior—either aggressive or withdrawing—seems to be unusual for his age and unusual in intensity or duration, you should begin at once to get what help you can. Most school systems have established procedures for calling in experts. The principal is normally and properly the first person you should consult. Do not delay because of over-confidence in your own abilities or fear that you might be considered an alarmist. *The sooner a child in trouble is helped, the better the prospect of a rapid and complete recovery.* If your system does not employ a school psychologist or a school social worker, and if there is no psychiatrist readily available, you may be able to secure help from your local Family Welfare Society or from the state departments of education, mental health, or welfare. Do not forget that the family doctor is familiar with all sorts of emergencies. If he cannot be of direct assistance he will know what steps to take.

MENTAL HYGIENE IN THE CLASSROOM

Therapy is the specialist's business, but mental hygiene is everyone's business. Your classroom practices can do much toward helping your pupils keep emotionally well. Here are some principles which are important guides.

Liking. Long before there was so much emphasis on the child's need to be loved, everyone said, "The good teacher likes children." You cannot love every child in your room. But you can try to respond warmly when a pupil shows he likes or admires you. He may be hunting for affection which he is denied at home, or he may be making a normal transition to independence of his family. You help him when you call him pleasantly by name, smile at him, and give him an occasional pat on the back, physically and metaphorically. And all of these things are even more important when you have a pupil who holds himself aloof.

Acceptance. Boys and girls often think that the way they feel and the way they behave must estrange them from their friends and other people. This is especially true of the bright child who feels different. You can help him by letting him know you know how he feels and that you think he is all right. Even when you disapprove something he does and have to con-

173

trol his behavior, he responds to an understanding, "I know how you feel, I've felt that way myself, but if we all gave way to our feelings we'd never get anything done." If you accept the intellectual activities of a bright child as desirable in themselves and for him, you reduce his feeling of being different and actually make it easier for him to associate with other children. But if you laugh at the words he uses, the books he reads, and his fondness for chess, you hurt him, perhaps irreparably.

Recognition. Recognition reinforces acceptance. The bright child thrives on working hard to achieve a goal which he knows you and the class respect. Achieving the goal is in itself satisfying, but it is even more satisfying to hear well-earned praise.

Security. Firm confidence that one is a fully accepted *member of the group* is the foundation of good adjustment. Here again the bright child's feeling of difference is a hazard. You can counsel him on how to avoid irritating his friends. You can show him the necessity for taking part in group activities, and especially in those in which he does not excel. And you can arrange for him to do things with children whom he likes and who share his interests.

New experiences. Exploring and adventuring grow out of security. The insecure child is afraid to venture on new projects. But he must have new experiences if he is to mature emotionally. So encourage your bright pupils to follow their natural bent and venture into new fields, intellectual and material.

Expression. Everyone needs to express his feelings. We have discussed how you help a child when you let him talk out his troubles to you. Play, dramatics, painting, writing, composing, and all kinds of creative activity are excellent means for bright children to express what they feel. The fact that the activity has a goal of its own, that it "sublimates" the feeling, is all to the good. You do not have to be versed in "play therapy" and "role-playing" to promote healthy and health-giving expression on the part of your pupils. Give them the opportunity, and teach them proper techniques when these will facilitate expression. Let a child, if he wishes, explain meanings which are obscure to you. But do not pry into hidden meanings or try to interpret them psychoanalytically.

Classroom atmosphere. If your classroom is a bright, cheerful, friendly place and you are a bright, cheerful, friendly, understanding teacher, you are building good mental health in your pupils. You may be formal or informal, provided that you enjoy your work, that you feel pride in seeing your pupils develop, and that you stand ready to help each one make the most of himself. One teacher writes:

> Despite the fact that so many people think of the gifted child as an unadjusted one, my experience has been to the contrary. I have known and worked with many gifted children who have been extremely happy well-adjusted individuals as children and have remained so. Dolly is an example. Now an adolescent, she is taking that difficult period in stride just as she has met and weathered other years in stride. Popular with her peers and with adults alike, she is kindly disposed to those not as alert as she. Talented in music, accelerated a grade, she leads a wholesome life because it is a balanced one.

XI

Character Development

*The Scholarship Committee [of students at Wood-
row Wilson High School, Middletown, Connecticut] has
been in existence since 1948. The nine students are selected by the Student Council with provision for con-
tinuity. The Committee sponsors fund-raising activities
and works toward an interest-bearing reserve. It formu-
lates and administers the standards for selection of candidates, and selects the winner. There has never been a
leak in information or a premature rumor. The faculty
have kept a "hands off" policy. They have a high regard
for student leadership and objectivity in the management of the endeavor. The experience noticeably enhances the social concern of student for student, gives
genuine experience in banking and investment procedures, and fixes responsibility on an adult decision-
making level. The pupils actually gain satisfaction in
terms of service.*

—Robert Stoughton, Re-
port on Provisions for the
Gifted, *Connecticut State
Department of Education
Bulletin.*[1]

Bright boys and girls who are high-achievers are commonly
characterized by their teachers as responsible, persistent, and full
of initiative.   They get along well with their fellows, and are
natural leaders.   A picture of good early development is drawn
by one sixth-grade teacher.

Cole is 11 years old and has an IQ of 139.   His grade levels on
the Stanford Achievement Test are 3½ to 4½ years ahead of his ac-

tual level. He has always been slight and small for his age but he is healthy and full of energy. He has a younger brother and sister, also very bright. His father left high school at the end of his junior year because his family needed financial support. He is a skilled mechanic and a foreman in the factory where he works. Cole's mother is a high-school graduate and was a clerk in a factory office before she was married. The parents know their children are bright. Both the father and mother have fine senses of humor. They do a great deal with the children. Each tries to spend some time alone with each child each week. Cole's father coaches him in baseball, plays chess with him, and takes him and his friends on Saturday excursions—sometimes to a museum, sometimes to a ball game.

Even when he was in kindergarten Cole was independent. Although he had to cross the railroad tracks, he begged his mother not to accompany him to and from school, and she didn't. His kindergarten teacher described him for the record as "bright but too serious." The first-grade teacher said he "is well-adjusted socially and emotionally and is very co-operative; works hard." He always received straight A's except in arithmetic and physical education, and since his fifth-grade teacher told him he'd have to know mathematics to be a scientist he's had an A in arithmetic, too.

He's known he wanted to be a scientist since he was 5. He says now he cannot decide whether he can help people more by becoming a doctor or a chemist. His parents have given him a microscope and a chemistry set. I've turned my old college chemistry books over to him. He's specially interested now in algae. He collects rocks and stamps, makes models of all sorts, is very creative with crayons, charcoal, paints, and clay. He reads a lot, mostly science and history. He enjoys making up poems and stories, has a lovely soprano voice, and plays the accordion. He often does extra work and reports on various subjects without being told to do so. He persists in anything he undertakes. Lastly, he is very much interested in a girl named Lily and enjoys square dancing with her.

He's only fair at baseball, but knows every rule of the game, and the other children often ask him to act as umpire. The children also choose him to be a discussion leader and a committee chairman. But he's a good follower in both sports and the academic groups—he's always ready to listen to others. He has a good sense of humor and can laugh at himself—as when he fell over the dog who was asleep behind third base.

Certain features stand out in this account of Cole. His home life is happy and his parents are handling him wisely. He has already decided on his general field of specialization (science), and, though he has an extremely wide range of interests and an almost uniformly high level of achievement, much of his reading and several of his activities are related to science. He has a sense of humor, despite having been a serious kindergartner. Lily is an indication that he will have a good heterosexual adjustment. The other children recognize him as a leader, but he is neither conceited nor bossy. The question is, how can one boy be developing so well while others, as bright or brighter, are underachievers academically and unpopular personally?

CONCEIT, SNOBBISHNESS, BOSSINESS

A junior-high-school girl writes: "I make friends easily, but after a while they think I am conceited and they are not friendly any more."

A bright child can find it very hard to meet his contemporaries on their own level and take an interest in what they say and do. It is not necessarily that the individual is conceited or that he feels superior in any way. On the contrary, he is more likely to feel inferior, because he longs to be one of the gang. But some of the time he is, as one teacher says of a pupil, "bored with everything he has to do and with everyone with whom he comes in contact and he shows he's bored and that's that. He presents a pathetic picture." And when a question in which he is interested does come up, he very probably knows the answer and gives it before anyone else can. Then he gets the reputation of being "cocky." The classmates of one gifted boy who always had the right answer ducked him in a pond. He asked why they'd done it: "I was right, wasn't I?" "That's it," was the reply; "you're always right." Years later, one of the boys who had ducked him was visiting a big mental hospital. The know-it-all, a patient, was assisting in the information booth.

We are not suggesting that cockiness is a symptom of incipient mental illness. But where a youngster is for any reason excluded by his group, he suffers a continuing emotional strain. He needs assistance in discovering the cause of his unpopularity and the remedy.

When a bright pupil shows signs of developing conceit, you can as a rule lead him to convince himself that conceit is foolish. One teacher, who has several very bright pupils working as an independent group in a regular class, writes: "One of the problems has been building tact among a few of the group. Only a few of them exhibited a tendency to deride the efforts of the less bright, and I simply pointed out to them in private that that was not an accepted method of behavior. Then I had them explain to me why it wasn't acceptable. They have not recently exhibited such an attitude here at school, and I am hoping it will carry over into other situations."

When a student strikes you as conceited, it may be hard not to belittle him, not to try to take him down a peg. A mother, who is also a teacher, writes: "In October I asked Sam's kindergarten teacher how he was getting along. She said he had won her completely and she wished she had more like him. I was very pleased. A month later I spoke to her again. 'Oh, Sam has straightened out beautifully.' 'Oh, I didn't know he was a problem.' 'Oh yes, he is much too enthusiastic. We have to tone him down. We have to make him conform, you know.' I was too annoyed to say anything." Sarcasm, toning down, and pressure for conformity may undermine the bright child's sense of worth. If he is to strive to live up to his abilities he must not be made to think he has none. He will not be conceited if you let him know that much is expected of him because he has much to give.

Sometimes the bright child makes the acute observation that his contemporaries dislike him because he prefers older children as playmates or otherwise shows he is old for his age. A girl writes: "I am a seventh-grader. My best friends are in eighth grade. Next year the eighth-graders will go to high school. I will be lost without them. The seventh-graders think I am a big snob. I'm not a snob. I like everyone, but if they think I'm snobbish they will not be friendly with me. Next year I will have no friends. What can I do to prove to them I'm not as snobbish as they think I am?" And a high-school boy writes: "I understand human nature to some extent and know how to get along with people. But I'm inclined to be moody, perhaps because I tend to act and think as an older person would. I often feel mentally too mature in tastes and ideas."

When a bright pupil's natural friendship for older boys and girls is reciprocated, and if he is otherwise qualified, you should consider recommending him for acceleration. In the meantime, try to get him to see the good qualities of slower students. Encourage him to engage in some activities in which the slower students equal or excel him. Have him use his abilities to help others.

The bright pupil in a class where his abilities are not challenged and where he has no worthy competitors tends to be bossy. Such pupils say of themselves, "I like to have my own way too much," and, "I like to run things." Often they say, "I'm always talking and give no one else a chance." These habits do not endear a pupil to his fellows or to his teachers. Thom and Newell speak of a boy who "tossed off his lessons without effort and then relieved his boredom by attempting to run the class, which annoyed the teacher and provided him with some interesting diversion." [2] A fifth-grade teacher writes:

Charlie is a brilliant child. However, he feels that you cannot have a decent discussion if you have to wait for everybody to have his say. He enthusiastically blurts out terrific contributions to the class. He has up to this point been a self-contained, lonely boy. I am so glad to see him contribute that I do not like to reprimand him for not waiting for the others. When I talk with him about anything from taking turns to improving his handwriting, he says, "I see your point, but it ruins discussion," or, "I see your point, but I can use a typewriter," and proceeds to do as he will. The other members of the class resent Charlie's "getting away with things." I have gone further in establishing a good relation with him than has any other adult outside the family. However, he is still very distant and hard to reach.

If talking privately with the precipitate, bossy pupil does not convince him that he is unfair to others and in danger of developing an unpleasant habit, try having the class as a whole consider the problems involved in a good discussion, and see if they will not agree on some guiding principles. If they do, the overtalkative pupil may follow these. Another device is to make the pupil the discussion-group secretary, with instructions to record the name of each speaker. If his appears too frequently, you have his own evidence to the point.

In any dealing with bossiness and overtalkativeness, remember that they may be symptoms of insecurity. The pupil may need the attention which he seizes. The wise procedure here, and a good one in any case, is to release the pupil sometimes from the discussion of topics he knows well and to enrich his program in a way that gives him scope for his energies. He can report to the class on a special topic of interest to them and so gain the recognition which he needs.

ALL-ROUND DEVELOPMENT

The bright child is always in danger of developing his personal intellectual interests at the expense of relationships with other children. He may set a difficult goal for himself and be very persistent in his effort to reach it. The early achievement of significant results, which an intense all-consuming interest sometimes produces, may justify one-sided as opposed to all-round development. The musical genius and the creative scientist perhaps should not spend time, which is inevitably limited, on amenities which do not even appeal to them. The sacrifice of human contacts will probably not be permanent, because as the individual grows in his specialty he will meet more and more people who can understand and appreciate him.

But we feel that anyone who is less than a genius stands to gain greatly if, as a child, he learns to get along with all sorts of people, if he participates actively in group sports and other extracurricular activities, and if he learns to use tools and to prepare himself for the mundane obligations of a family man— or housewife. Not only will he become a better-rounded personality, but his intellectual work will also profit because he will be better adjusted; he will feel more secure, more self-confident, and more a member of the group. The good effects start immediately and last through life.

PROMOTING CHARACTER DEVELOPMENT

In an important book, *Children's Social Values*,[3] Arthur W. Foshay and Kenneth D. Wann discuss how the teachers in Springfield, Missouri, studied their pupils' responsibility ("follow-through"), independence, initiative, considerateness, sharing, and democratic behavior. The teachers discovered that these traits were "related to the child's group acceptance and his feeling of his own importance" and to his feeling of security. The well-adjusted, self-confident, secure children were superior in the traits. The child who was insecure in his group membership, the one who felt inferior, and the one who was emotionally insecure, because of difficulties at home or for any other reason, behaved in ways that revealed a lack of these traits.

The Springfield teachers found that a pupil gained in responsibility and other desirable traits as he was helped to a higher standing in the group and to a feeling of greater security. They also found that they had underestimated the extent to which the class's opinion of a child and his opinion of himself were favorably affected by teacher approval. When a teacher expressed approval of a pupil, the group tended to reflect this approval and accept him, and his feeling of importance increased. When teachers gave a pupil opportunities to be of service, his feeling of security increased. They were aware that giving responsibility and praising generously were time-honored methods, but felt that sometimes these are given only lip service and that sometimes they are not applied in the case of the child who might benefit most.

Character Development

Dale B. Harris and his colleagues in the Laboratory for Research in Social Relations at the University of Minnesota have made a special study of responsibility and its development and have published a series of reports.[4, 5, 6, 7]   They say that responsibility tends "to be positively correlated with such aspects of adjustment as good family relations, good school marks, and leadership." This is in agreement with the Springfield studies. On the development of responsibility, Harris says, "There is little evidence that routine tasks, such as washing dishes, caring for pets, house cleaning, preparation of food, repairing the house, are associated with an attitude of responsibility." In other words, a child who regularly does his chores proves himself responsible, but merely assigning chores to an irresponsible child will not make him responsible.

No one changes his character traits automatically. The pupil who rarely shows initiative and rarely carries out what he has agreed to do must *learn* new and positive ways of behaving. The conditions prerequisite to learning hold here. The pupil must believe he can learn, he must intend to learn, he must try to learn, he must see that he is progressing, and he must feel satisfaction when he progresses.

You must, therefore, if you are to promote good character development, attach such values to desirable traits as will convince the pupil that they are in fact desirable to him. For example, he must be convinced that "honesty is the best policy." Private conferences with the pupil, group discussions of, e.g., why behaving responsibly is the right course in a given situation, the example of admired adults—his parents, you, his favorite heroes—all serve to inculcate a trait. Along with a growing belief that it would be good to behave in a certain way, the pupil needs many opportunities to behave in that way. When he does, you must praise him and do what you can to see that he wins approval from the group. When he fails to behave as he should, you help him see any undesirable consequences.

There is always a question of how to generalize a lesson learned under particular circumstances. A pupil may keep at the chore of cleaning the blackboard until he has removed every trace of chalk but never finish sweeping the floor when it is his turn for this job.   He may work and work to get the right answer to a mathematics problem but never concentrate on his spelling.   Luckily, bright children are quick to make generalizations.   You can help them by holding class discussions of proverbs ("If at first you don't succeed, try, try again"), fables ("The Hare and the Tortoise"), and a trait as an abstract ideal ("persistence").   Ask the class to cite examples from their own experience.   Drive the moral home by reference to a famous man's life (Bruce and the spider).

Of course, there are parallels between schoolwork in one year and the next, and between school and life, and many of these are so close that transfer is automatic.   The child who is offered and takes opportunities to engage in activities which require initiative, responsibility, and persistence is learning how to carry out similar activities in the future.   Experience does teach.

The great merit of instructional techniques which involve projects, units, and the problem-solving approach is that they afford exercise for all the traits which we have been discussing. If they are used from the beginning, as they are in Cleveland's Major Work Classes and in Colfax' Workshops, there is every hope that the majority of the pupils taught by them will develop well.   The student who comes to them late will need careful induction, especially if he does not have an established goal or at least a powerful interest which will be served by his studies—but better late than never.

Extracurricular activities, including chores, have been a perennial means of giving pupils scope to display good character traits.   One teacher writes:

Roberta, age 13, Grade VII, IQ 130, does neat, accurate work and her assignments are done way ahead of most of the others.   She loves to read, but if she thinks she can be of any service she is right there asking me how she can be of use.   This year she took entire charge of the school insurance collection.   She went to each teacher's room each day, and if the teacher had neglected any detail, e.g., grade or room number missing on the form, Roberta would attend to it if she could. If not, she'd return and ask the teacher. When polio shots were to be given she distributed the forms, listed the pupils, and stapled the permission slips to the forms. After the shots were given she made a list of all the pupils who were absent.

We believe that activities like this can be undertaken with profit by all bright pupils and that, when teachers express their appreciation of work well done, the experience actually helps develop good traits. Teachers have long known that giving a misbehaving pupil a special duty helps reform him, both by giving him a chance to earn recognition and by teaching him to discipline himself.

SPORTS AND EXTRACURRICULAR ACTIVITIES

The bright child's feeling that he is not as good at sports as at studies may keep him from realizing that he could nonetheless be very good. If he does not expect to succeed he will not try very hard and he may not try at all. Point out to boys and girls who are normally healthy and not underdeveloped physically for their age how well bright youngsters can do in sports. If you can give examples that are familiar to your pupils, so much the better. If not, here are two pertinent news items. The Wabash College track team has won 41 out of 52 meets in 6 years, and has set 2 state and 8 college records. During that time 4 of the 6 captains have been members of Phi Beta Kappa. The Bronx High School of Science, limited to superior students, has won all but 7 of its swimming meets in 10 years. One graduate has been captain of the Columbia swimming team, and other graduates have competed at City College, New York University, Cornell, Colgate, Colorado, Massachusetts Institute of Technology, Michigan, Rensselaer, Swarthmore, and Union.

The American emphasis on spectator sports, and particularly the prominence of basketball as a high-school sport, narrows the opportunity for secondary-school students to participate.

When a team consists of five players and a squad is limited to fifteen or twenty members, the natural athlete gets all the exercise. The nonathletes may not even walk to school. Jean Mayer, of Harvard's School of Public Health, has pointed out that, in comparison with European boys and girls, American youths are, on the average, underdeveloped physically just because so many of them are spectators rather than players. The bright student will be quick to appreciate Mayer's point and to see the value of tennis, swimming, golf, and other sports which he can continue after he graduates from high school. He may even take to heart Mayer's remark that, "boring though they may be to some, humble calisthenics are still the most convenient way to get into shape and stay fit." [8]

The undersized or physically handicapped bright child need not despair of athletic success. Doris Hart was crippled as a girl, but in 1955 won both the Wimbledon and the United States tennis championships in ladies' singles. The struggle to overcome a handicap can be the best of all training in persistence, because the child wants to succeed, makes progress, and feels satisfaction in the result. One first-grade teacher tells of a well-set-up gifted girl who is cross-eyed. "But she's working systematically and patiently with a private doctor to overcome the difficulty—and this attitude is typical of her approach to any problem."

Participation in extracurricular activities apart from athletics is a natural road to recognition for most bright students. In 1955, the 97 honor students in the senior class of Garfield High School, Seattle, had participated in an average of 8.1 extracurricular activities apiece.[9] If you have a student who needs more standing with the group, lead him to talk about the extracurricular activities in which he might do well. Try to steer him into one that engages a fairly large number of students. And be sure that he knows the value of being a good follower.

There are scores of nonacademic accomplishments which bright youngsters can acquire if they will and which will be of value now in helping them get along with their fellows and later in family living and as recreational interests. Knowing how to use the common tools, to cook, to sew, to dance, to draw and paint, to sing, to play an instrument—all these and many more are cultivated by bright boys and girls without any special talent for them. When your school offers subjects like these, advise your bright pupils to take them, either as electives or as extra subjects. When no instruction is available in school, encourage the pupils to take advantage of any local hobby groups there are and, if their families can afford it, to take private lessons. More than one bright student would have been happier if he had been a good dancer in his teens.

LEADERSHIP

Bright children who live up to their promise will be called upon throughout their lives to serve as administrators and leaders. They will need to be fully matured emotionally. They will need to know how to help people set worthy goals and work together to attain them. And the world has much to gain if they grow up to cherish high ideals.

Responsibility for forming ideals is shared by the school, the family, the church, the press, and other agents which mold public opinion. We are not minimizing the school's share in this responsibility when we point out that the school has a unique opportunity to teach the techniques of working in and for a group and of carrying through with group-made plans. And we are not minimizing the importance of having good civic leaders, including good school administrators, when we say we think it is a mistake to consider only public office in discussions of leadership. Most of our leaders in the United States serve their apprenticeship, not in government, but in a profession or business.

You can teach many things which good leaders and good administrators should know. These range from specific fundamentals, like the rules of order, to abstract principles, like the rights of minorities. Every time you hold a group discussion, whether you teach in first grade or in college, you have the opportunity to give your pupils practice in exchanging opinion, in expressing themselves in public (so important for the bright but shy), and in the art of reaching right decisions. Every group project represents, in a microcosm, the processes of administration. If you help your pupils evaluate discussions and projects by criteria of good government, you train them to apply these in broader fields. And, as always, if you can lead them to generalize just how and why fundamental principles hold true in varying situations, you increase the probability that the principles will guide their conduct. There are many books which will help you think through the problems and methods of teaching leadership, ground you in the techniques of leadership, and propound philosophies of government.[10, 11, 12, 13]

The good discussion leader must himself refrain from dominating the group and must see that no one else does. He has to be sure that everyone has an opportunity to criticize and to make suggestions so that the results reflect the best thinking of the group as a whole. But he does more than enforce Robert's rules of order. He has to think quickly, analytically, and efficiently. Otherwise there is great danger that the group will lose the benefit of some individual criticisms and suggestions, even if there is an efficient secretary taking minutes. True group thinking develops best when the leader can, at the proper moment, restate the problem or summarize the plans with all accretions and deletions of value but in the simplest possible phrasing. This requires high intelligence and much practice in thinking on one's feet.

Some high schools conduct courses in leadership. These are primarily for students who are officers in student government and other extracurricular organizations, but they may be open as electives as well. The good teacher of a leadership course takes his students far beyond a textbook study of formalities, methods, and principles. He has them analyze the workings of the student organizations, with special reference to the way goals are established and affairs administered. He integrates his course with the students' study of English, mathematics, and history. He has them visit local and state legislative meetings and interview both elected and civil-service officials. He arranges for them to study small and large business concerns to discover how policies are determined. He holds out to them the ideal of service in their own occupations and in Church and State.

In the meantime, the students are learning by doing. A modern high school affords a large number of students the opportunity to serve as officials of one kind or another. If the organizations are conducted democratically, and if there is a sincere attempt to evaluate procedures and results, the active members may learn as much as their elected officials. But practice in self-government should not be left to chance. If you are a home-room teacher, you should consider organizing your room as a committee of the whole and letting the students manage the thousand and one collections, questionnaires, and announcements which fall to your lot. The home room is an especially good training ground in leadership, because positions can be rotated and because the relatively small group can consciously evaluate performancc as a means of learning and with little risk of rancor.

Many young people's organizations, both those affiliated with the school and those which are sponsored by outside groups, give students responsibility on a high level. For example, one Neighborhood House recruits superior students from secondary schools as sports and group leaders in a recreation program in a slum district. The paid director supervises them, but they are responsible for making and carrying out plans with their own teams and groups. Members of the National Association of Future Teachers of America learn to take charge of classes. In one Pennsylvania school, when a bus mishap made all the teachers late, members of the NAFTA took over on their own initiative. When the regular teachers arrived, the school was running quietly and smoothly.

Elementary schools could probably extend pupil responsibility much further than they customarily do. The AAA traffic patrol has demonstrated how capable pupils vested with authority can be. Some elementary schools have systems of student government, complete with house of representatives and senate. Miami's Westview Elementary School has a Future Teachers Club as part of the enrichment program for bright sixth-graders. The members teach the first and second grades for fifteen minutes four or five times a week. They make their own plans and, though they are under supervision, they are responsible for everything except punishment. They have a "faculty" meeting with their sponsor once a week. The club rules are: "Attend meetings regularly. Wear official FTC badge at all times. Be kind and considerate to children. Set a good example to others. Keep up lesson plans. Conduct yourself with dignity and modesty and do not brag or lord it over others."

IDEA MAN

Much educational writing about leadership is quite properly devoted to the democratic process. There is danger, however, of losing sight of the contributions which bright individuals can make by social invention. Industry thrives on inventions of new products and of new solutions to old problems of manufacture. Men and women who have been educated to think critically and constructively about problems in human relations have a similar role to play in improving society. If Binet and Terman and other psychologists had not developed mental measurements, educational administration would still be floundering in a morass of conflicting personal opinions. The person who has a new idea which solves a local traffic problem is as much a leader as the mayor who takes up the idea and sees it through the town council. Thomas Jefferson was a successful practical politician, but he was a political philosopher, too. The Constitution was hammered out democratically in a convention, but it was the idea of men of learning and vision.

XII

Educational Guidance

The highlight of forty years of teaching has been starting Tony on his way to college. He was the brightest fifth-grader I'd ever had. When I told his family he should go to college, they laughed at me. Tony was to be a shoemaker, like his father. When I insisted, they said they didn't have any money. I rashly said it would never cost them a cent. It never has. He always won full scholarships, right through graduate school. Now he's a nuclear physicist in a good job with a big company.
—A Teacher.

Have you ever tried to make a high-school sophomore make a decision?
—A Teacher.

Every bright child should have all the education he can profit from. As a rule, he should go to college. The talented child should receive professional training either in college or a technical school or in both.

Young people who do not take a college degree automatically cut themselves off from most professions. The degree is a prerequisite for admission to schools of law, medicine, dentistry, and divinity and for graduate study in any field. Engineers and teachers must have four years of college training, and very often graduate work as well. More and more financial and industrial corporations are giving preference to college graduates in employment in the divisions from which they draw their junior executives. College graduates, as a group, earn more money, win promotion faster, and serve in more-responsible

191

positions than do most people who have not been to college. Part of the superior success of college graduates comes through a process of selection. The weak are weeded out. But there can be no doubt that in most cases a college education helps the individual develop. He learns to study, to seek information and apply it, and to express himself. And, perhaps above all, he gains in perspective and sets high standards for himself. So when a bright student cannot or will not go to college or stay in college, everyone stands to lose.

GUIDANCE IS NEEDED

The fact that each year 500,000 of our better students fall by the educational wayside was mentioned in Chapter I. Lack of money and lack of motivation were cited as the principal reasons. Good educational guidance can help students overcome the financial obstacles and convince students who now see no reason why they should go to college of the desirability of obtaining a college degree. And good guidance can help each student pick the courses in school and college which, all things considered, would be best for him. How effective guidance can be is suggested in a study of 9,689 superior seniors from 478 high schools.[1] Of the 4,920 boys, 66 per cent of those who had discussed college with a guidance counselor intended to go, but only 21 per cent of those who had not.

THE ROLE OF THE CLASSROOM TEACHER

If students are to receive more guidance, classroom teachers must give it. Less than one-fifth of the high schools in the United States have any staff member who gives half or more of his time to guidance. In the schools where guidance is available, the ratio is one counselor to every 524 students. Commenting on the shortage of guidance personnel, Henry Chauncey, president of the Educational Testing Service, has said, "It seems inevitable that more and more of the guidance functions will fall to the lot of the home room teacher. This is by no means a last resort; there is a growing feeling that she should be the keystone of the guidance process because she is in close contact with the student and gets to know him well." [2]

We would add to this that guidance ought to be a continuous process and one of the duties of all teachers from kindergarten through graduate school. The principal techniques of guidance should be taught to all prospective teachers. Teachers in service who have not studied guidance in a course will find it helpful to read one of the many good books in the field.[3, 4] Since classroom teachers will not ordinarily have the specialist's knowledge or experience, they ought to have a specialist on whom they can call for advice. But, day by day and year by year, the pupil depends most on his regular teacher.

CUMULATIVE GUIDANCE

Long-range, continuing guidance, what we might call cumulative guidance, helps the pupil in several ways. When his successive teachers co-operate, there is less chance of mistakes in judgment about the pupil's general ability and specific aptitudes. The advice he receives is the product of group thinking and therefore probably superior to any that one teacher or counselor acting alone could give. When the bright elementary-school pupil and his family have their attention called to the desirability of his going to college, they get used to the idea and they may save money to help finance his higher education. Each teacher is made aware of plans that have been considered for the child and can correlate these or advise changes with due regard to his development. And, as a bonus, teachers find it refreshing and stimulating to emerge from the confines of their own classrooms and exchange information about their pupils' backgrounds and progress.

In small schools the teachers, under the leadership of the principal, can talk over each bright pupil's problems and plans in a teachers' meeting. In a large school, and when a pupil shifts from elementary to junior high to high school, a co-ordinating committee on the bright and gifted performs a very useful service. For example, the Atchison, Kansas, public schools have a permanent committee consisting of the director of special education, two administrators, two high-school teachers, and two elementary-school teachers. This committee studies the children throughout public school and follows them after graduation from high school. It maintains regular contact with every teacher who has any pupil with an IQ of 130 or above, and meets about once a year with teachers who have pupils with IQ's between 120 and 130. The committee members receive additional pay for the extra time this work takes, and they are provided with office space and secretarial help.

There is grave danger that bright and talented students will be lost in the shuffle which accompanies transfer from elementary school to junior high, and from junior high to senior high. Sixth-grade teachers should make it a duty to see the seventh-grade teachers of their bright and talented pupils early in the school year. Junior-high-school principals can facilitate this by inviting sixth-grade teachers to a faculty meeting for the discussion of problems of articulation. High-school teachers of the difficult electives—mathematics, science, the foreign languages—ought to talk with each bright student about his choice of course. Each department should have a committee which maintains liaison with junior-high-school teachers and makes itself responsible for studying both the cumulative records and the preliminary choices of courses. When a bright student proposes dropping a subject which he ought to continue, an understanding teacher should talk with him. The student may be underrating his own abilities. He may not know how dropping a subject will affect his future. The teachers of art and music should follow similar procedures to guide talented boys and girls.

ESTABLISHING COLLEGE AS A GOAL

The aforementioned study of 9,689 bright seniors showed that 85 per cent of those who were children of doctors expected to go to college, but only 25 per cent of those who were children of semiskilled laborers. Only part of this differential can be traced to the greater financial resources of the professional family. A good part, at least, is due to the fact that many laborers and their children never visualize the possibility of college, while the doctor, himself a college graduate, expects his children to go and they grow up looking forward to it.

Relatively large numbers of high-school graduates who live in college towns go on to college. Presumably the presence of the college has the same effect as a collegiate background in the family. For example, 46.2 per cent of the 551 boys and girls who graduated with the class of 1955 at Hillhouse High School, Yale's neighbor in New Haven, went on to college. In that year the national average for all high-school graduates was about 25 per cent. But only 18 of the Hillhouse boys went to Yale. The students' attention is not directed so much toward a particular institution as toward an idea.

The earlier the idea of going to college can be planted, the more likely it is to bear fruit. In whatever grade you teach, if you have a pupil who seems to you of college caliber, find out what plans he and his family have for his higher education. If it looks as though he will not go to college, talk with the pupil and if possible with his parents. Points to make include the child's ability, the way a college education would help him develop his major interests, the financial advantages of a college degree, college as a prerequisite to the professions, the standing of colleges in your neighborhood, the cost of attending college and ways to finance the cost. Point out the college graduates whom the family knows or knows about—their clergyman, their doctor, any prominent graduate in the community. Do not forget to tell of your own experiences in deciding to go to college, of the good times you had there, and of what it has meant to you since.

Make a special effort to interest girls in a college education. More girls than boys graduate from high school, but twice as many men as women graduate from college. If we could increase the number of women graduates we would do much to lessen the shortages in teaching and the other professions. Point out to girls that women college graduates have a marriage rate as high as the national average for women and a lower divorce rate. They are better equipped to earn their living before marriage and, in case of need, after marriage. Most important, the personal and cultural development which comes from four years of higher education will be a continuing asset for them and their children.

GENERAL EDUCATION AS PREPARATION FOR COLLEGE

Whether or not a pupil is now planning on college, you should try to see that he takes the courses and acquires the knowledge that will prepare him for college. Then, if he eventually wants to go, he will be ready.

Just as well-planned enrichment broadens a pupil's knowledge of a specific subject and introduces him to additional subjects, so a well-planned course of study avoids narrow specialization. Most liberal-arts colleges, technological institutes, and teachers colleges now require all students to take a considerable number of courses in the liberal arts. There is general agreement with the ideals expressed by President Harold W. Dodds of Princeton in his 1956 Commencement address, in which he said, "We shall maintain the creative and generating power of liberal learning broadly conceived." Even after specialization in a technical field has started, the wise student puts general training in his subject ahead of details. Richard T. Whitcomb, designer of the wasp-waist fuselage for jet airplanes, addressed the

1956 winners of the Grumman Scholarships for students whose major interest is in aviation. He advised them to acquire a solid foundation in the fundamental laws of science. "Learn to handle problems rather than the details of current problems," he said; "the things being taught now will be obsolete by the time you graduate."

Long before college, a bright pupil needs to be guided away from too exclusive a specialization. If he is not, he may early in elementary school begin to concentrate his hobbies, his free reading, and his enrichment activities on a narrow subject. There is special danger of a potential engineer's thinking that he can learn all he wants by going to a vocational school, and so cutting off his chance of attending an engineering college.

The pupil who explores a variety of subjects discovers whether or not any one of them has a deep appeal for him. If he already has a major interest, he tests its strength by becoming familiar with rival fields. If in each of the four years of high school he takes mathematics, science, a foreign language, English, and social studies (the five studies are the components of most schemes of "general education"), he can satisfy the entrance requirements of any engineering school or liberal-arts college and so be free to postpone his choice of an institution. When the curriculum does not permit his scheduling five subjects a year, he can still meet the requirements of most institutions, regardless of type, if he takes three years of a foreign language, two of science, and four of mathematics, in addition to the usual English and social studies.

A student should always familiarize himself with the requirements of the college he favors, and should keep himself posted on any changes that are made from year to year. Seventh grade is not too soon for a bright student to write for college catalogues and begin to study them. Tell him to do this for himself and not leave it to you or his parents or the guidance office. If he finds out that he can get into a particular college without taking a foreign language, point out to him that the college in question will give credit for three or four courses in a language and that other colleges, one of which he may later prefer, demand them.

RECOMMENDING A PRIVATE SCHOOL

Parents frequently fear that if their child continues in public school he will not be able to get into college. This idea persists, though practically all the undergraduates in the best state universities are from public schools and in most of the Ivy League institutions public-school graduates outnumber those from private schools. Moreover, public-school graduates usually do much better scholastically in college than do private-school graduates. At Yale, where half the students come from private schools, 32 of the 40 members elected to Phi Beta Kappa from the class of 1956 had prepared wholly at public schools. The scholastic superiority of public-school graduates has been confirmed by research studies at Yale, Harvard, Minnesota, and other institutions.

Socially and athletics-wise, private-school graduates excel public-school graduates at Yale, that is, more of the private-school graduates belong to clubs and make teams. But the public-school graduates at Yale, that is, more of the private-tracurricular activities, from football to the Junior Promenade Committee. The chairman of a recent promenade committee was a public-school graduate. A public-school graduate, a Negro, was one of the most popular football captains Yale has ever had.

You can give inquiring parents these facts about the general situation, and you can warn them that some private schools are pretty weak. Our book *Bright Children: A Guide for Parents* goes into the problem in more detail and sets up criteria to help parents decide between public and private school and select a private school if they so wish.[5] You cannot help them do the latter unless you happen to have personal knowledge of a given school or are willing to take the time to visit several. But you can talk with them frankly about your own school. Tell them whether or not the graduates of your high school are successful in obtaining admission to the colleges of their choice, and about their scholastic and extracurricular achievements in college. And you can tell the parents how their child compares with the graduates whom you describe.

A well-considered decision to send a boy through public high school is reported in the following case:

Vic's father, a professor of physics at the University, took his B.S. and Ph.D. degrees there. Vic's mother took a B.A. at Smith and an M.A. at California and taught English at California before she was married. Vic has an IQ of 135. When he was in the eighth grade, his parents decided he would be challenged more if he went to a private day school. This is an excellent school, but they soon found that the work there was as easy for Vic as that in the eighth grade of public school had been. Vic missed his old friends and wanted to come to our high school, and his parents agreed. He's working hard now. His course is planned for five subjects each year—English, French, history, mathematics, and science. We're lucky to be able to offer a fourth year of French and the calculus, and he hopes to enter the University with advanced credit in both French and math. He wants to win a scholarship because he expects to go to graduate school and says that before he finishes his education his three younger brothers will be in college, too.

Not all public high schools have as good a college-preparatory curriculum as Vic's. Many do not offer four years of mathematics or any physics or chemistry. If your school is one of these and if you have a student who needs the missing courses for college entrance or for his own development, you should certainly consider suggesting that he be sent to private school. Other conditions that might make transfer to a private school desirable include lack of intellectual competition, acute sibling rivalry, and severe emotional strains in the home. You probably will not feel free to suggest that a pupil go to private school unless you know the parents fairly well or unless a case seems so unusual to you that you would feel guilty if you did not try to bring about a change.   Of course, if parents ask for advice, you should say what you think, honestly and frankly.   You can be entirely loyal to your school and to the principle of free public education and still know that for a given pupil under given circumstances private school might offer great advantages.   The best private schools are liberal in giving scholarships to outstanding youngsters.   They are not prejudiced against a youngster because of race, color, or creed.

One teacher tells how she came to recommend a private school for a gifted boy and what happened.

I first met Oliver in the nurse's room.   He was 4 years old and just starting our two-year kindergarten.   There was a twinkle in the nurse's eye when she saw me.   "Tell Miss Farwell about it, Oliver." He held out a red little arm and said, "The rash is not contagious. It is an allergy to tomatoes.   I'll stop at my friend the druggist's on the way home.   He will give me the ointment the doctor prescribed. When mother comes home she will give me the money and I'll take it to him."   My interest in Oliver was born that minute and has never waned.

Oliver's father was a day laborer.   His mother was a waitress. From the time he started kindergarten, he had his own doorkey and got his own lunch.   The family lived in an "old-law" rat-infested tenement.   The mother and father were divorced when Oliver was 5. She remarried but continued working.   Oliver has one half sister.

When he was in kindergarten he used to relate the day's news to the teacher.   His mother read the paper to him each morning. His memory was astonishing.   And even at 4 he could relate number concepts to his own environment.   When I saw him dressed in a new rain outfit he told me how much each item cost and how hard his mother worked to earn the money.

By first grade he was reading everything in sight.   He had the same teacher through Grades I and II.   She asked him to join her Sunday School class.   She says he plunged into religion as he did into any new subject.   It has remained a vital influence in his life.

A Binet-Stanford test was given in Grade II.   Oliver's IQ was 160.   The examiner still remembers how mature he was.

Oliver came into my class when I was teaching a combination fourth and fifth grade.   He was 9 at the time.   With the principal's permission I put him in the fifth grade.   This meant he'd enter Grade VI at the age of 10 years 1 month.   But we all felt that there

was no real competition for him in our school. Also, things were
not going well at home. Oliver was struggling over the moral problem of his mother's remarriage, which was against the tenets of his
religion. He worked through that, but was still upset.

I made friends with Oliver's mother by repeatedly visiting the
home. The tenement was awful, but their four rooms shiningly
clean. Oliver had a room to himself, the most attractive in the
flat. Here was all that was dear to his heart: bookshelves filled
with his own books, the volumes of the encyclopedia which he had
won as a radio "quiz kid," a dictionary "like yours," an atlas, globe,
and maps. He had a typewriter his mother had given him for
Christmas after consulting me about it.

Oliver's mother told me he was growing irritable and difficult
to handle. She had tried to help him with a problem and he'd said,
"Mother, you simply have not had enough education to help me.
You can't possibly understand what I'm trying to do." She wondered if there was any way she could send Oliver away to school.
I told her about a competitive examination for a scholarship to a
six-year school. She agreed to let Oliver try. He won it.

That was twelve years ago. Oliver is now in his second year
at Harvard Medical School. He comes to see me whenever he is in
town. I've asked him about how he felt at some of the crises in
his life. He can't remember early details but knows that by the
time he reached my room he sensed a gap between himself and his
classmates. He was different and seemed to grow more different
each month. He loved his mother (and still does, devotedly) but
had the idea that she had no appreciation of his needs and of what
he hoped to do in life. He remembers my decrying his ambition to
be a sports writer and his pointing out John Kieran's accomplishments as an ornithologist and philosopher. The first months at private school were hell. The other boys soon discovered his background and were cruel to him. He cried himself to sleep every
night. But he made up his mind to make friends and soon discovered that others were lonely too. He took part in all the extracurricular activities he could. By junior year, he says, he felt no differences between himself and the other boys. He knew the differences
existed but they didn't bother him.

He won a scholarship to Harvard and did very well there. He
was on the staff of the *Crimson* and popular with his fellow members
of Eliot House. I asked him why he hadn't made Phi Beta Kappa.
I wish I could quote all he said. In effect, it was, "I thought out
the problem of scholarship. I felt that the university had a tre-

mendous wealth to offer its students: books in Widener Library; public lectures by the world's great men; plays to see; friends to make. I wanted to maintain a high average but I didn't want to sacrifice the richness of life. If I had done less I might have made Phi Beta Kappa, but I felt life was to be lived."

FINANCING COLLEGE

The cost of attending college varies from a minimum of about $500 a year in a local publicly supported college with a minimal tuition fee to about $2,500 in some of the private colleges for women. In addition to the cost, the student and his parents may have to consider that the young person loses four years of wages which would have eased the family's burdens. But even at a cost of $10,000, four years of college are a good investment. The relatively high earnings of the college graduate may be due to the superior average ability of the college group. But since employers prefer the graduate, the degree is worth while.

Foresighted families begin to accumulate funds for educating their children as soon as the children are born. If you feel that the parents of a bright child might have difficulty sending him through college, suggest that they consult immediately both their bank and their insurance agent. The bank can tell them how much they will have to save each year to have given sums available during the child's college years. Some banks make a specialty of "save-for-college" accounts. Insurance companies have policies which will provide for a child's college expenses even if a parent dies and payments are stopped. Any insurance agent will be glad to explain the advantages of such a plan. When you are suggesting savings and insurance, point out that, though a pupil may win a scholarship, most scholarships do not pay all expenses.

Many colleges and universities now give scholarship assistance to a large percentage of their undergraduates. The regular policy has been to devote part of the income from each increase in tuition to aiding students who would suffer hardship from having to pay the higher amount. The older institutions have accumulated large endowments for scholarships. In some Ivy League colleges, 50 per cent of the undergraduates are receiving scholarship aid and are also eligible for low-interest scholarship loans. Vassar reports that in 1953 17 per cent of its student body, 241 out of 1,408, were on scholarship and that the scholarship students proved their worth by winning almost half of the scholastic honors.

Each year brings great increases in the number and the size of unrestricted scholarships, which allow the winners to attend the colleges of their own choice. Industry, aware that industrial development depends on a continuing supply of college-trained recruits, is establishing large grants. For example, in 1955 the Sears, Roebuck Foundation and Time, Inc., joined with the Ford Foundation in setting up the National Merit Scholarships, which total $1,000,000 a year.

There are so many sources of scholarship funds, and the picture is changing so rapidly, that each community should have a community scholarship committee with representatives from the schools and from industry. The high-school guidance counselor should be a member. The committee should keep an up-to-date file of all publications which list available scholarships, such as *You Can Win a Scholarship.*[6] The value of complete and up-to-date information is illustrated by the many "name scholarships." For example, in 1884 a man named Leavenworth left Yale a fund to pay $600 a year to a student in need of aid whose last name is Leavenworth. This scholarship was vacant in 1955–56. The scholarship committee should be in contact with local and national business corporations which offer aid. And it should encourage gifts from residents of the community so that it will have funds to assist outstanding students who do not receive other awards. Incidentally, the recommendation of a good community committee carries greater weight with most college officials than does a recommendation from the school alone.

The competition for scholarships is so severe that it is easy to overlook the colleges' competition for the best students. A really topnotch high-school student can do a certain amount of "shopping around," though several leading colleges have now combined to set up a clearinghouse which determines how much aid a student needs and what he should be offered. The collaborating colleges adhere to this figure so the student may pick the college he really wants to attend. When the good student has a choice between colleges of equal merit he should try to find out what the prospects are for scholarships in the later years. Some institutions deliberately channel their funds into scholarships for freshmen, hoping they will take care of themselves through the last three years.

Bright boys and girls often earn a good part of their college fees. Oliver, described earlier in this chapter, worked summers when he was in preparatory school and worked all through college. Vic was saving his baby-sitting fees and already had a sizable bank account. But few can or should count on earning their whole way. As Oliver said, "Life is to be lived."

CHOICE OF A COLLEGE

If you are advising a youngster about his choice of a college and if, one way or another, he can afford to attend any one he wishes, you should give main weight to how the college provides for his special interests. If he has already made up his mind to enter a profession in which much of the technical training is customarily given in college rather than in graduate school, e.g., engineering or music, the problem is greatly simplified: comparatively few of the more than 1,800 colleges in the United States give technical training of a specific type. But when a student's interests are broad and when he either has no definite vocational plans or expects to receive his professional training after graduation, e.g., in medical school or law school, any one of several hundred colleges offers adequate instruction.

For many students, the first decision will be between a junior college and a four-year college. *If possible,* the bright student should plan to go to the four-year college from the beginning. He should certainly take a bachelor's degree. Most colleges integrate their courses, and a transfer student is at a disadvantage when he enters an advanced course. Moreover, much of the social life in any American college follows a pattern set in the first two years. Unless a student's intellectual interests are intense enough to compensate for the lack of a normal share in extracurricular activities, he is happier if he can spend his four undergraduate years in the same institution. If, for reasons of economy or any other reason, a student does go to a junior college, he should make provisional arrangements for transfer to a specific senior college. Then he can be sure of the latter's requirements for admission to an upper class and he can co-ordinate his junior-college courses with those he hopes to take in his last two years.

Most of the famous universities, both private and state, have good teachers, libraries, and laboratories. They are not necessarily at the top in every field, but they are safe. A goodly number of small colleges actually surpass the larger in the quality of instruction and the availability of books and laboratories. A million books in a stack closed to an undergraduate are not of much use to him. Moreover, he will use a medium-sized library in his dormitory more than he will a main reading room one block away. But unfortunately a great many small institutions are not much more than old-fashioned academies with fixed curriculum, ill-trained teachers, a textbook type of instruction, and grossly inadequate facilities.

The principle that "the individual must choose for himself" holds firmly in the case of choice of a college. A student who accepts his father's pushing or a teacher's recommendation has a ready out when he does not want to work. One who makes his own choice has to do well in order to justify himself. But you can help by pointing out possibilities and by suggesting criteria.

Your school library should have the American Council on

Education's two volumes *American Universities and Colleges* [7] and *American Junior Colleges*. [8] The former describes 969 accredited universities and colleges and 2,016 accredited professional schools; the latter, 531 accredited junior colleges. The student should read the accounts of institutions in which he is interested and then send for the catalogues of those which seem best for his purposes. The catalogue will let him see whether the courses in fields he likes are varied enough and numerous enough to satisfy him. He should be on his guard against courses in brackets—"[not offered in 1970]" or "[offered only if elected by 10 students]." A visit to the college is strongly recommended. One brilliant high-school senior wanted to go West to college. He narrowed his choice to Reed, Stanford, and Pomona. After visiting all three, he said, "Reed didn't have enough student life. Stanford had too much. Pomona was just right." (The judgments are his, not ours. We think very highly of all three.) The visit should include inspection of dormitories, classrooms, and laboratories as well as the stadium. Talks with a few faculty members can be very revealing.

The location of a college is to be taken into account. We know one not-so-bright student who went to a Canadian college because he liked to ski; when he got there he found it located in the midst of a city on a level plain. Colleges in big urban centers offer advantages in the way of museums, concerts, the opera, and the theater, to say nothing of restaurants where the student can hear French or Greek spoken by natives and eat the national dishes. Colleges far from home add breadth of experience. And there are Canadian colleges where the winter sports as well as the science and philosophy departments are superb.

When cost and nearness are deciding factors in a student's choice, we hope you will call his attention to state teachers colleges in your state and in neighboring states. Teachers colleges are now paying their faculties better than are many private institutions; they are building good laboratories and have good libraries. Many are residential colleges, complete with dormitories and football teams. They seem to us to offer a superior education at the lowest possible cost. The student who is talented in art or music may well find better instruction in a teachers college than he will in any old-line university or in many a special school. And he will be able to earn a living by teaching his specialty, when many of his talented contemporaries will be leading a hand-to-mouth existence.

ARTICULATION WITH COLLEGE

The number of bright students who drop out of their freshman year at college—sometimes as much as 25 per cent—constitutes one of the greatest wastes in education. Granted that this is mainly the responsibility of the college, there is lots you can do to soften the impact of the first weeks and months.

Almost every college has graduates in every state. The alumni registrar will be glad to send you or the student the names of alumni who live near you. These alumni will surely be glad to meet and talk with the student.

One college club in a small city makes a custom of arranging college visits for high-school seniors. The members, between them, have a wide acquaintance in a large number of colleges and can see that the student is met by a member of the faculty and shown around. These voluntary cicerones often become friends later. At least the new student feels he has someone to whom to turn in case of need. High-school teachers have similarly wide contacts and could well follow this club's example. Some schools run chaperoned trips to different institutions. The college officials may co-operate more fully with a school official than with an individual student and his parents. But, in any case, do what you can to help a student visit the college of his choice at least once in the year before he enters. He will feel much more at home when he actually starts.

The trials, both scholastic and social, of college freshmen are not much different now from what they were in your day.

A study of 500 freshmen in 27 leading colleges [9] shows that, while most of them praise their high schools and their colleges, they find fault with both. They complain about the way the high school taught English composition, the reading skills, the use of the library, and note-taking. They say they were unused to doing the quantity of reading and writing demanded in college. They did not know how to budget their time and to organize study. They were unprepared for the freedom of college life and for the responsibility the colleges expected them to exercise both in academic work and in their social contacts. Some were gravely disturbed by problems of drinking, sex, snobbishness, and anti-intellectualism.

Talk frankly with your students about what to expect when they start college: the freedom and responsibility, the load of work, the types of people they will meet, and the problems of dating, drinking, and sex. If a student is forewarned that some of his college classmates are sure to abuse their freedom, he will be better prepared to manage his own affairs wisely. And do not forget to mention the cultural side. One old alumnus is still grateful to a high-school teacher who praised a college art gallery. No college instructor ever mentioned its existence.

A NOTE ON MILITARY SERVICE

The probability of military service confuses a great many high-school boys. And high-school girls may wonder if the Waves would not be a good way to get employment and further training at the same time.

The official attitude of all the services stresses the desirability of good students' continuing their education through college and graduate school. Deferments are regularly granted for this purpose. When a student is in any doubt, he should secure the official literature from the nearest recruiting officer.

The services have published a handbook to help high-school teachers guide their students. This can also be secured through a recruiting officer, or you can write to the Pentagon or to your congressman for it. You should own a copy and study it. You will note that the services offer excellent training in a wide variety of specialties, and that the ambitious student can enroll for extra courses offered by the Information and Education Service—a $40,000,000-a-year program. A newspaper story tells of a sailor who had joined the Navy on graduation from high school. He kept taking courses and in thirteen years earned the degrees of B.S., M.S., and Ph.D. in psychology. He explained, "I saw a poster that said, 'Join the Navy and Learn.' I took them at their word."

XIII

Vocational Guidance

Cultivation of talent and an interest in an engineering career should begin in the higher elementary grades.

—John T. Rettaliata, President, Illinois Institute of Technology.[1]

A boy who wants to study science and who will make personal sacrifices to study it, is far more likely to turn into a good scientist than one who has to be persuaded to study it. . . . The world also needs leaders in many other fields.

—James R. Killian, Jr., President, Massachusetts Institute of Technology.[2]

It seems to me that older people do not think of us and the future together. They are only interested in the present and at most a year into the future. Sometimes I become engrossed in my future life and then people refer to it as daydreaming. If only they could understand how much it means to us, I'm sure they'd be glad to discuss our problems with us.

—A High-School Junior.

Three general principles should govern the employment of the bright, gifted, and talented: the individual's occupation should give scope for the full exercise of his ability and talent; it should be of intense personal interest to him; and it should serve the common good.

THE GUIDANCE COUNSELOR

The trained guidance counselor has detailed knowledge of the duties involved in the main types of occupation. He is likewise expert in the giving and interpreting of achievement, aptitude, and interest tests. He has experience in interviewing youngsters. He can lead them to see in which occupation they might use their abilities to the best advantage and in which ones they might suffer from their disabilities or dislikes. In this way the counselor helps the individual to choose for himself. The individual remains personally responsible for the decision.

If your school has a guidance counselor you will of course co-operate with him in every way. He will be glad to have all the information you can give him about a student's interests, abilities, aptitudes, and character. And he will want the student to talk problems over with you, both before and after the counseling interview.

If there is no guidance counselor in your school, there may be a guidance clinic within reach. A list of accredited clinics is available from The American Personnel and Guidance Association, 1534 O Street, N.W., Washington 5, D.C. Find out whether the most convenient clinic accepts high-school students for vocational guidance, and how much it charges. The professional counselor has so much to offer all students, and especially the undecided student, that every effort should be made to take advantage of available services.

When you cannot get expert advice for the student, you will have to do what you can without it. As a matter of fact, your close knowledge of the student's ability and character, your experience as a teacher, and your common sense combine to make you an excellent adviser. You will be on safe ground as long as you confine yourself to helping the student see how his particular abilities and disabilities accord with the evident demands of an occupation, and then leave the decision to him.

SUITABLE OCCUPATIONS

The individual who earns his living at an occupation that does not give scope for the exercise of his abilities may be very unhappy. But there is no occupation that is unsuitable for a person just because he is bright or gifted. Genius can make a career in any field. You may laugh at first-graders who say they want to be policemen. But consider the achievements of Dr. J. Edgar Hoover and the requirement that the F.B.I.'s operatives be lawyers or certified public accountants. Consider too that the world's great chefs are bright and talented, have undergone rigorous professional training, and are creative artists in their own right. (Might not the shortage of chefs be more of a threat to civilization than the shortage of scientists? We should gladly exchange the atom bomb for a *bombe noisette* concocted by a *cordon bleu.*)

Nonetheless, when a bright teen-age boy seems inclined to an occupation in which college graduates do not normally engage, try to make him see the importance of being very sure of his choice. To what extent will he be able to use his abilities? If he is successful, what will his position be in twenty years? Will he be satisfied with the pay and the recognition?

A rough guide to suitable occupations is afforded by the actual occupations which college graduates favor. Of the men in Terman's study of genius, 46 per cent were engaged in a profession, 26 per cent in business or executive work, and 20 per cent as salesmen, real-estate and insurance agents, clerical workers, or workers in skilled trades.[3] Of the members of the Yale class of 1946, ten years after graduation, more than 45 per cent were engaged in a profession, 17 per cent were in sales and insurance, and 16 per cent in manufacturing, finance, advertising, and military service.[4]

Of the 40 members of Phi Beta Kappa in the class of Yale

1956, 35 expected to continue their studies in graduate school. Of these, 9 were going to law school, 7 to medical school, and 1 to divinity school. Eighteen were going to do graduate work in the fields of the liberal arts or sciences, as follows: 7, physics; 2, foreign languages; 2, mathematics; 2, literature (including one "literature and music"); 2, economics; 1, history; 1, anthropology; and 1, biology. Of the 5 who were not going to graduate school, 2 were going directly into teaching, 1 into insurance, 1 into business, and 1 was undecided. (One of the prospective graduate students in mathematics said that after taking his Ph.D. he expected to work for an insurance company.) These figures are notable not only for the preponderance of professional work among the choices, but also for the fact that only one of these seniors had not decided on his occupation. In contrast, an estimated 22 per cent of the total class had not made definite choices by the spring of senior year. The possession of a vocational goal may, to some extent at least, have motivated the outstanding scholastic achievements of the Phi Beta Kappa members.

Teaching claims a fortunately large percentage (about 28 per cent) of female college graduates, both married and unmarried, who are employed. Large numbers are also occupied as office workers, partly because this is traditionally woman's work and partly because it makes a convenient temporary job for those who are waiting to marry. But the day has long passed when teaching and office work were the only fields open to women. The Smith College Vocational Office reported that in 1956 they received more than two hundred calls for science majors at starting salaries of $4,500 to $5,000 a year. However, only 8 seniors entered scientific work, as compared to 66 in office work and general business, 43 in teaching, 20 in advertising and editorial work, and 17 in banking and insurance. You can certainly advise a teen-age girl who asks you about a career in science or business that both fields are wide open.

PROCRASTINATORS

As we said in discussing motivation, many high-achievers, both scholastically and professionally, make their vocational choices early. This may tempt you to urge the late decider to make up his mind. But pressure may make an already worried youngster desperate and not bring him to any certainty.

The worry over uncertainty is the principal harm of long indecision. The youngster who can cheerfully continue in the general-education courses which were described in the last chapter does not positively have to make a decision about an occupation until he graduates from college. He may even try one or two fields before he finds the right one. John Enders, who shared the Nobel prize for his part in propagating the polio virus, did not begin graduate work in biology until he was 28. But for every one who makes a successful shift there are hundreds who would like to change but cannot.

If you have a student who is worrying over the choice of a vocation, or hesitating as to whether he should commit himself (for example, by going directly from high school to a college of engineering or a school of art), do all you can to arrange an interview for him with a trained guidance counselor. If this cannot be done, encourage him to talk to you about the subjects which he likes best and least and the implications these have for his choice. You might also have him take the Kuder Preference Test. If you do, go over with him the directions for giving and interpreting the test. This will help him understand the way the results should be used.

THE OCCUPATIONS COURSE

Most junior high schools and a few high schools give a formal course in occupations as part of the curriculum. Many high schools have informal courses or club programs and invite representatives of different occupations to speak to the students. In theory, a good occupations course ought to give many students clues to what they would like to do, or, and this is almost as important, what they would not like to do. But in fact, many bright students say that the course is the least interesting and least helpful of any they have taken. The usual difficulty seems to be that too much time is devoted to occupations which the bright students know they do not wish to follow, and too little time to the few occupations which have an appeal. We believe the course would be more profitable if the classes taking it were grouped according to ability and if they were taught by a method which allowed each youngster to concentrate on a few vocations. Then he would learn a considerable amount about those in which he was interested and something of a number of others from the reports of his fellow students.

VERIFYING A CHOICE

Lots of youngsters isolate themselves from any real thought about a career by saying confidently, "I want to be a writer"—or a doctor, or lawyer, or an Air Force pilot. They have a ready answer to anyone's questions, even their own. But when the time comes to make a crucial decision, they find they have no solid basis for their choice. They quickly abandon their old ambition and have nothing to put in its place.

Your knowledge of a student's strengths and weaknesses in his various school subjects makes it possible for you to help him stop dreaming and face reality. For example, the boy who says he wants to be a journalist but whose themes are always dull, ungrammatical, poorly organized—and late—may yet learn to be a writer. Show him how his present mistakes would disqualify him for work as a novelist, journalist, or advertising copy writer. Tell him how he can improve. Quote Stevenson on the value of exercises in imitation, and Sheridan's "Easy writing's curst hard reading." If he then puts his mind on learning the fundamentals and begins to practice writing he may be serious in his choice. If he does not improve, see if he can tell you how he expects to overcome his disabilities and his disinclination to do the necessary work.

When it seems to you that a student's tentative choice is a good one, is work which is worthy of a bright individual and which the particular student could do well, encourage him to find out all he can about it. Practical information is available in the guidance monographs which exist for virtually every occupation. If the student cannot find what he wants in the school or public library, suggest that he write to The Science Research Associates, 57 West Grand Ave., Chicago 10, Ill. They publish an excellent series. Note that the student should himself hunt out the book or write the letters, rather than leave it to you to do. If he acts for himself he will have more interest in the outcome.

The youngster who thinks he may be interested in a specific occupation does well to talk with someone who is engaged in it. Men and women are usually glad to talk about their work, to describe their everyday duties, and give interested youngsters an on-the-job demonstration. Some community committees on the gifted have made a specialty of arranging this type of guidance conference. If there is no list of people who are willing to cooperate, you can probably think of a qualified person among your friends. Or the student may know one. In either case, suggest that he write and ask for an interview. He should let the adult know what kind of advice he needs: i.e., about duties, training, openings. He should be serious enough about entering the field to have done a good deal of investigating on his own. Only then will he be able to appreciate the adult's comments and to know what questions to ask. This test of serious interest is important from all points of view. If every student who had an idle thought of studying law tried to call on the town's leading lawyer, the lawyer soon would withdraw the privilege.

PART-TIME EMPLOYMENT

The student who can get an after-school or summer job in line with a vocational interest is extremely fortunate. The job will probably be very minor, and perhaps less lucrative than lawn-cutting or baby sitting. But the youngster will see enough of the humdrum routine side of a business or profession to keep him from having falsely romantic ideas. He will gain some familiarity with the different kinds of work which go on in an office or plant, and he will learn the everyday terms that are used. When he is ready for full-time employment, prospective employers with whom he has interviews will welcome his ability to understand their descriptions of openings. And he will know whether a job which he may be offered is what he really wants. Furthermore, there is always the chance that the student and his temporary employer will develop a mutual liking that will result in permanent employment later.

One of the best city editors whom we know began work as a newsboy for his present paper. By the time he had finished college he had been given part-time employment in every department of the paper, sometimes running errands and sometimes doing odd jobs. He spent his college vacations as a relief reporter while the regular reporters took their vacations. When he graduated he was able to start as a full-fledged reporter. He moved up quickly.

A few able and enterprising youngsters manage to set themselves up in business. If you know any who have done this, ask them if they are members of Junior Achievement, Inc. This is an organization which helps boys and girls model their business on the lines of a regular corporation. Each junior company is given a sponsor. One high-school group in Houston, Texas, formed the Metal Engineering Company to make charcoal grills. They cleared $593.93, and received awards from their sponsor (the Humble Oil Company) and from the New York Stock Exchange. Information can be secured from

Junior Achievement, Inc., 345 Madison Ave., New York, N. Y.

About one-quarter of all high-school students hold jobs outside of school hours. A 1956 survey of forty-six Connecticut high schools showed that 37.7 per cent of the juniors and 55.5 per cent of the seniors were employed. Even when students' work is not prevocational, they can derive many benefits. The money they make may help pay their college expenses. Being able to earn gives them a feeling of self-confidence. And the awareness that carelessness means no work and no work means no pay is a great builder of responsibility.

The drawback to a student's holding a job during the school year is the amount of time it takes. According to the Connecticut survey, 17.5 per cent of the seniors were employed from 21 to 30 hours a week. Because a paid job usually takes precedence, a student may cut down on study or on extracurricular activities. He may try to do everything and overwork badly. When you know a student has a paid job, talk with him about his schedule. Do not discourage employment, but give him a sense of proportion so that he will not slight study and school affairs in favor of his job. He will not like to be told that he is only young once—he may now think it once too often—but he can see the virtue of an occasional good time.

The Future Nurses Club, the Future Teachers Club, the 4-H Club, and similar organizations give some bright students an opportunity to try out their interests. When a student is interested directly or indirectly in an occupation related to such a club, encourage him to join. For example, a future scientist might learn something about practical laboratory work while testing the acidity of soils as a member of the 4-H Club.

RESEARCH

Bright and gifted students with an intense interest in a subject may not visualize the vocational possibilities of research. They may think that the only way they could earn a living as a specialist would be by university teaching, and may not feel that they would be good teachers.

You can make the young chemist, physicist, mathematician, or engineer aware of the research openings in industry by showing him the advertisements in the financial and employment sections of a metropolitan newspaper. The demand seems insatiable. Industries are also eager for psychologists and economists. The United States civil service employs practically every type of specialist from agronomists to zymologists. The airlines need more meteorologists. And the increasing number of senior executive officers in big corporations who hold the Ph.D. degree shows that the research specialist can find room at the top, financially as well as intellectually.

The youngster who might make a career in research needs educational as well as vocational guidance. He should plan early to take a doctor's degree. He has to be sure that the college he attends has the facilities and offers the courses that he will need, and that the best graduate schools accept its students. Only 8,995 doctoral degrees were conferred in 1954. We could have used 100,000 individuals with graduate training. The main hope of securing more in future years rests upon good guidance by classroom teachers.

THE SERVICE PROFESSIONS

Bright and gifted youngsters are typically idealistic, and most of all they cherish the ideal of service. But our American civilization stresses money as the symbol of success. Many able young men and women enter fields, such as that of medicine, in which both objectives can be attained. But many forgo riches and find true wealth in serving others.

If you are happy as a teacher, you can with good conscience encourage bright youngsters who want to become teachers. And you can speak confidently of the rewards of serving others when young people ask about becoming, for example, librarians, social workers, or clinical psychologists. We recognize that not only the call of service but also increased salaries, better working conditions, and more opportunities for research and creative work are necessary to attract more people to these professions, and we are confident that improvement in these respects can be obtained. But they will never be the real reward.

That teachers, at least, do find satisfactions in their work is shown by a study which we have made of 125 teachers' replies to the questions: When and why did you decide to become a teacher? Do you regret it? Do you advise your good students to become teachers?

Only 7 of these teachers had even occasional feelings of regret. Three typical opinions are: "After twenty-six years I can truthfully say I've loved every minute"; "I've only taught three years but I can't wait for September"; and "If I regretted going into teaching, I certainly would not remain."

If everyone were as happy in his vocation as these teachers are, the world would be a better place. So their replies as to when and why they decided on their profession offer valuable clues to guidance.

Well over half of these teachers had wanted to be teachers since before they graduated from high school. More than a quarter made the decision when they were in elementary school. Remarks like, "I can't remember when I didn't expect to teach," are common. One teacher writes: "I used to come home from kindergarten and play teacher." Of a total of 29 late deciders, 12 made up their minds as seniors in college, 5 while they were in the Army, and 12 after trying other kinds of work. (Of the 7 who had regrets, 3 were among the 12 who decided as college seniors.) These figures accord with the principle that, whereas an early vocational decision is desirable, a late decision is not necessarily a handicap.

The two leading reasons for becoming a teacher were a liking for children and a desire to be of service. A large number of the replies also mention the influence of example. One teacher writes: "I decided to be a teacher before ever going to school.   Then 'heroine worship,' the personality of a very wonderful first-grade teacher, confirmed my predisposition." Another says, "My seventh-grade teacher, a nun, was a living personification of everything associated with scholarship and an understanding love of children."

The "predisposition" to teaching was thoroughly tested by many of these teachers before they made their final decision. One writes: "Baby sitting convinced me.   I liked it so much that I did all I could.   And I began teaching Sunday School as soon as they would let me."   Certainly an actual trial, even though the conditions are not those of responsible employment, is about the best test of a vocational interest.   Several of the late deciders deliberately kept open minds until they had had a period of practice teaching.   And one Army veteran writes: "In my Army camp, I served as librarian and did a good deal of instructing and gradually realized how much I liked to teach."

The answers to the question, "Do you advise your good students to become teachers?" show that these teachers have a good grasp of the principles of guidance.   They know that the individual must decide for himself but that the adviser can help him gauge his abilities and interests.   A typical reply reads: "I don't urge any student to become a teacher unless he shows some interest.   When one does, I encourage him to consider all sides of the question: his own personality (not just being a good student), his sense of humor, and his liking for children.   I want him to think of other things he might do, too.   But I make it very clear that I love to teach and am glad I am a teacher."

XIV

Working with Parents

"Children are not always as bright as parents think they are."
"Parents are not always as dumb as children think they are."
"Where do teachers come in?"
—Overheard at an Institute on the Gifted.

I have a conference with each child's parent as soon as possible after school opens. Before each conference I review the child's record card and make note of things to praise and points on which I'd like more information. The parents always throw new light on the children's characteristics. It certainly helps me in my teaching.
—A Teacher.

The old slogan, "Home and school should work together," has special significance in the case of bright and talented children. The exchange of information and the co-ordination of plans facilitate practically every feature of a sound educational program. Accurate early identification, enrichment, motivation, mental hygiene, educational and vocational guidance are all promoted by close co-operation between parents and teachers.

Unfortunately, communication between home and school is severely limited by the practical situation. Teachers and parents do not have much free time in common and both have many obligations. Fathers rarely meet their children's teachers unless the children are in trouble. Good will and careful planning are necessary to break down the barriers. You will find helpful discussions on the problem and on methods in James L. Hymes's *Effective Home-School Relations* [1] and in Grace Langdon and Irving Stout's *Teacher-Parent Interviews*.[2]

CONFERENCES

A surprising number of elementary-school teachers manage to have private conferences with the parents of all of their pupils. High-school teachers can hardly find time to meet the parents of every one of their students, but they can and do confer with the parents of the youngsters in their home rooms. Considering what a large proportion of parent-teacher conferences are about low marks or disciplinary difficulties, those about bright students' achievements and plans can be a great relief.

Face-to-face talks with parents are worth all the time and trouble involved. One teacher writes: "The chief value of these conferences is the insight they afford me into the child's background and personality. They help establish a friendly relation between home and school." This teacher arranges to meet parents before school in the morning and during the noon hour as well as after school in the afternoon. He occasionally visits a child's home in the evening and in one case went to the father's place of employment to talk with him. The conferences average about 20 minutes each—a total of about 12 hours for the 34 children in the room. In addition, he and all the other teachers in his school hold semiannual group meetings with the parents of their pupils. These meetings are held in school time and the pupils are dismissed.

The parent's first question in a routine conference is apt to be, "How is Johnny getting along?" This gives you a chance to put the parent at his ease, because you can surely find something nice to say about the child's work. It also leads naturally into the question of how bright Johnny is. Your comments on the child's progress and ability will probably start the parent talking. Take time to listen. Make a mental note of information that should be in the record. Once rapport has been established you can raise any question which you may have—for example, about hobbies, siblings, homework, or plans for the future.

The wide range of topics that can be usefully discussed in a parent-teacher conference is shown by one teacher's report on conferences with the parents of fifteen bright children. In a number of cases, parents gave him important information that was not in the record. For example:

I hadn't known that George's father was blinded in the war. He's never been able to see George. He's now away from home taking a rehabilitation course. (George's work is satisfactory but he has been fighting a good deal. I'll give him more attention and I suggested he be taught to box.)

Fred's father is dead. That explains why his mother is so anxious. I reassured her warmly about his work.

It turned out that Maria's family spoke only Italian at home. I told the mother that Maria wasn't reading as well as I knew she could and suggested that since Mrs. Antonio spoke English so perfectly she should speak to her more often in English at home—I was sure it would help her in her reading—but not to put aside Italian entirely.

Three of the fifteen conferences described by this teacher concerned physical handicaps of which the parent had not been aware. Surprisingly, two of these were speech handicaps, and the conferences resulted in work by the parents and children with the school speech specialist. The third was a visual defect. The parent took the child to an oculist, who prescribed glasses. The child "adjusted nicely and his work improved greatly."

Two of the cases were of children whose school behavior changed for the worse soon after the birth of a baby brother or sister. In each case the teacher's suggestion that the school-age child be given more attention was gratefully accepted by the parents and worked well. Of another case the teacher wrote:

Working with Parents

Bob has a high IQ but was doing badly. I met with his parents. After tactful questioning they admitted that perhaps the fault could be that Bob's work was usually compared with the work of an older sister who is very responsible and always turns in excellent papers. Right here could be the answer to Bob's lack of interest and "What do I care" attitude. The parents agreed to help Bob with his homework, to show more interest in what he did in school, and above all to stop comparisons. I promised to give him more individual attention whenever I could. There's been a good change in Bob's attitude and work.

Another bright boy had not been reading as well as his record indicated he should. The teacher wrote:

Jake was referred to the remedial-reading teacher for special help. Soon after that I noticed that he was biting his nails and seemed very nervous and unhappy. I called in the parents. They said they'd engaged a tutor for Jake, that they didn't know we had a remedial-reading teacher. We hadn't known about the tutor, a former teacher whose methods conflicted with ours. Poor Jake was being told one thing at home and another in school and was naturally upset. We were all of us to blame for not conferring sooner. They agreed to let the tutor go, and everything straightened out nicely.

The remaining conferences described by this teacher were initiated by the parents to tell the teacher how pleased they were that their children were so happy and progressing so well. But each of the conferences resulted in an exchange of information which both the teacher and the parents valued.

In general, parents of bright children are co-operative and eager for help. Your professional knowledge of child development often lets you give them advice on points that might not have occurred to them. At least you can call their attention to some of the standard books for parents. When you have any reason to believe that there is a serious problem involved, you can suggest that they consult a specialist. Most often the problems that are worrying them and the difficulties of which you are aware are matters on which you are competent to advise. The fact that you teach thirty or more boys and girls each year gives you a breadth of experience that parents seldom equal. We have records of parents who were helped by teachers' advice on grade placement, acceleration, TV programs, bedtime, school behavior, attendance, recreation, playing football, transfer to private school, choice of college, choice of occupation, good books for children, and a wide variety of difficulties and successes in different school subjects.

How grateful a parent can be for a chance to talk over a problem and secure advice is shown by the report a mother, who is also a teacher, wrote after a conference:

> I spent half an hour with Katrine's teacher, Mrs. T., going over K's achievement-test scores and cumulative record. I came away with a much better understanding of K's strengths and weaknesses (high verbal, low arithmetic) and of what she should take in high school. I had a wonderful sense of working together with a fine capable teacher for my child's benefit. This teacher is experienced and motherly and loves every one of her pupils. Through many years in town she knows families, histories, and aspirations. Her conferences, like her teaching, emphasize her love of children. There was no talk of acceleration—K is very happy in the class and the group is exceptionally able—but rather of enrichment and of what each of us could do. Mrs. T. said, "This is the kind of conference I love to have and the kind of child it's a pleasure to teach." On my part, I know K is a pupil willing and happy to learn, but I know, too, the place good teaching plays in her happiness and achievement.

Home visits are an eminently satisfactory way of holding a friendly conference. They show your interest in a child as nothing else does. Parents and child are proud to welcome you. You gain firsthand knowledge of the child's background. He has a chance to show you his books and collections and tools. When you and the parents meet in their home you prove that school and home are working together. The values of home visits are so well-established that some school systems give teachers time off to make the visits. If you are not lucky enough to work in a system like this, at least try to accept any invitation to visit that a child or parent gives.

File in the pupil's cumulative-record folder any nonconfidential information that parents give you which might be useful to his future teachers.   Include a note on what you have told the parents about the child's ability.   Describe any attitude to the child or the school that seems unusual, for example, a tendency to exploit the child or antagonism to the school.   Indicate whether or not the parents expect the child to go to college.

DISCUSSING A PUPIL'S INTELLIGENCE WITH HIS PARENTS

You want both the pupil and his parents to know that he is bright.   Otherwise everybody concerned might be content with mediocre achievement and fail to make suitable educational and vocational plans.

The pupil is rarely left in doubt of your opinion of his ability.   Your praise of his achievements, your talks with him about his plans, your refusal to accept inferior work, and your suggestions for extra work combine to give him the conviction, "I can if I will and I'd better."   But the pupil, particularly the young pupil, will probably not discuss with his parents what you think of his powers, and if he did they might consider it childish boasting.

A report card which gives you a chance to comment on a pupil's ability and to indicate whether or not he is working up to it leads parents to consider how intelligent their child is. But they almost surely think mainly in terms of how well he is doing now and, except in the case of parents who are already eager for a child to go to college, do not realize the opportunities which superior intelligence opens up.

If you actually talk with the mother or father, you can be sure that they grasp both the problems and the possibilities of brightness.   The amount and kind of information you give them will depend on their education and attitude.

As a rule you are wise to avoid the use of terms like IQ and mental age.   Experience has shown that parents are extremely sensitive about IQ's but that they do not have any idea of the limitations of tests or of the insignificance of minor differences in scores. You can avoid misunderstanding and still convey conviction if you will confine yourself to "bright" or "very bright" or, in the case of a nonacademic talent, "clever." Both parents and pupils regularly refer to a superior student as "a bright kid" or "clever with his pencil." Back up your opinion with anecdotes about how well he reads or remembers or how quickly he thinks. Specific detail gives life and meaning to your statements.

When parents are very bright themselves, and especially when they are also well-educated, they may have trouble realizing that a bright child of theirs is anything out of the ordinary. Their plans for his future are likely to be sound. But bright parents may not understand that their child has any feeling of being different from his less gifted age mates. They may not be doing all they could to help him develop a well-rounded personality. They may take good marks at face value and not understand that the child is getting all A's without working as hard as he should. Your observation of the child in the classroom and at play gives you information on all of these points. When you feel that parents do not share your knowledge, talk with them frankly.

REPORT CARDS

The report is one of the oldest and still probably the most prevalent means of communication between school and home. Skillfully used, it serves several good purposes well. But some forms of report can do a good deal of harm if you do not guard against the dangers.

One school that was organizing special classes for bright pupils prepared the way by a series of parents' meetings. There was cordial agreement between parents and teachers on every point except report cards. The parents insisted that the traditional form be used, complete with numerical grades for each subject and for deportment. The school very wisely acquiesced, particularly as each parent promised to come to school semiannually for a conference.

Parents and students sometimes raise the question of how the newer systems of reporting affect a student's chances for college admission and for a scholarship. They fear that a student who has "a straight A record" in a school which marks on a five-letter system and without regard to effort may be preferred to one whose record notes what he might have done better. They may oppose placement in a high-ability group because they think the pupil will not receive as good marks as he would in a regular class. But most college committees on admission are far more influenced by a student's scores on standardized achievement tests and aptitude tests than by school marks. They are quick to note when a candidate's record shows he is in a high-ability group. They give great weight to teachers' recommendations. If parents or students are nervous about the marking system you use, suggest that they write to a college or two and inquire about it. If your experience indicates that any college to which your school sends graduates prefers a marking system different from the one you are using, it is only fair for the office to equate the grades when sending on a transcript.

Regardless of the type of official report, try to talk with each pupil individually about his report before you send it home. Get him to tell you what he thinks he has been doing well and what he might have done better. Give him your opinion on both points, and, if improvement in any subject or harder work or more home study is called for, make some joint plans for the weeks ahead. Some schools have each pupil write a brief summary of his report-card conference with the teacher, he and the teacher both sign it, and it is made a part of the report. This method, whether it is used separately or in connection with letter grades, has the merit of avoiding one danger in the generally helpful written report—it keeps the teacher from using stereotyped phrases that, by repetition, become almost meaningless.

Parents give more thought to a note from you that accompanies a report than they give to the recorded grades. If your official report does not provide for rating in terms of ability, or at least for rating on effort, work habits, and progress, you will want to comment on these. If your report has to be critical, try to temper it with some praise. If you think the pupil has a problem that you and his parents should discuss, ask them to telephone you and arrange a conference.

Many schools hold parents' nights or group conferences either to issue reports or soon after the reports are sent home. In high schools, each teacher stays in his own room and the parents seek out those of their youngster's teachers with whom they wish to talk. One elementary school conducts a "get acquainted" meeting in early October and subsequent conferences after each marking period. A teacher from this school writes:

Our principal plans these conferences with the whole staff to discuss what we want to accomplish and how we can best do it. The children take home cordial notes of invitation well in advance. The hour is set for 3–4 P.M. Children are dismissed, but the playground is supervised so that, if necessary, they can wait for their mothers. In line with the procedure we've worked out, I greet the parents and ask each one to find her child's desk. (Fathers seldom come.) On each desk is a folder with samples of the child's work. I explain the aims and objectives of the curriculum for my grade. I leave plenty of time for discussion, and there are always some good questions that let me give additional information and clarify some points. The conference certainly sets up a cordial home-school relationship. All but 9 of my 32 children had parents at this year's meeting, and the parents of 6 of these made appointments to talk with me later, either before school or during the noon hour. Marking-period conferences are scheduled every six weeks, but only those parents with whom I specially want to talk are invited. At the end of the year I have an individual conference with the parent of each child in my room to review the child's work and talk about the next year.

PARENTS' MEETINGS AND STUDY GROUPS

If your school is making any special provision for its bright and talented pupils, giftedness is a good topic for a P.T.A. meeting. Plans for the meeting should be based on the probability that a large proportion of the audience will have children who are not exceptionally bright and on the certainty that all parents want to know how everything that happens in school may affect their children. The safe approach is through emphasis on how methods which provide for individual differences help all children. Identification, particularly means which parents can use to estimate their children's ability, is of particular interest to parent groups. Other good topics are the world's need for educated brain power and what parents can do to enrich a child's early education and to plan for seeing him through college and professional school. The suggestions given in earlier chapters and those at the end of this chapter may be helpful.

Some school systems, either directly or through the P.T.A., have organized study groups for parents. There is a good chance that one for parents of bright children can be formed by setting it up on a city-wide basis. Or giftedness can be included as a part of a more general subject like child psychology. In some cities, college or university extension courses on bright children are open to both teachers and parents.

Parents who join together to study along a line of common interest gain a great deal not only from books and lectures but also from meeting and talking with each other. A difficulty which parents face in raising children is that their experience is mainly confined to their own children. Parents of bright children are further handicapped when the children are brighter than the neighbors' and when the parents themselves did not go to college or did not have other experiences which they would like their children to have. Comparing notes with other parents in a like situation enhances security and gives courage to institute far-reaching plans.

PARENTS' MISTAKES

One great advantage of the study group is that the mistakes parents are likely to make can be discussed in an impersonal atmosphere. For example, when a group considers the dangers of comparing a bright boy with his more responsible sister, no member of the group feels directly accused. The leader of a group can spend several sessions on a topic, or at least come back to it later when a parent for whom a lesson has struck home raises questions. The group will be mainly composed of people who want to learn and who are therefore willing to change their ways.

When you are trying to help an individual parent correct mistakes, you have to move slowly and tactfully. Even when a parent asks for advice about a problem which you are sure you could help solve, he may react very defensively when you tell him the truth. Remember that if you can only let him talk out his troubles he may himself see the right solution. If he does, he will be far more willing to apply it than he would be to follow any rule you might lay down. When a parent makes a constructive suggestion, reinforce it by stating your approval, by saying, for example, "That's a good idea of yours, having Tommy do his homework in private."

Books help many parents. Your public librarian will be glad to tell you what books the library has about child care and about specific problems. A parent is more likely to read a book which you recommend by name than he is to go to the library and make inquiries himself. Government pamphlets, e.g., *Your Child from 6 to 12*,[3] and the books by Gesell and Spock have contributed to the physical and emotional health of millions of children. Our own *Bright Children: A Guide for Parents* takes up the major mistakes which parents of bright children make: faulty discipline, exploitation, forcing beyond capacity, overprotection and spoiling, and favoritism.[4]

THE LOWER-CLASS HOME

Although our public schools pride themselves on offering equal opportunities to all children, the bright child from a lower-class home suffers from several disadvantages. Perhaps the gravest of these is the limit which the parents unconsciously place on their expectations for a child. They may have hopes that he will better himself, but these hopes are often confined to his doing better than they have in their line of work or to his making more money. They may not know that their child is exceptional and that, granted a good education, "the sky is the limit." They may even profess a scorn for book learning of any kind.

When the parents have little or no education, the home often lacks the books, magazines, record collections, and pictures which play such an important part in forming a child's taste and his attitude to intellectual activity. And because most of the homes in the neighborhood are similarly lacking in good cultural influences, the child who shows a glimmering of interest may be regarded as queer by other children and their parents. Even if the mores of the group do not taboo reading and study, there is no readily available adult model to inspire the child.

Crowded quarters and the family's need for each child's help may interfere with reading, study, and hobbies. There is little room, less privacy, and no time for anything but the necessities of life. One teacher writes: "Vespucci School is located in a low-income neighborhood. Most of the seventh- and eighth-grade boys hold jobs after school, and the girls are needed to assist working mothers with 'dishes and diapers.' This means the children have little time after school hours to pursue hobbies and special interests."

Under these circumstances you have to exert extra effort to help your bright pupils. Make friends with the parents. Convince them that their child is exceptional and that they should do all they can for him and that they must not stand in his way. Point out specific ways in which they can help him enrich his

233

out-of-school life. Lead them to look ahead to the time when he may be practicing a profession.

Remember the great influence which adult models have on a child's development. Try to give the child a feeling of the meaning that books and the profession of teaching have for you. See if you can get his clergyman interested in him. Arrange for him to join the Scouts. If there is a community center with well-educated leaders, see that he spends some time there and ask the leaders to give him special attention.

PROMOTING PARENTAL INTEREST IN THE SCHOOL

When you talk with a group of parents or confer with parents individually, stress the good effects on the child of their taking an interest in the school.

Both father and mother, and most especially the father, should take time to talk with a child about what happens in school. They need not, probably should not, question him in detail about what he does each day, but when he wants to talk they should listen. Their own attitude to education in general and the child's present schooling in particular forms his attitude. Discourage them from boasting about how bad they were in school, either in behavior or in their studies or both. Encourage them to speak well of learning and to express admiration for people who have made their way in the world by studying hard. The story of Lincoln's reading by the firelight gains force when a child senses his parents' approval of it.

If you send a good paper home, you give the parents an extra opening to praise the child. Hymes recommends an occasional one-or-two-line note from you about how fine a review a student has given or about how well he has done some specific task.[5] The note does not take long to dash off, and the spontaneity gives it appeal. If the student has been talking at home about the review or task, everyone will be extra pleased by your attention.

Working with Parents

Ask parents to keep you posted about unusual events so that you can give the child a word of congratulation or of sympathy. Tell them how important it is to let you know at once if they notice any sudden change for the worse in the child's attitude to school. Sometimes a difficulty that could be straightened out quickly in the beginning is not discovered until the pupil has a deep aversion to school. For example, one bright boy, somewhat young for his class, came to the point where he begged not to be sent to school. He would not explain why to his parents. They finally consulted his teacher, who quickly discovered that two older boys from a higher grade were systematically bullying him. The older boys were transferred to a junior high school, but it took the younger boy a long time to regain his self-confidence.

Parents should realize how their plans for the future may affect a child's schooling. For example, if they are to move to a neighboring district in October, it might be wise for the child to start in his new school in September rather than transfer later. More specifically, the bright child's parents should share with you their hopes and plans for the child's education and vocation. This makes it easy for you to be sure that they are aiming high enough and lets you advise them about choice of courses.

When parents have a friendly interest in what the school is doing, they can assist in numberless ways. Parents of one girl taught a Polish folk dance to a social-studies group which was doing a project on Poland, and provided authentic costumes. A machinist whose son's science group was studying steam power made the class a working model of James Watt's original engine. Another father took a group of boys on a weekend trip to New York to visit the Museum of Science and the Hayden Planetarium.

You can often point out how parents can supplement the school's program by what they do with and for the child outside of school. To some extent what they do will depend upon their means, but many could afford to do more and would do more if you made some suggestions. Possibilities include more trips and excursions on weekends and in the summer, space and equipment for hobbies, a personal typewriter, the beginnings of a personal library (including reference books), and private lessons in music, dancing, and sports. In fact, parents can and should carry further everything the school starts, whether it is an enrichment project or vocational guidance.

XV

The Challenge

The general objects . . . are to provide an education adapted to the years, to the capacity, and the condition of every one, and directed to their freedom and happiness. . . . We hope to avail the state of those talents which nature has sown as liberally among the poor as the rich, but which perish without use, if not sought for and cultivated.
—*Thomas Jefferson*, Notes on Virginia.

From the time of Socrates and before, thoughtful teachers have reasoned that the salvation of civilization depended on educating all children and educating the brightest to become leaders. Plato called education "the one sufficient thing," and proposed that the most intelligent and capable children be trained to become the guardians of his Republic. Sir Thomas More said that in his Utopia "all children are instructed in learning" and some are chosen to be scholars, namely, those "in whom from their very childhood they have perceived a fine wit, a unique ability, and a mind apt to good learning."

We in the United States have far surpassed the designs of the philosophers in establishing and maintaining universal schooling. But we have fallen far short of the ideal of identifying our bright and talented children and providing them with an education adapted to their capacity. As a result we are faced with dire shortages of teachers, scientists, and other professionally trained people.

237

There is no immediate remedy.   The low birth rate in the Thirties and the high birth rate in the decade 1946–1956 mean that there are not enough young people with the requisite ability to supply the demands in every field.   But today boys and girls crowd our schools, and the brightest among them will rescue our tomorrows if only we give them the instruction and the guidance that they deserve.

Consider what would happen if:

> All teachers made a systematic attempt to identify all bright and talented children.

> All teachers used methods that helped all children make the most of their abilities.

> All teachers continued to think, study, and experiment with a view to improving the teaching of the bright and talented.

> All parents and all communities organized all of their resources with a view to providing the best schooling for the bright and talented.

> All the bright and talented were educated to apply their gifts in the service of humanity.

Notes

I. CALLING ALL TEACHERS

[1] Paul Witty, "How to Identify the Gifted," *Childhood Education,* Vol. 29, No. 7 (March 1953), 312–16.

[2] *Teachers for Tomorrow,* Bulletin No. 2 (New York: The Fund for the Advancement of Education, 1955). Obtainable from the Fund, 655 Madison Ave., New York 21, N. Y.

[3] Norma E. Cutts, ed., *School Psychologists at Mid-Century* (Washington, D.C.: American Psychological Association, Inc., 1955), p. 4.

II. IDENTIFICATION

[1] James Bryant Conant, *The Citadel of Learning* (New Haven: Yale University Press, 1956), pp. 43–44.

[2] Lewis M. Terman and Melita H. Oden, *The Gifted Child Grows Up,* Genetic Studies of Genius, Vol. IV (Stanford, Cal.: Stanford University Press, 1947).

[3] Catharine Morris Cox [Miles], *The Early Mental Traits of Three Hundred Geniuses,* Genetic Studies of Genius, Vol. II (Stanford, Cal.: Stanford University Press, 1926).

[4] Paul F. Brandwein, *The Gifted Student as Future Scientist* (New York: Harcourt, Brace and Company, Inc., 1955).

[5] J. P. Guilford, "Creativity," *The American Psychologist,* Vol. 5, No. 9 (September 1950), 444–54.

[6] Arnold Gesell, *The Child from Five to Ten* (New York: Harper & Brothers, 1946).

[7] *Vineland Social Maturity Scale* (Minneapolis, Minn.: Educational Test Bureau, Educational Publishers, Inc., n.d.).

[8] Charles Watters Odell, *How to Improve Classroom Testing* (Dubuque, Iowa: Wm. C. Brown Company, 1953).

[9] Florence L. Goodenough, *Measurement of Intelligence by Drawings* (Yonkers-on-Hudson, N. Y.: World Book Company, 1926).

[10] Beatrice Lantz, *Easel Age Scale* (Los Angeles: California Test Bureau, 1955).

III. ENRICHMENT: PURPOSES AND PLANS

[1] Elizabeth Stevenson, *Henry Adams* (New York: The Macmillan Company, 1955).

[2] *Time,* Vol. LXVII, No. 14 (April 2, 1956), 63.

[3] Ruth Strang, "Psychology of Gifted Children and Youth," in *Exceptional Children and Youth,* ed. William M. Cruickshank (Englewood Cliffs, N. J.: Prentice-Hall, Inc., 1955), p. 491.

[4] *Curriculum Development in the Elementary Schools,* Curriculum Bulletin No. 1, 1955–56 Series (New York: Board of Education of the City of New York), pp. 42–60.

IV. ENRICHMENT: METHODS AND CONTENT

[1] Kurt Lewin, Ronald Lippitt, and Ralph K. White, "Patterns of Aggressive Behavior in Experimentally Created 'Social Climates,' " *Journal of Social Psychology,* Vol. 10 (May 1939), 271–99.

[2] Brandwein, *The Gifted Student as Future Scientist, op. cit.,* pp. 51–52.

[3] Theodore Andersson, *The Teaching of Foreign Languages in the Elementary School* (Boston: D. C. Heath & Company, 1953).

[4] *Education of the Gifted* (Washington, D.C.: Educational Policies Commission, National Education Association, 1950), p. 63.

[5] New York State Counselors Association, *Tips* (Albany, N.Y.: Delmar Publishers, Inc., 1956).

[6] Robert J. Havighurst, Eugene Stivers, and Robert F. DeHaan, *A Survey of the Education of Gifted Children,* Supplementary Educational Monographs, No. 83 (Chicago: University of Chicago Press, November 1955).

[7] Theodore Hall, *Gifted Children: The Cleveland Story* (Cleveland, Ohio: The World Publishing Company, 1956).

V. UTILIZING COMMUNITY RESOURCES

[1] *The Gifted Child* (Palo Alto, Cal.: Unified School District, 1955).

[2] Havighurst, Stivers, and DeHaan, *A Survey of the Education of Gifted Children, op. cit.*

[3] *Ibid.,* pp. 56–57.

[4] *Educators Guide to Free Films,* 16th ed. (Randolf, Wis.: Educators Progress Service, July 1956).

[5] Metropolitan School Study Council, *Fifty Teachers to a Classroom* (New York: The Macmillan Company, 1950).

Notes

VI. SPECIAL GROUPS

[1] Walter B. Barbe and Dorothy E. Norris, "Special Classes for Gifted Children in Cleveland," *Exceptional Children*, Vol. 21, No. 2 (November 1954), 56.

[2] George V. Sheviakov and Fritz Redl, *Discipline for Today's Children and Youth* (Washington, D.C.: Association for Supervision and Curriculum Development, National Education Association, 1944), p. 57.

[3] Walter B. Barbe, "Evaluation of Special Classes for Gifted Children," *Exceptional Children*, Vol. 22, No. 2 (November 1955), 60–62.

[4] Dorothy E. Norris, "Tailor-Made for High IQs," *NEA Journal*, Vol. 42, No. 5 (May 1953), 276–77.

[5] Merle R. Sumption, *Three Hundred Gifted Children* (Yonkers-on-Hudson, N. Y.: World Book Company, 1941).

[6] Hall, *Gifted Children, op. cit.*

[7] Hedwig O. Pregler, "The Colfax Plan," *Exceptional Children*, Vol. 20, No. 5 (February 1954), 198–201, 222.

[8] James M. Dunlap, "Gifted Children in an Enriched Program," *Exceptional Children*, Vol. 21, No. 4 (January 1955), 135–37.

[9] Gertrude Howell Hildreth, *Educating Gifted Children at Hunter College Elementary School* (New York: Harper & Brothers, 1952).

[10] Havighurst, Stivers, and DeHaan, *A Survey of the Education of Gifted Children, op. cit.*

[11] Helen Erskine Roberts, *Current Trends in the Education of the Gifted* (Sacramento: California State Department of Education, October 25, 1954).

[12] Paul H. Holcomb, "A Program for the Gifted," *Exceptional Children*, Vol. 19, No. 5 (February 1953), 201.

[13] J. Wayne Wrightstone, "The Career High School," *Educational Leadership*, XIII, No. 4 (January 1956), 236–40.

[14] Brandwein, *The Gifted Student as Future Scientist, op. cit.*

VII. ACCELERATION

[1] Terman and Oden, *The Gifted Child Grows Up, op. cit.*, pp. 264–81.

[2] Noel Keys, "The Underage Student in High School and College," in *University of California Publications in Education*, Vol. 7, No. 3 (Berkeley: University of California Press, 1938), 147–271.

[3] Sidney L. Pressey, *Educational Acceleration: Appraisal and Basic Problems*, Bureau of Educational Research Monographs, No. 31 (Columbus: Ohio State University, 1949).

Notes

[4] D. A. Worcester, *The Education of Children of Above-Average Mentality* (Lincoln: University of Nebraska Press, 1956).

[5] Jack W. Birch, "Early School Admission for Mentally Advanced Children," *Exceptional Children*, Vol. 21, No. 3 (December 1954), 84–87.

[6] *Survey: Gifted Child Education in California* (n.p.: State Advisory Council on Educational Research, December 1955). Obtainable from California Teachers Association, 693 Sutter St., San Francisco 2, Cal.

[7] Elizabeth Morrissy, Walter Sondheim, Jr., and J. Trueman Thompson, "The Superior Child in the Baltimore Public Schools," *Baltimore Bulletin of Education*, XXXI, No. 5 (June 1954), 1–13.

[8] Havighurst, Stivers, and DeHaan, *A Survey of the Education of Gifted Children, op. cit.*, pp. 49–50.

[9] *Bridging the Gap between School and College* (New York: The Fund for the Advancement of Education, 1953). Obtainable from the Fund, 655 Madison Ave., New York 21, N. Y.

[10] Roberts, *Current Trends in the Education of the Gifted, op. cit.*, p. 36.

VIII. THE FUNDAMENTALS

[1] *What Research Says to the Teacher* (Washington, D.C.: National Education Association, 1953).

[2] Ralph C. Preston, "Inefficient Readers among Superior College Students," *School and Society*, Vol. 69, No. 1792 (April 23, 1949), 299–300.

[3] Glenn Myers Blair, *Diagnostic and Remedial Teaching* (New York: The Macmillan Company, 1956).

[4] N. E. Cutts and Nicholas Moseley, "Bright Children and the Curriculum," *Educational Administration and Supervision*, Vol. 39, No. 3 (March 1953), 168–73.

[5] Henry S. Dyer, Robert Kalin, and Frederic M. Lord, *Problems in Mathematical Education* (Princeton, N. J.: Educational Testing Service, 1956).

IX. MOTIVATING THE UNDERACHIEVERS

[1] Strang, "Psychology of Gifted Children and Youth," *op. cit.*, pp. 475–519.

[2] Terman and Oden, *The Gifted Child Grows Up, op. cit.*, pp. 157–59.

[3] Robert J. Dowd, "Underachieving Students of High Capacity," *The Journal of Higher Education*, Vol. 23, No. 6 (June 1952), 327–30.

Notes

[4] Jesse A. Bond, "Analysis of Factors Adversely Affecting Scholarship of High-School Pupils," *Journal of Educational Research*, XLVI, No. 1 (September 1952), 1–15.

[5] J. C. Gowan, "The Underachieving Gifted Child a Problem for Everyone," *Exceptional Children*, Vol. 21, No. 7 (April 1955), 247–49.

[6] Terman and Oden, *The Gifted Child Grows Up, op. cit.*, p. 157.

[7] J. Jeffery Auer and Henry Lee Ewbank, *Handbook for Discussion Leaders*, rev. ed. (New York: Harper & Brothers, 1954).

[8] Robert S. Woodworth, *Psychology*, 4th ed. (New York: Henry Holt and Company, Inc., 1940), p. 366.

[9] Viktor Lowenfeld, *Creative and Mental Growth*, rev. ed. (New York: The Macmillan Company, 1952).

[10] Conant, *The Citadel of Learning, op. cit.*, pp. 45–46.

[11] Gordon W. Allport, *Becoming* (New Haven: Yale University Press, 1955), p. 51.

X. MENTAL HYGIENE

[1] Terman and Oden, *The Gifted Child Grows Up, op. cit.*, pp. 108, 110–11.

[2] Leta S. Hollingworth, "The Child of Very Superior Intelligence as a Special Problem in Social Adjustment," *Mental Hygiene*, XV, No. 1 (January 1931), 1–16.

[3] Douglas A. Thom and Nancy Newell, "Hazards of the High I.Q.," *Mental Hygiene*, XXIX, No. 1 (January 1945), 62.

[4] M. L. Fallick, Mildred Peters, Morton Levitt, and Ben O. Rubenstein, "Observations on the Psychological Education of Teachers in a School-based Mental-Hygiene Program," *Mental Hygiene*, XXXVIII, No. 3 (July 1954), 374–86.

[5] Thom and Newell, "Hazards of the High I.Q.," *op. cit.* pp. 72–74.

[6] Eveoleen N. Rexford, Maxwell Schleifer, and Suzanne Taets van Amerongen, "A Follow-Up of a Psychiatric Study of 57 Antisocial Young Children," *Mental Hygiene*, XL, No. 2 (April 1956), 196–214.

[7] Thom and Newell, "Hazards of the High I.Q.," *op. cit.*, pp. 68, 69.

[8] Norma E. Cutts and Nicholas Moseley, *Better Home Discipline* (New York: Appleton-Century-Crofts, Inc., 1952), pp. 110–32.

[9] Thom and Newell, "Hazards of the High I.Q.," *op. cit.*, p. 71.

[10] Ruth Cunningham and Associates, *Understanding Group Behavior of Boys and Girls* (New York: Bureau of Publications, Teachers College, Columbia University, 1951).

[11] Blair, *Diagnostic and Remedial Teaching, op. cit.*, pp. 364–66.

[12] Norma E. Cutts and Nicholas Moseley, *Practical School Discipline and Mental Hygiene* (Boston: Houghton Mifflin Company, 1941), pp. 123–26.

Notes

XI. CHARACTER DEVELOPMENT

[1] Robert Stoughton, *Report on Provisions for the Gifted,* Connecticut State Department of Education Bulletin (Hartford: September 1954).

[2] Thom and Newell, "Hazards of the High I.Q.," *op. cit.,* p. 70.

[3] Arthur W. Foshay, Kenneth D. Wann, and Associates, *Children's Social Values* (New York: Bureau of Publications, Teachers College, Columbia University, 1954).

[4] Betty L. Mitton and Dale B. Harris, "The Development of Responsibility in Children," *The Elementary School Journal,* Vol. 54, No. 5 (January 1954), 268–77.

[5] Dale B. Harris, Kenneth E. Clark, Arnold M. Rose, and Frances Valasek, "The Measurement of Responsibility in Children," *Child Development,* Vol. 25, No. 1 (March 1954), 21–28.

[6] Dale B. Harris, Kenneth E. Clark, Arnold M. Rose, and Frances Valasek, "The Relationship of Children's Home Duties to an Attitude of Responsibility," *Child Development,* Vol. 25, No. 1 (March 1954), 29–33.

[7] Dale B. Harris, "How Student-Teachers Identify Responsibility in Children," *The Journal of Educational Psychology,* Vol. 45, No. 4 (April 1954), 233–39.

[8] Jean Mayer, "Muscular State of the Union," *New York Times Magazine,* November 6, 1955, p. 17.

[9] Herlin Slocomb, "The Myth of Neglect: Bright Students' College Records," *The Clearing House,* Vol. 29, No. 6 (February 1955), 346–48.

[10] Howard Lane and Mary Beauchamp, *Human Relations in Teaching* (Englewood Cliffs, N. J.: Prentice-Hall, Inc., 1955).

[11] Thomas Gordon, *Group-Centered Leadership* (Boston: Houghton Mifflin Company, 1955).

[12] William M. Sattler and N. Edd Miller, *Discussion and Conference* (Englewood Cliffs, N. J.: Prentice-Hall, Inc., 1954).

[13] Nicholas Moseley, "Politics in City-School Administration," *The Elementary School Journal,* XXXIX, No. 1 (September 1938), 36–45.

XII. EDUCATIONAL GUIDANCE

[1] Charles C. Cole, Jr., *Encouraging Scientific Talent* (New York: College Entrance Examination Board, 1956), p. 159.

[2] Henry Chauncey, *Annual Report to the Board of Trustees, 1954–5* (Princeton, N. J.: Educational Testing Service, n.d.), p. 31.

[3] Raymond N. Hatch, *Guidance Services in the Elementary School* (Dubuque, Iowa: Wm. C. Brown Company, 1951).

Notes

[4] Ruth Strang, *The Role of the Teacher in Personnel Work*, 4th ed. (New York: Bureau of Publications, Teachers College, Columbia University, 1953).

[5] Norma E. Cutts and Nicholas Moseley, *Bright Children: A Guide for Parents* (New York: G. P. Putnam's Sons, 1953), pp. 141–81.

[6] Samuel C. Brownstein, Mitchel Weiner, and Stanley H. Kaplan, *You Can Win a Scholarship* (1956). Obtainable from Barron's Educational Series, Inc., 343 Great Neck Road, Great Neck, N. Y.

[7] Mary Irwin, ed., *American Universities and Colleges*, 7th ed. (Washington, D.C.: American Council on Education, 1956).

[8] Jesse P. Bogue, ed., *American Junior Colleges*, 4th ed. (Washington, D.C.: American Council on Education, 1956).

[9] Burton P. Fowler, "College Freshmen Tell Their Story," in *Selection and Guidance of Gifted Students for National Survival*, ed. Arthur E. Traxler (Washington, D.C.: American Council on Education, 1956), pp. 91–101.

XIII. VOCATIONAL GUIDANCE

[1] John T. Rettaliata, *President's Report*, For the Year Ending August 31, 1955 (Chicago: Illinois Institute of Technology), p. 13.

[2] James R. Killian, Jr., Address at the White House Conference on Education, November 28–December 1, 1955.

[3] Terman and Oden, *The Gifted Child Grows Up, op. cit.*, p. 172.

[4] Samuel W. Matthews, Richard D. Schwartz, John S. Hartshorne, Barton H. Lippincott, eds., *Decade of Decision* (n.p.: Yale Class of 1946, 1956). Obtainable from Paul V. R. Miller, Jr., Treasurer, Yale Class of 1946, Ivyland, Pa.

XIV. WORKING WITH PARENTS

[1] James L. Hymes, Jr., *Effective Home-School Relations* (Englewood Cliffs, N. J.: Prentice-Hall, Inc., 1953).

[2] Grace Langdon and Irving Stout, *Teacher-Parent Interviews* (Englewood Cliffs, N. J.: Prentice-Hall, Inc., 1954).

[3] *Your Child from 6 to 12*, Children's Bureau Publication No. 324 (Washington, D.C.: Federal Security Agency, Social Security Administration, 1949).

[4] Cutts and Moseley, *Bright Children: A Guide for Parents, op. cit.*

[5] Hymes, *Effective Home-School Relations, op. cit.*, p. 185.

APPENDIX I

Bibliography

The books described below deal with the broad field of education of bright and gifted children. Books dealing mainly with special subjects or with methods of individualized instruction are listed in Appendix III. In both places books and pamphlets rather than articles have been selected, as being more readily available to teachers.

BIBLIOGRAPHIES

Education Index, The. Lists current books and articles under "Children, Gifted."

Gowan, John Curtis, and May Seagoe Gowan, *An Annotated Bibliography of Writings on the Education of the Gifted Child.* Separate issues: 1955, 1956. Obtainable from John Curtis Gowan, Los Angeles State College, Los Angeles, Cal.

Jewett, Arno, *The Rapid Learner in American Schools: A Bibliography,* Secondary Education Circular No. 395. Washington, D.C.: U.S. Department of Health, Education, and Welfare, Office of Education, May 1954. Of particular value to high-school teachers.

Martens, Elise H., "Annotated Bibliography on Gifted Children," in *The Gifted Child,* ed. Paul Witty. Boston: D. C. Heath & Company, 1951.

SELECTED WORKS

Birch, Jack W., and Earl M. McWilliams, *Challenging Gifted Children.* Bloomington, Ill.: Public School Publishing Company, 1955. A pamphlet for classroom teachers in elementary and secondary schools; it includes suggestions for enrichment in different subjects at all levels.

Appendix I

Cole, Charles C., Jr., *Encouraging Scientific Talent.* Princeton: College Entrance Examination Board, 1956. A study of America's able students who are lost to college and of ways of attracting them to college and to science careers.

Connecticut State Department of Education, *Education for Gifted Children and Youth: A Guide for Planning Programs,* Bulletin No. 77. Hartford, Conn.: The Department, 1956. A pamphlet with sections on identification, enrichment, special classes, acceleration, and on the roles of lay and professional people in initiating programs.

Cutts, Norma E., and Nicholas Moseley, *Bright Children: A Guide for Parents.* New York: G. P. Putnam's Sons, 1953. A general guide for parents, with chapters on early identification, out-of-school educational activities, public and private schools, and guidance.

Educational Policies Commission, *Education of the Gifted.* Washington: D.C.: National Education Association, 1950. A pamphlet on the role of the gifted in a democracy, the current waste of talent, and means of identification and instruction.

Fund for the Advancement of Education, *Bridging the Gap between School and College.* New York: The Fund, 1953. A consideration of articulation of school and college, with reports on projects for early admission and for admission with advanced standing.

General Education in School and College, A Committee Report by Members of the Faculties of Andover, Exeter, Lawrenceville, Harvard, Princeton, and Yale. Cambridge, Mass.: Harvard University Press, 1952. A practical report on the content of a liberal education during the last two years in high school and the first two years in college.

Hall, Theodore, *Gifted Children: The Cleveland Story.* Cleveland: The World Publishing Company, 1956. A brief account of the Cleveland Major Work Classes, with a vivid description of actual class periods.

Havighurst, Robert J., Eugene Stivers, and Robert F. DeHaan, *A Survey of the Education of Gifted Children.* Chicago: University of Chicago Press, 1955. Introductory sections on identification, motivation, the use of community resources, and methods, and descriptions of programs in more than fifty schools and communities in the United States.

Hildreth, Gertrude Howell, *Educating Gifted Children at Hunter College Elementary School.* New York: Harper & Brothers, 1952. A detailed account of the selection of pupils for a special school and of methods of instruction.

How to Educate the Gifted Child. By the Committee on Exceptional Children and the Reporters of *Exchange* Magazine. New York: Metropolitan School Study Council (525 West 120th St.), 1956. A pamphlet with firsthand accounts of teachers' experiences with

Appendix I

ability groups and enrichment, and a teacher's check list for the identification of the gifted.

Jewett, Arno, J. Dan Hull, and Others, *Teaching Rapid and Slow Learners in High Schools,* Bulletin 1954, No. 5. Washington, D.C.: U.S. Department of Health, Education, and Welfare, Office of Education. An analysis of the techniques which 795 high schools use in teaching rapid and slow learners in English, social studies, mathematics, science, home economics, and industrial arts.

Kough, Jack, and Robert F. DeHaan, *Teacher's Guidance Handbook: Part I, Identifying Children Who Need Help.* Chicago: Science Research Associates, Inc., 1955. Lists of characteristics useful in identifying children with scientific ability, talent in the fine arts, leadership abilities, and mechanical skills, as well as the generally gifted, the mentally handicapped, the physically handicapped, and those with emotional problems.

Nicola, Ethel, and Diane Witte, *The Rabbit With a High I.Q.* New York: Bureau of Publications, Teachers College, Columbia University, 1955. Amusing illustrated verses favoring enrichment over acceleration.

Passow, A. Harry, Miriam Goldberg, Abraham J. Tannenbaum, and Will French, *Planning for Talented Youth.* New York: Bureau of Publications, Teachers College, Columbia University, 1955. A pamphlet, the first prepared by the staff of the Talented Youth Project of the Horace Mann–Lincoln Institute of School Experimentation, which summarizes and interprets theory and research and raises questions to stimulate research in schools.

Philadelphia Suburban School Study Council, Group A, *Guiding Your Gifted: A Handbook for Teachers, Administrators and Parents.* Philadelphia: The Educational Service Bureau, School of Education, University of Pennsylvania, 1954. A general handbook for teachers, administrators, and parents.

Roberts, Helen Erskine, *Current Trends in the Education of the Gifted.* Sacramento: California State Department of Education, October 25, 1954. An account of the author's visits throughout the United States to elementary schools, secondary schools, and colleges which have special programs for the bright and gifted.

Scheifele, Marian, *The Gifted Child in the Regular Classroom.* New York: Bureau of Publications, Teachers College, Columbia University, 1953. A pamphlet with chapters on the methods and content of enrichment and on the teacher's role.

Strang, Ruth, "Psychology of Gifted Children and Youth," in *Psychology of Exceptional Children and Youth,* ed. William M. Cruickshank, pp. 475–519. Englewood Cliffs, N. J.: Prentice-Hall, Inc., 1955. A treatment of the characteristics of gifted children, with special emphasis on mental hygiene.

Appendix I

Terman, Lewis M., and Melita H. Oden, *The Gifted Child Grows Up, Genetic Studies of Genius*, Vol. IV. Stanford, Cal.: Stanford University Press, 1947. An analysis of the educational and vocational histories and the general adjustment of the 1,500 subjects through the average age of 35; the major research work in the field.

Traxler, Arthur E., ed., *Selection and Guidance of Gifted Students for National Survival*. Washington, D.C.: American Council on Education, 1956. Chapters on crucial issues, selection, scholarships in private schools and in colleges, adjustment to college, and on the reading of gifted students.

Witty, Paul, *Helping the Gifted Child*. Chicago: Science Research Associates, Inc., 1952. An illustrated pamphlet on how adults can discover and help youngsters with superior ability.

————, ed., *The Gifted Child*. Boston: D. C. Heath and Company, 1951. Chapters, by authorities in the field, on many phases of the education of the gifted.

APPENDIX II

Tests

If you do not have expert guidance in choosing tests, you will find help in the book by J. Wayne Wrightstone, Joseph Justman, and Irving Robbins, *Evaluation in Modern Education* (New York: American Book Company, 1956). The catalogues of test publishers are also very helpful. The names and addresses of a few of the leading companies which specialize in tests are given below. Many of these, e.g., the World Book Company, the California Test Bureau, and the Psychological Corporation, are glad to send to teachers free materials about the choice and use of tests. The catalogues describe the services which the companies offer, e.g., scoring tests and analyzing results on a fee basis. Some of the companies, including the California Test Bureau and the Psychological Corporation, counsel students and adults on an individual basis.

Because new tests and new revisions of old tests are constantly coming out, be sure your choice is made from a new catalogue. The tests which are listed below are to be regarded as samples of types which you yourself can give, rather than as recommendations of the particular tests. Orders for tests should be written on official school stationery.

There are a few points to keep in mind when you are choosing tests for bright and gifted youngsters:

Pick a test which is difficult enough to show what the student can do. For example, in testing a fourth-grader, a test designed for Grades IV, V, and VI is better than one designed for Grades II, III, and IV.

Appendix II

If a test has alternate forms, pick a form which has not been given in your school before. If the test has never been given in your school, start with the first form.

Never coach a child on a test, and never give the parents test blanks which they might use to coach a child. Coaching defeats the purpose of a test, because the norms are based on the scores of children who have not been coached.

Study carefully the directions for giving the test and follow them meticulously. Any deviation from the directions destroys the uniformity of conditions which is presumed when the norms are established.

Remember that test results are to be interpreted with caution. Mistakes in giving the directions and in scoring, and misunderstandings on the student's part, are common and invalidate the results. A series of test results is more reliable than a single test result.

The cumulative record should contain full information about each test a student takes: the exact name and form of the test, the date given, the chronological age of the student and his grade level at the time, and the name and title of the person who gave the test. The record should make it clear whether the result entered is a raw score, a percentile ranking, a grade level, a mental age, or an IQ.

TEST PUBLISHERS

California Test Bureau, 5916 Hollywood Boulevard, Los Angeles 28, Cal.

Committee on Diagnostic Reading Test, Inc., 419 West 119th St., New York 27, N. Y.

Educational Test Bureau, 720 Washington Ave., S.E., Minneapolis, Minn.

Educational Testing Service, 20 Nassau St., Princeton, N. J.

Houghton Mifflin Company, 2 Park St., Boston 7, Mass.

The Psychological Corporation, 522 Fifth Ave., New York 36, N. Y.

Public School Publishing Co., 204 West Mulberry St., Bloomington, Ill.

Science Research Associates, 57 West Grand Ave., Chicago 10, Ill.

Western Psychological Services, 10655 Santa Monica Boulevard, West Los Angeles 25, Cal.

World Book Company, Yonkers-on-Hudson, N. Y.

Appendix II

READING READINESS TESTS

Harrison-Stroud Reading Readiness Tests, K-I, Houghton Mifflin Co.
Metropolitan Readiness Tests, K-I, World Book Co.

GROUP TESTS OF MENTAL ABILITY

California Test of Mental Maturity, K-Adult, California Test Bureau.
Cooperative School and College Ability Tests, VII–XIV, Educational Testing Service.
Differential Aptitude Tests, VIII–XII, Psychological Corp.
SRA Primary Mental Abilities Tests, K-Adult, Science Research Associates.

GENERAL ACHIEVEMENT TESTS

(These come in "batteries" containing a test in each of the subjects commonly taught in the grades for which the test is designed. Some also include a test of work-study skills. The tests for a particular subject are usually available separately.)

California Achievement Tests, I–XIV, California Test Bureau.
Cooperative Achievement Tests, VII–XVI, Educational Testing Service.
Iowa Every-Pupil Tests of Basic Skills, III–IX, Houghton Mifflin Co.
SRA Achievement Series, II–IX, Science Research Associates.
Stanford Achievement Test, I–IX, World Book Co.

DIAGNOSTIC TESTS

(The separate tests in the achievement batteries can also be used to diagnose a student's difficulties.)

Diagnostic Reading Tests, VII–XIII, Committee on Diagnostic Reading Test, Inc.
Durrell Analysis of Reading Difficulty, I–VI, World Book Co.
Gilmore Oral Reading Test, I–VIII, World Book Co.
Brueckner Diagnostic Arithmetic Tests, IV–VIII, Educational Test Bureau.
Buswell-John Diagnostic Test for Fundamental Processes in Arithmetic, Public School Publishing Co.
Los Angeles Diagnostic Tests, Fundamentals of Arithmetic, II–VIII; Reasoning in Arithmetic, III–IX, California Test Bureau.

TESTS OF STUDY HABITS

Brown-Holtzman Survey of Study Habits and Attitudes, IX–XVI, Psychological Corp.
Wrenn Study Habits Inventory, IX–XVI, Western Psychological Services.

APPENDIX III

Methods

Almost all educational magazines, including those devoted to specific subjects, carry articles about the bright and gifted. Topics range from accounts of small projects to surveys of methods and curriculums. A few minutes a week devoted to examining professional magazines keep you posted. There are tremendous numbers of books about all phases of teaching. The following list gives a few titles of books that include practical methods of individualizing instruction in large classes. The books have been chosen from those that describe books and materials which bright pupils find interesting. The NEA pamphlets in the series *What Research Says to the Teacher* contain brief accounts of modern methods and excellent brief bibliographies. They cost only $.25 each.

GENERAL

Alexander, William M., and Paul M. Halverson, *Effective Teaching in Secondary Schools*. New York: Rinehart & Company, Inc., 1956.

Baxter, Bernice, Gertrude M. Lewis, and Gertrude M. Cross, *Elementary Education*. Boston: D. C. Heath & Company, 1952.

Curriculum Development in the Elementary Schools. Board of Education, City of New York, 1955.

Dale, Edgar, *Audio-Visual Methods in Teaching* (rev. ed.). New York: The Dryden Press, 1954.

Faunce, Roland C., and Nelson L. Bossing, *Developing the Core Curriculum*. Englewood Cliffs, N. J.: Prentice-Hall, Inc., 1951.

Hanna, Lavone A., Gladys L. Potter, and Neva Hagaman, *Unit Teaching in the Elementary School*. New York: Rinehart & Company, Inc., 1955.

National Society for the Study of Education, *Adapting the Secondary-School Program to the Needs of Youth,* The Fifty-Second Yearbook, Part I. Chicago, The Society, 1953. Distributed by the University of Chicago Press.

Noar, Gertrude, *The Junior High School—Today and Tomorrow.* Englewood Cliffs, N. J.: Prentice-Hall, Inc., 1953.

Ojemann, Ralph H., *Personality Adjustment of Individual Children,* What Research Says Series, No. 5. Washington, D.C.: National Education Association, 1954.

Otto, Henry J., ed., *Curriculum Enrichment for Gifted Elementary School Children in Regular Classes.* Austin: The University of Texas, 1955.

Rothney, John W. M., *Evaluating and Reporting Pupil Progress,* What Research Says Series, No. 7. Washington, D.C.: National Education Association, 1955.

Strang, Ruth, *Guided Study and Homework,* What Research Says Series, No. 8. Washington, D.C.: National Education Association, 1955.

Trow, William Clark, *The Learning Process,* What Research Says Series, No. 6. Washington, D.C.: National Education Association, 1954.

ART

D'Amico, Victor, *Creative Teaching in Art* (rev. ed.). Scranton, Pa.: International Textbook Co., 1953.

Erdt, Margaret Hamilton, *Teaching Art in the Elementary School.* New York: Rinehart & Company, Inc., 1954.

Lowenfeld, Viktor, *Creative and Mental Growth* (rev. ed.). New York: The Macmillan Company, 1952.

———, *Your Child and His Art: A Guide for Parents.* New York: The Macmillan Company, 1954.

ENGLISH AND THE LANGUAGE ARTS

(See also Reading, Reading Lists.)

National Council of Teachers of English, *English Language Arts in the Secondary School.* New York: Appleton-Century-Crofts, Inc., 1956.

———, *Language Arts for Today's Children.* New York: Appleton-Century-Crofts, Inc., 1954.

Reports and Speeches of the Second Yale Conference on the Teaching of English. New Haven: Master of Arts in Teaching Program, Graduate School, Yale University, 1956. The teaching of writing and the teaching of poetry.

Appendix III

FOREIGN LANGUAGES

Andersson, Theodore, *The Teaching of Foreign Languages in the Elementary School.* Boston: D. C. Heath & Company, 1953.

Cornelius, Edwin T., *Language Teaching: A Guide for Teachers of Foreign Languages.* New York: Thomas Y. Crowell Company, 1954.

HANDWRITING

Freeman, Frank N., *Teaching Handwriting,* What Research Says Series, No. 4. Washington, D.C.: National Education Association, 1954.

MATHEMATICS

Brown, Kenneth E., and Philip G. Johnson, *Education for the Talented in Mathematics and Science,* Bulletin 1952, No. 15. Washington, D.C.: U.S. Department of Health, Education, and Welfare, Office of Education, 1953.

Fehr, Howard F., *Teaching High-School Mathematics,* What Research Says Series, No. 9. Washington, D.C.: National Education Association, 1956.

Gordon, Garford G., *Providing for Outstanding Science and Mathematics Students,* Southern California Education Monographs, No. 16. Los Angeles: University of Southern California Press, 1955.

Hickerson, J. Allen, *Guiding Children's Arithmetic Experiences.* Englewood Cliffs, N. J.: Prentice-Hall, Inc., 1952.

Morton, R. L., *Teaching Arithmetic,* What Research Says Series, No. 2. Washington, D.C.: National Education Association, 1953.

National Council of Teachers of Mathematics, *Emerging Practices in Mathematics Education,* Twenty-Second Yearbook. Washington, D.C.: The Council, 1954.

National Society for the Study of Education, *The Teaching of Arithmetic,* Fiftieth Yearbook, Part II. Chicago: University of Chicago Press, 1951.

MUSIC

Mathews, Paul W., *YOU Can Teach Music.* New York: E. P. Dutton & Company, Inc., 1954.

Nye, Robert E., and Bergethon Bjornar, *Basic Music for Classroom Teachers: An Activities Approach to Music Fundamentals.* Englewood Cliffs, N. J.: Prentice-Hall, Inc., 1954.

Thompson, Carl O., and Harriet Nordholm, *Keys to Teaching Elementary School Music.* Minneapolis, Minn.: Paul A. Schmitt Music Company, 1950.

Appendix III

READING

(See also English, Reading Lists.)

Gates, Arthur I., *Teaching Reading,* What Research Says Series, No. 1. Washington, D.C.: National Education Association, 1953.

McKim, Margaret G., *Guiding Growth in Reading in the Modern Elementary School.* New York: The Macmillan Company, 1955.

Reading for Today's Children, Thirty-Fourth Yearbook of the Department of Elementary School Principals, National Education Association (*The National Elementary Principal,* Vol. XXXV, No. 1, September 1955).

Robinson, Helen M., ed., *Promoting Maximal Reading Growth among Able Learners,* Proceedings of the Annual Conference on Reading Held at the University of Chicago, 1954, Vol. XVI. Chicago: The University of Chicago Press.

READING LISTS

("There are more book lists for children than there are children."— Arbuthnot. The four lists given here are helpful, but you should consult your librarian.)

Adamson, Catherine E., *Inexpensive Books for Boys and Girls* (3rd ed., rev.) [through Grade VIII]. Chicago: American Library Association, 1952.

Arbuthnot, May Hill, and Others, *Children's Books Too Good To Miss* (rev. ed.) [through age 14]. Cleveland: The Press of Western Reserve University, 1953.

Children's Catalog [through Grade IX]. New York: H. W. Wilson Company, 1909–51, with supplements.

Secondary Education Board, *Junior Book List* [through Grade IX]; *Senior Book List* [Grades X–XII], annuals. Obtainable from Secondary Education Board, Milton 86, Mass.

SCIENCE

(See also Mathematics.)

Barnard, J. Darrell, *Teaching High-School Science,* What Research Says Series, No. 10. Washington, D.C.: National Education Association, 1956.

Blough, Glenn O., and Albert J. Huggett, *Elementary-School Science and How to Teach It.* New York: The Dryden Press, 1951.

Brandwein, Paul F., *The Gifted Student as Future Scientist.* New York: Harcourt, Brace & Company, 1955.

Appendix III

Cole, Charles C., Jr., *Encouraging Scientific Talent*. New York: College Entrance Examination Board, 1956.

Conant, James B., *On Understanding Science*. New Haven: Yale University Press, 1947.

Richardson, John S., and G. P. Cahoon, *Methods and Materials for Teaching General and Physical Science*. New York: McGraw-Hill Book Company, Inc., 1951.

SOCIAL STUDIES

Carpenter, Helen McCracken, ed., *Skills in Social Studies*, Twenty-Fourth Yearbook (1953) of the National Council for the Social Studies. Washington, D.C.: National Education Association, 1954.

Michaelis, John U., *Social Studies for Children in a Democracy* (2nd ed.). Englewood Cliffs, N. J.: Prentice-Hall, Inc., 1956.

Reports and Speeches of the First Yale Conference on the Teaching of the Social Studies. New Haven: Master of Arts in Teaching Program, Graduate School, Yale University, 1956. The U.N. Charter, Problems of Minorities, the 14th Amendment.

Tooze, Ruth, and Beatrice Perham Krone, *Literature and Music as Resources for Social Studies*. Englewood Cliffs, N. J.: Prentice-Hall, Inc., 1955.

SPELLING

Horn, Ernest, *Teaching Spelling*, What Research Says Series, No. 3. Washington, D.C.: National Education Association, 1954.

APPENDIX IV

Needed Research

You may not think of yourself as a research worker. But you have exceptional opportunities to locate essential problems in teaching, to collect firsthand data, and to form and try out hypotheses. You and your 1,000,000 colleagues in United States classrooms are potentially the greatest research team in the world.

The problems listed below are but a few to which better solutions are needed if we are to improve the teaching of bright and gifted children. As in the case of all research, advances on one front will bring advances on all fronts. For example, anything that you discover about the motivation of superior students will improve our knowledge of motivation in general. A. Harry Passow and his colleagues, in *Planning for Talented Youth,* list many topics about which we need more information. You and your fellow teachers might use Passow's suggestions as a guide to "action research." Whether you work alone or with the other teachers in your school or as a member of a city, state, or national committee, you will find that research is good fun in itself and that it increases your interest in teaching.

Write up any study that you think may be generally valuable and submit it to your favorite educational magazine. If one editor turns you down, try another. There are more than two hundred educational publications indexed in *The Education Index* and countless local and state publications. You will like to see your ideas in print, and other teachers will like to try them out. Moreover, every good account that appears in print adds to the data that other workers can use to establish new theories.

If you want to find out what others have done, you will find current books and articles on the bright and gifted listed in *The Education Index* under "Children, Gifted." Research in the field was reviewed in the June 1944 issue of the *Review of Educational Research* (Vol. XIV, No. 3, pp. 224–30) by Elizabeth L. Woods, and in the December 1953 issue (Vol. XXIII, No. 5, pp. 417–31) by T. Ernest Newland.

Only the teacher can observe pupils in a normal classroom setting. And education desperately needs more detailed accounts of how bright children and all children act and react under given conditions. Your observations will have added value if they become a part of an extended case history, if you or a pupil's later teachers can see whether the way he behaves in one year can be used to predict how he will behave in later years in school and in life. Education also needs much more in the way of information which will help account for changes in pupil behavior. What makes a lazy student into a worker, and vice versa? As matters now stand we seem to know more about the characteristics of the pupil who is either generally superior or generally inferior than we do about what causes shifts.

SOME PROBLEMS

Identification. How often and why do screening devices like group tests fail to identify the bright and gifted? How often and why are bright children from underprivileged homes misjudged by their teachers?

The curriculum. What are the best methods of enrichment? What type of project—class, group, individual—produces the best results under what conditions? How do pupils in an enriched program compare with others on total achievement?—on the fundamentals?—in creativity?

Organization. How have ability grouping, acceleration, and chronological grouping affected pupils? Why?

Motivation. What differing patterns of motivation are there among high-achievers? What ways are there of giving a child a mental set to achieve?—to exercise his creative talents? What accounts for the "drop outs" among bright high-school and college students?

Mental hygiene. Granted the general superiority in the mental health of bright students as a group, what are the most frequent specific causes of strain and of failure to adjust? What are the most frequent danger signals?

Guidance. What proportion of bright students of given ages have made a vocational choice? What proportion of these carry out their vocational plans by securing appropriate education?—by actually engaging in the chosen vocation? What happens to "drop outs"?

The challenge. What are the attitudes of teachers, parents, students, and the community to the education of the bright and gifted? How are changes in individual and group attitudes effected?

INDEX

Index

Index

Index

Index

Index

Index

Sibling rivalry, 160–62, 199, 232
Skills, 43
Skipping. *See* Acceleration
Slower pupils, helped by bright, 68, 145
Smith College, 213
Snobbishness, 178–81
Social development, 29–30, 111
Sociograms, 165, 172
Solitariness, 171 (*see also* Adjustment; Mental hygiene)
Spanish, 56, 97 (*see also* Foreign languages)
Specialization, danger in, 197
Specialized high schools, 98–99
Special teacher of gifted, 51, 73, 98
Spelling, 119–20, 123, 126, 147, 257
Spock, Benjamin, 232
Sports, 109, 111, 171, 185–87
Springfield, Mo., 182, 183
Stamford, Conn., 73, 79
Stanford-Binet Test. *See* IQ
Stivers, Eugene, 76, 98
Stoeckel Trust, 78
Strang, Ruth, 48, 132
Strauss, Lewis L., 4
Student day in city government, 68, 87
Study, 50, 59–60, 122, 133, 252
Summer classes, 84–85
Sumption, Merle R., 96
Supervisor of gifted, 51, 73, 98

T

Talent, defined, 3
Talkativeness, 181
Talking, age of beginning, 29
Tape recorder, 127
Teachers:
    of high-ability groups, 100–101
    shortage of, 5
    supplementary, 58, 79, 81, 82–83
Teaching, as a career, 213, 220–21
Terman, Lewis Madison, 18, 104, 132, 133, 190, 212
Tests, 250–52
    achievement, 30–32, 36
    aptitude, 36, 42
    diagnostic, 123
    and enrichment, 46–47
    of fundamentals, 71, 121
    in identification, 30–32, 93–94
    intelligence, 30–35, 36

Tests (*Cont.*)
    teacher-made, 33
    See also Examinations; Psychological examination
Texts, basal, 40
Thinking, 19, 44
Thom, Douglas A., 155, 157–58, 159
Traits, 17–26
Transportation on field trips, 65–66
Tyler, Ralph, 70
Typing, 56–58, 97, 147

U

Underachievers, 131–52, 225
Underprivileged, 8, 74, 233–34
Understanding, need of, 42–43
Units, 49, 96, 253–54
University City, Mo., 97

V

Van Kleeck, Edwin, 5–6
Vassar College, 203
Vision, defects of, 15
Vocabulary, 14, 18–19, 27, 29
Vocational guidance. *See* Guidance, vocational
Vocations. *See* Guidance; Occupations

W

Walking, age of, 29
Wann, Kenneth D., 182
Westinghouse Science Talent Search, 86
What Research Says to the Teacher, 121
Whitcomb, Richard T., 196–97
White, Ralph K., 55
Withdrawal, 27, 164–66, 171 (*see also* Daydreaming; Mental hygiene)
Witty, Paul, 2
Worcester, D. A., 106
Workbooks, 127–28
Wrightstone, J. Wayne, 99, 250
Writing, creative. *See* Creativity

Y

Yale University, 56, 78, 104, 114, 198, 203, 212–13
You Can Win a Scholarship, 203
Your Child from 6 to 12, 232

268